INNER JOURNEYS

INNER JOURNEYS

A Guide to
Personal and Social Transformation
Based on the Work of Jean Houston

Jay Earley, Ph.D.

SAMUEL WEISER, INC.
York Beach, Maine

First published in 1990 by
Samuel Weiser, Inc.
Box 612
York Beach, Maine 03910

Library of Congress Cataloging-In-Publication Data
Earley, Jay, 1944–
        Inner journeys : a guide to personal and social
    transformation based on the work of Jean Houston / Jay
    Earley.
        1. Self-actualization (Psychology) 2. Social change.
    3. Spiritual life. 4. Houston, Jean.   I. Title.
    BF637.S4E37 1990
    158'.1—dc20   90-27198
                                                        CIP

ISBN 0-87728-704-X

Cover painting is entitled "Liberation,"
© Rob Schouten, 1990.
Used by kind permission of the artist.

Typeset in 11 point Goudy by World Composition Services
Printed in the United States of America by
Baker Johnson, Inc.

Dedicated to my parents
for love and caring
which I didn't fully appreciate at the time.

Contents

Section Four:
Life Purpose

Section Five:
Empowerment

Section Six:
The Spiritual Realm

Section Seven:
Organizing and
Designing Exercises

About the Author

Jay Earley has a Ph.D. in computer science from Carnegie-Mellon University and was formerly on the computer science faculty of the University of California at Berkeley. He also has a Ph.D. in psychology from Saybrook Institute and is currently a psychotherapist in private practice on Long Island. He has been active in the peace movement, leading workshops which integrate psychological, spiritual, and social concerns. He is especially interested in the psychology of social transformation and how to empower people to make their contribution. He also gives talks and workshops on interpersonal relationship skills, self-esteem, and finding your life purpose.

Foreword
by Jean Houston

A S THIS BOOK goes to press, we are witnessing much speculation on the meaning and methods of millennial consciousness. We move daily between glasnost and claustrophobia. Current affairs seem more mythic than real, and many of us, whether we are nations or individuals, are coming to see our lives as variations on the theme of the *Hero with a Thousand Faces*. We are haunted by a call to a larger life. "It's Time to Wake Up Now!" If we refuse this call, we are beset by a nausea of self-disgust and trivialization. Reluctantly agreeing to the call, we find unusual and unexpected allies between and within ourselves, new arenas of brain, mind and feeling. When we cross the threshold into the realm of internal, amplified power, we are invariably swallowed in the belly of the whale. There we are rewoven for higher life and deeper journey.

Then it begins: the road of trials, a dreamscape of challenges wherein we meet our shadows. We face the goblins and monsters of our old betrayals and self-doubts. As we go through the initiations and dyings we encounter the fact and necessity of death in life as our constant companion and discover that our renewal is always at hand. Then, if we allow the deeper journeying to take its course, we meet the Beloved of the soul and we are no longer alone. We return to the world of the ordinary bearing the extraordinary, the companion of extended reality, ready and willing to renew the wasteland of the everyday with the findings of the external world within.

We are citizens of two worlds, and celebrate the fact that we inhabit a reality larger than our aspirations and more complex than all our dreams. The traditional journeys of the hero and heroine have always seemed to us exclusive and aristocratic—out of reach. But we live in a time of planetary consciousness and unfoldment where we are beginning to realize that we are all travellers on a heroic journey. The personal particulars of our own lives reflect and realize the universal of a great life and great story. Everyone is a traveller. Everyone is a godseed. We have moved beyond heroics. We are coming Home.

Is it any wonder then that many are coming to experience a significantly different order of personal reality than the one known in the past? Many people live through something like five to ten times the amount of "experience" of their ancestors of two hundred years ago. But many have been psychologically wounded in ways that their ancestors, living in fixed realities and given social structures, could have neither imagined nor even sustained. It takes strong healing forms to minister to this much experience and this much wounding. It takes wisdom to devise a variety of healing experiences that can speak to the depths and intensities that modern folk contain.

In *Inner Journeys*, Jay Earley has done this with richness and elegance, addressing the plenum of human possibility. Never avoiding the pathos, always present to the shadows that rise, he plays the role of a goodly Hermes, guide to the mysteries of the depths, the one who takes us back to our holy sources and shows us how to avail ourselves of the healing gifts that await us there. With remarkably fine and lucid instruction and guidance, he creates an environment that the reader can enter and there discover a path to the possible human. Drawing upon and often improving my work, he facilitates the discovery of sensory, psychological, symbolic and spiritual capacities within the self.

Empowerment, that much needed quality, is raised to a high art in Earley's work. He shows how the human heart can go to the lengths of god. With skillful means, he takes us into our polyphrenic self—our many different, creative selves—the potential key to humanity's extended health and longevity. Most importantly, he evokes the relationship between person and planet, between personal and social transformation, psychological and spiritual development.

Inner Journeys is a new kind of ministry. It speaks deeply to the fact that given the multiplication of novelty, variety and quantity of experience in present day living, we are simply not the same people that we were before. Indeed, there appears to be occurring a collective reorientation in the global mind, what I have referred to as the rising of the depths occasioned by the coming of planetary consciousness. With leaky margins and diaphanous membrane between cultures and economies, shared natural resources and shared pollution, migrating populations and cross-cultural styles, this new consciousness has been hastened by the emergence of our own inner realities, the bleed-through from our own geopsychic realms. Earley's work demonstrates in the most practical and yet luminous manner that everything is reciprocal: the growing world psyche is the occasion for the growing of more developed psyches in our own brain/mind systems.

We and the world are flowering simultaneously. As the earth is becoming for many sacred once again, we are moving toward becoming the gods for whom once we yearned. But even the gods themselves must outgrow—in pattern and in principle—the archaic strata of previous ages before a new day, a good day, a god day, can dawn. *Inner Journeys* is a guide for godding.

Introduction

WHAT IS YOUR LIFE really all about? In addition to the natural pursuit of security, pleasure, love, and recognition, what gives your life meaning? When the give and take of everyday life fade for a moment—in the middle of the night, in the sauna, walking alone in the woods, meditating—when you think about deeper questions, what moves you? When you feel a need to be part of something larger than yourself, what calls to you? Come with me on a journey to explore these issues, and perhaps learn how to help others do the same.

These questions arise for people when their basic needs have been met and they are looking for something more from life. They arise during mid-life and during times of crisis and transition. They arise as people grow psychologically and become interested in the spiritual realm. And they arise when people start taking the planetary crisis personally and asking what their response could be.

This book has grown out of my own search for meaning in life and is intended to help people discover, explore, and deepen theirs. It derives from my experience taking people on what I call Inner Journeys. This work is based on the approach of Jean Houston, world renowned psychologist, workshop leader, spiritual teacher, and evocateur of human potential. Inner Journeys work is my way of bringing some of Houston's immensely valuable contributions to the public through my particular lens, that of psychotherapy and planetary concerns.

Inner Journeys work helps to heal psychological pain from the past and foster self-support and personal power, but more importantly it aims at developing the higher human faculties: creativity, love, wisdom, spiritual opening, life purpose, and the ability to serve as an agent of planetary healing. We all have great unexplored depths in our psyches, which are the wellsprings of these faculties. In Inner Journeys we explore these depths, evoke the hidden potential, enhance the conscious connection, and empower people to live and act from these places. Inner Journeys work also fosters a heartfelt sense of bonding and community among the members of a group, supporting each person's growth and serving as a model for the larger sense of connection our world so desperately needs.

This book is intended for two audiences: (1) For those of you who want to explore your life purpose and develop your own higher faculties, it provides a guided tour through the major issues of Inner Journeys work and exercises that will take you on your own Inner Journeys. Even though Inner Journeys work has been developed primarily in a group setting, the exercises in this book can be done (with small modifications) on your own or with a friend. (2) For professionals who would like to incorporate this work into your current practice, it describes in detail how to organize and facilitate an Inner Journeys group.

Inner Journeys work combines powerful group exercises with follow-up individual work in the group setting. The exercises consist of combinations of guided fantasy, trance, expressive movement, ritual, and personal contact, set to evocative music. The individual work involves experiential, process-oriented psychotherapeutic exploration using all of the above modalities. The individual work is made available to people after each group exercise, so that if any participants are not able to complete the exercise on their own or if important material comes up that needs to be processed, they can receive guidance from the leader.

A central theme of this approach is integration: integration of the potency of group exercises with the individual attention of psychotherapy; integration of a variety of different modes of exploration—imaginal, movement, ritual, interpersonal; integration of the healing work of therapy with the growth and transcendent orientation of spiritual practice; and integration of the inner world of these approaches with the outer world of social and planetary concerns.

The Exercises

The exercises are structured experiences that take you deep inside your psyche, to places rarely visited. Some help you to heal old pain, so that you are freed from the inhibitions of chronic patterns. Some help you to develop or improve your relationship with yourself—that bond of primal importance. Others encourage you to discover new and different parts of yourself and to learn how these parts can relate to each other harmoniously.

In some exercises you connect with another person, sharing an experience together, supporting and empowering each other, learning to relate in deep ways that go beyond our usual modes of interacting. In others you connect with the whole group, playing and laughing together, affirming and celebrating each person, or melding together in shared communion for a time.

There are some exercises in which you contact higher, wiser, and perhaps divine parts of yourself. There are others which help you tap into the reservoir of love that is in all of us, waiting to be freed—love for others, for yourself, for the earth, and for all of creation. And there are some which take you to the spiritual realm, where you might contact an archetypal presence or experience union with a larger reality.

At times you investigate your life purpose, that deeper sense of direction and meaning for your life. At times you explore how to manifest this, feeling your personal power, projecting your action in the world. At other times you deal with your personal relationship to the planetary crisis, feeling your compassion for the pain in the world, envisioning a better future, and discovering what your particular contribution to that future might be.

Through it all there is respect for the integrity of your personal journey, for the wisdom of the deep psyche, for life and the great mystery that surrounds us. And there is caring, for ourselves, for each other, for humanity, and for the planet.

Sample Journeys

Following are some examples of inner journeys that people have taken. Put yourself in their place; imagine how you would feel.

Imagine sitting in your living room chatting with a person who turns out to be yourself. You spend some time getting to know this person who might be a very special friend, who has been through a lot with you and will never leave you. You realize how much you have ignored this relationship with yourself, and you feel an intense yearning for that deep connection. You realize, in a flood of tears, that the love you have been looking for outside yourself was there inside all the time.

• • •

You experience yourself as a great eagle soaring through the heavens, feeling the strength of your mighty pinions and seeing the vast sweep of the earth below you. You express this experience through movement—dancing, gliding, whirling—as you are lured on into your power. From this perspective you look down on the landscape of your life and are awed to see a pattern emerging. The next step on your path is staring you in the face, and you are a little frightened, but ready to meet the challenge.

• • •

You are sitting across from a group member you hardly know, making eye contact. You see their pain and their joy, their needs and their strengths, and you sense them seeing the same in you. Your most subtle emotions are met and reflected in their eyes.

You see into the essence of their being, and your heart opens to them. You are struck by the realization that this is possible with anyone.

• • •

A woman takes an inner journey to meet her shadow, the part of her that she has disowned because it seemed unacceptable. Her shadow turns out to be a kind of repulsive slime. In order to reown her shadow, she becomes the slime and begins to explore who she is in that shape. She finds herself wanting to ooze over things, experiencing a desire for intimate physical contact. She suddenly realizes that the slime represents her disowned neediness, and she feels like a baby, sobbing in pain for lack of touching and nurturing. The group members respond to her need, respectfully touching her, holding her, caressing her, and she opens like a flower, feeling shaken and deeply filled.

• • •

A man travels deep inside himself where he encounters the goddess Gaia, the living earth. He sees how we are harming her through environmental carelessness and threatening her with nuclear weapons, and he hears her call for help. Profoundly moved, he goes outdoors and finds a leaf, which for him represents the fragile beauty of the earth. He walks in a procession with the others in the group, holding the leaf and contemplating his calling. In his turn he comes to a sacred circle of stones and places the leaf in the center, declaring, "I dedicate myself to the healing of the planet."

Context

The question of meaning and purpose in our lives is shaped by the current social and historical context. We live in a time of profound change. Our current worldview, which is based on science and reason and which treats everything as a machine to be analyzed and controlled, has brought us tremendous gains in knowledge, freedom, and comfort, but it has also brought about its own demise.

The tremendous explosion of our technical power, our population, and our ability to exploit the earth poses a whole new set of issues that our industrial worldview is no longer adequate to comprehend. It has outlived its usefulness, and our continued attempts to apply it to our current problems are simply making matters worse. Similarly our current lifestyle based on material consumption and personal ambition, which once made so much sense in fueling our drive toward mastery of the environment, is now contributing to the problems and dangers at hand.

As a result, our society is breaking down. This is causing tremendous stresses and dangers, and it is also allowing for the possibility of a transformation to a whole new social structure and worldview. Not only are we faced with major world issues such as nuclear war, terrorism, and global climate change, but our psyches are being affected. We are seeing huge increases in drug addiction, alcoholism, suicide, and other mental problems. There are increases in crime, violence in schools, and corruption and deception in government. The nuclear family is breaking down and more and more people are living in isolation from meaningful personal and community ties.

Most of us are deeply enmeshed in our own personal problems and do not see that they are actually symptoms of the larger societal breakdown. We are so busy dealing with our own difficulties that it seems overwhelming to take on the problems of the world as well. When you are in pain, it's hard to concentrate on things which otherwise might concern you. To even consider the larger problems invites fear and a sense of powerlessness before the immensity of the task.

Yet when you are able to reframe your own difficulties as part of the larger issues of our time and join with others in confronting them, you become revitalized. You are relieved of that sense of guilt and inadequacy we often feel when we think we are the only one with a problem. Hope is kindled and a sense of shared responsibility, and your creative energy flows freely. You must still work through your own issues, but you can align your own struggles with society's so that your personal transformation contributes to social transformation and vice versa. You are then lifted out of yourself into a larger, more meaningful context, and a sense of deeper purpose emerges.

A new worldview and way of life appropriate to the current historical situation is beginning to surface. Our collective psyche is erupting with signs and portents of this new way of being: from the new systems science to the burgeoning interest in consciousness, from the self-help movements to the rise of women, from ecological awareness to the emergence of the global village. We don't know what it will be finally, but we have hints that this new outlook is built on a foundation of cooperation, interconnectedness, and an interest in the inner life, and that it is interlaced with cultural diversity, human scale institutions, and reverence for the earth. This doesn't mean discarding all the advantages of science, analytic thought, and technology, but rather integrating them with the new emerging values to serve human goals rather than ruling them.

The narrowness of our current view of what it is to be human has restricted many of us to linear, unfeeling, disconnected, and competitive ways of being. In answer to the needs of the time we are called on to develop ourselves to the fullest as well as to work to change society. We are called on to embody the values and sensibilities of the new society that is trying to be born and to discover that deep sense of life purpose and vision impelling us to create a new world.

We are not called on to do this alone or in isolation, however. Vast numbers of people in this country alone are hearing this call in a wide variety of ways and responding with changes in their lives and values. Daniel Yankelovich, the pollster, estimated in 1981 that about 20 percent of the population had strongly adopted the new values and that 80 percent were somewhat affected by them.[1]

Jean Houston

Jean Houston is one of the major figures of our day calling our attention to the dangers and opportunities of this time of transition. She provides us with the vision and the tools to develop ourselves, discover our deeper purpose, and engage in the work of transformation.

Perhaps her most important quality is her vision; she sees the big picture. In a time when narrow specialization is the rule and we have an explosion of information to cope with, we desperately need people who can see from the widest possible perspective, who can understand holistically the human being, the planetary situation, and the cosmos. Jean Houston is such a person, and to my knowledge the one with the most range and depth of vision.

Sometimes after telling someone that my work is based on Jean Houston's work and having them ask me who she is, I feel tongue-tied. She is hard to characterize. Her work is so broad, it doesn't fit into any of the narrow compartments that we are used to.

To put it in one sentence, Jean Houston relates the complexity of the human psyche to our social and historical context and to the larger spiritual dimension. She understands and integrates insights from a wide variety of disciplines—psychology, mythology, history, philosophy, anthropology, literature—and from her vast knowledge of religions and cultures worldwide. She weaves these threads together through the medium of myth to enchant us with stories about how the call of our times relates to our personal journeys toward growth and wholeness.

---

[1] Daniel Yankelovich, *New Rules* (New York: Bantam, 1981).

From her unique vantage point, what does Houston see? She understands the current crisis of social transformation, the rhythms of awakening that are stirring in our collective psyche, and how these relate to past times of ferment and change. She views psychology from a mythic and a spiritual perspective, which enobles our personal struggles and lifts them to their proper universal dimension. She sees the human being as an integrated physical, mental, emotional, social, and spiritual system with a vast untapped potential for higher functioning in all these areas. She harvests and celebrates the great spiritual traditions of our past while recognizing the need for the emergence of a new one that can meet the challenge and complexity of our present time.

Background

Early in her career as a college professor in philosophy, religion, and psychology, Jean Houston participated in LSD research and began to observe and chronicle the structure and complexity of the psyche. The results of this research are described in *The Varieties of Psychedelic Experience*, [2] which she wrote with her husband, Robert Masters.

In 1965, she and Robert Masters established the Foundation for Mind Research, where they experimented with ways to conduct similar explorations without using drugs. They developed a wide variety of techniques for eliciting the depths of the psyche and expanding people's modes of functioning. These are described in their books *Listening to the Body*[3] and *Mind Games*,[4] both of which describe detailed exercise programs that can be undertaken by the reader. Inspired by the work of Moshe Feldenkrais, *Listening*

---

[2] Robert Masters and Jean Houston, *The Varieties of Psychedelic Experience* (New York: Delta, 1966).

[3] Robert Masters and Jean Houston, *Listening to the Body* (New York: Delta, 1978).

[4] Robert Masters and Jean Houston, *Mind Games* (New York: Delta, 1972).

to the Body contains exercises for the psychophysical re-education of the body and nervous system. *Mind Games* contains a carefully crafted sequence of exercises for the development of the mind and psyche using primarily trance and guided fantasy.

Since 1975 Houston has offered their research findings to professionals and laypersons in workshops and trainings throughout the world. She maintains a vigorous schedule, traveling a quarter of a million miles a year, giving keynote speeches and leading seminars for a multitude of conferences and organizations.

In her workshops Houston leads experiential exercises for large groups of people, weaving together approaches and techniques from a wide variety of sources into a creative blend that is uniquely her own. She draws from brain and mind research, physiology, bodywork, psychotherapy, and meditation. She uses drama, dance, storytelling, and the visual and performing arts. She adapts concepts, rituals, and spiritual technologies from religions and mythologies worldwide.

All these are designed to help us unlock our unused potential: to free the body; to sharpen our senses, perceptions, and memory; to awaken us to our multidimensional consciousness; to develop intuitive and visionary ways of knowing; to spark our full creativity; to contact our deep sense of meaning and purpose; to experience our unity with the cosmos. She has a profound belief in the great possibilities in every person, and faith that these can be realized if that person is acknowledged and empowered. Perhaps most important, she has the genius to manifest this on a large scale, to create exercises that reveal to people their depths and potentials, thereby igniting the growth process.

Portions of this extensive body of work are described in two more recent books. In *Life Force: The Psychohistorical Recovery of the Self,*[5] she correlates five stages of human development with five eras of human history, and then presents

---

[5] Jean Houston, *Life Force: The Psycho-Historical Recovery of the Self* (New York: Delta, 1980).

exercises and rituals for passing through each stage. In *The Possible Human*[6] she elucidates a beginning set of exercises for developing our full potential in a variety of areas.

Her workshops include lectures as well as exercises, but for Houston, a lecture is more like a performance. She is a trained Shakespearean actress, a consummate storyteller, and a passionate public speaker. A strong believer in multi-modal education, she lives out her beliefs, using music, story, song, humor, and dramatic interludes to enliven and enrich her cognitive presentations.

In recent years Jean Houston's work has taken new and exciting forms. She heads a three year Training Program in the Cultivation of Human Capacities, which prepares people to use her work professionally in the educational and healing arts, with a Ph.D. option. She also leads a modern Mystery School, a spiritual training program drawing from a wide variety of ancient traditions and modern disciplines. This program contains the cutting edge of her newest ideas and processes for the more advanced levels of spiritual development.

Her book, *The Search for the Beloved: Journeys in Sacred Psychology*,[7] describes the importance of the mythic journey for personal growth and elucidates the process of spiritual opening through union with the "beloved of the soul." A series of smaller books are to follow, each one exploring a particular myth, complete with exercises for taking you through your personal version of the mythic story. The first of these is *Godseed: The Journey of Christ.*[8]

Her energy and commitment to personal and social transformation are enormous. In 1984 our present planetary crisis led her to initiate a workshop entitled "The Possible Society." Designed

---

[6] Jean Houston, *The Possible Human* (Los Angeles, CA: J.P. Tarcher, 1982).
[7] Jean Houston, *The Search for the Beloved: Journeys in Sacred Psychology* (Los Angeles, CA: J.P. Tarcher, 1987).
[8] Jean Houston, *Godseed: The Journey of Christ* (Warwick, NY: Amity House, 1987).

to be inexpensive and draw large numbers of people, this work-shop was presented throughout the world. The sessions spawned a Possible Society organization which is carrying on this work in other forms. Houston has also entered into a collaboration with the Institute for Cultural Affairs, an organization that does com-munity organizing of the poor and disenfranchised in both the United States and third world countries.

Her work has influenced a vast array of people, who have taken her ideas, her processes, and her vision into their profes-sional lives and begun to alter and reshape our institutions. Jean Houston has reached influential people in education, psychother-apy, medicine, religion, gerontology, government, community development, business, and academia. She is truly a prophet of social transformation and a global midwife of the emerging society.

Inner Journeys work is based heavily on Houston's approach. Some of the exercises are my renderings of exercises she has designed. In others I weave bits and pieces of her exercises into my own creations. All the exercises have been designed using the style and form of Houston's exercises, and my whole perspective and underlying philosophy have been strongly influenced by her.

Inner Journeys work, however, is based on only a portion of Houston's contributions. I make little use of the mythic sensibility so important to her work. My emphasis is more psychological. I do not employ her earlier psychophysical research or her more recent work with drama. I emphasize the methods of guided fantasy and personal interaction, and the goals of psychological healing, life purpose, and social transformation. Where Houston has the gift to inspire large groups of people, I prefer to apply my skills as a psychotherapist in small groups where there is more opportunity for individual attention. Though Houston deserves much of the credit for Inner Journeys work, her achievements are not to be judged in any way by the limits you may discover in this book.

How This Book Evolved

I started out my work life as a computer scientist, doing research and teaching on the faculty at the University of California at Berkeley. Although I enjoyed this work and made significant contributions to my field, my sense of life purpose led me in a different direction. I was uncomfortable with many of the ways computers were being used in this society in the service of bureaucracy and the military and I wanted to devote my life to something I valued. I had developed an avid and abiding interest in personal growth and consciousness, and in 1973 I became a psychotherapist.

After becoming established and proficient as a psychotherapist, I found myself not entirely satisfied with the influence I was having on the world through the usual therapy framework. I wanted to work with people more directly on issues of growth and meaning, and I wanted to influence the larger societal issues that were becoming apparent to me.

In 1982 I was introduced to Despair and Empowerment work, created by Joanna Macy and others.[9] This approach combines psychology, spirituality, and political concern in workshops that enable people to deal constructively with their responses to the nuclear threat. This was a wonderful discovery for me: I could combine my therapy skills with my interest in planetary issues.

Soon after I started attending workshops given by Jean Houston. I was captivated by her approach, my own growth took a leap forward, and my interest in spiritual matters blossomed. I began leading Despair and Empowerment workshops that also incorporated Jean Houston's approach. This was the beginning of Inner Journeys work. I discovered to my delight that I seem to have a natural talent for designing and leading exercises of this

---

[9] Joanna R. Macy, *Despair and Personal Power in the Nuclear Age* (Philadelphia, PA: New Society Publishers, 1983).

kind, and that it taps deep creative energies in me. This work is as much an artistic endeavor for me as it is a therapeutic or political one.

I became involved with Psychotherapists for Social Responsibility, a Bay Area organization of therapists who banded together in response to the nuclear threat. I also joined Interhelp, a national network inspired by despair and empowerment work and devoted to dealing with the emotional and spiritual aspects of global issues. These two groups have given me a sense of community with others concerned with the planetary crisis, and continuing inspiration to carry on my work for social transformation.

I soon realized that I could lead Inner Journeys groups oriented toward personal and spiritual growth as well as toward social transformation. In fact, I found that the two areas were not as separate as they first appeared. These groups gave me the opportunity to work with people on the most advanced growth levels dealing with issues of life purpose and spiritual connection. It was a very exciting further integration of my interests.

Since 1983 I have been involved in a peer support group which grew up around Jean Houston's work. In this group we take turns leading psycho-spiritual exercises, as well as sharing our personal journeys and metaphysical meanderings. This group has been a wonderful source of friendship, community, and support, and has given me the opportunity to experiment with Inner Journeys work as it has developed.

In 1984 I wrote a paper describing some of my social transformation exercises, which received praise from many quarters. A year later, I was encouraged by my support group to expand this into a book containing all of my workshop exercises and a full description of Inner Journeys work. After two years and much sweat and tears, this book is the result.

I have developed approximately fifty Inner Journeys exercises; nineteen of them are described in this book. A full chapter is devoted to each exercise, including a discussion of the issue explored by the exercise and a detailed description of how people have responded to it, with quotes from group members. I have chosen these exercises for the book because they cover a wide range of essential growth issues, they have been tested and refined to my satisfaction, and I have recorded enough comments from participants to provide a clear idea of their effects.

The exercises are divided into six sections dealing with the larger themes of this work: developing a relationship with yourself, opening the heart, social transformation, life purpose, empowerment, and the spiritual realm. Do not be misled into thinking that the only exercises which deal with a given theme are those which are placed in its section. Most exercises have multiple themes. For example, even though only two exercises are listed under Social Transformation, nine exercises actually deal with that theme. In the introduction to each section is a listing of all the exercises related to that topic.

The next section describes how to use the exercises. This is followed by the nineteen exercise chapters. Chapter 20 discusses the larger growth trajectories in a person's life and how the exercises fit into these patterns. Chapters 21 and 22 are oriented toward group leaders and describe how to structure workshops and groups and how to design exercises.

Non-Sexist Language

There are many solutions for the problem of using male pronouns for indeterminate gender. The best one, of course, is to rephrase the sentence so as to avoid the problem. However, there are always a few cases where this is not possible without awkwardness. For these cases, I have chosen to use the solution that we naturally and unconsciously use in spoken language: the third person plural. Thus, I use "they" instead of "he or she," "them" instead of "him or her," etc. I consider this not an incorrect use of grammar, but rather an anticipation of the direction in which the language is moving.

How to Use the Exercises

THIS BOOK IS DESIGNED to be of value even if you don't intend to actually do the exercises. The body of each exercise contains rich and evocative material that explains and deepens the issue introduced in the chapter. Read the exercises slowly and think about how the concepts apply to your life. You may even want to do the exercises (within limits) as you read them, taking time to stop and go through the processes as you go along.

After each exercise, there are descriptions of what other people have experienced doing the exercise. These provide concrete examples to make the concepts more real and to give you a sense of the variety of different experiences possible. You will probably discover that you identify with some people's experiences, that some of them speak to things you have gone through or questions you are facing. This will enrich your understanding of the issue presented in the chapter.

You can get even more out of the book if you do the exercises. There are a number of ways to arrange this.

On Your Own. Record the directions on tape with appropriately timed pauses, then play them back when you actually do the exercise, thus becoming your own leader. This is the most difficult method; it is only recommended if you are dedicated to working in a solitary way and have the motivation to prerecord the directions. If you choose this mode, be careful when recording the directions to time the pauses correctly. Think ahead to what will be happening later when you are doing the exercise.

With a Friend. Whenever you get together with a friend, you can explore the book by leading each other in exercises. Take turns leading each other through a particular exercise, with one being the leader and the other the participant, and then switching roles. This is intimate and fun and relatively easy to arrange.

A Peer Group. You can meet with a group of friends to explore this work together. Share the leadership by having each person take a turn at leading an exercise. This is the most rewarding way, but requires you to gather a group of interested people. If this proves difficult, you might start with just one friend and then gradually add more people over time.

Since the exercises were originally designed and used in group settings, I have written the directions for a group. However, most of the exercises can be done individually or with a friend with little or no change. In some cases, further directions for working alone or with a partner are given under particular exercises.

Most of the exercises are enjoyable and safe for everyone. However, some of them encourage you to access memories, images, or feelings which could be unsettling for people whose psychological stability is questionable. If this is true of you and you are not currently in psychotherapy, it would not be wise to do the exercises except under the guidance of a therapist.

The rest of this chapter contains detailed suggestions on how to use the exercises to the best advantage. You may want to skim this first, reading it in detail later when you are actually ready to do them.

Participants' Outlook

The attitudes discussed in this section will help you get the most out of the exercises. These should be discussed at the beginning of a group or workshop and explained to new group members when they join.

For best results, approach the exercises with openness and a willingness to let go, to surrender and give yourself over to the process. This requires trust—trust of the exercises, the leader, the group, and trust in yourself. I understand that this may not be fully present when you are first introduced to these exercises or to a new group or leader. Just let go as much as you are able.

Each person has a different optimal pace for an exercise, and different ways of imaging. In addition people are at different points in their development, and each person has a unique path in life. Even though each exercise is designed to connect with as many people as possible, you will sometimes find that the directions do not quite fit you. Feel free to modify the exercise in any way that seems right for you. You may change an instruction slightly to mesh better with your process, or you may go off in an entirely different direction for a while. If you do this, check back in from time to time to see if you can reconnect with the exercise.

If an exercise does not seem to be working for you, it is easy to slip into a judgmental attitude—judging yourself or the leader or the group or the exercise. It works much better to adopt an accepting attitude, going along with the exercise, maintaining an open mind, and waiting to see what will happen. You may find that at one moment you feel disconnected from an exercise, and then a few moments later you are unexpectedly moved by it. Avoiding judgments allows room for this to happen more easily. Afterwards you can critically evaluate the exercise, when it will not interfere with the experience.

Guided Fantasy

Most, if not all, of the guided fantasies are done in trance. This simply means you are in an altered state of consciousness where material from your unconscious and the deeper levels of your psyche is more readily available to you. Trance can be thought of as a deeper state of relaxation. You retain alertness and control, but you have access to more of your psyche.

The best attitude to adopt for guided fantasies is a combination of letting go and staying focused. Letting go allows images from your unconscious to emerge freely. Don't try to control the images (except for the degree of control implicit in the directions). It's important not to doubt or discard the images that spontaneously emerge. You might be inclined to do this for a variety of reasons:

1. You don't understand them. This is actually a plus; some of the most important images are not understood at first.

2. They seem too obviously associated with recent events or well-known images. Remember that their significance for you in this fantasy may be very different from the conventional meaning.

3. They seem evil or unacceptable to you. Please trust that the image has come up for a good reason and that you don't need to fear your unconscious.

The other ability important to guided fantasy is staying focused. This keeps you on track with the leader's directions and with the thread of your own journey. During a fantasy it is easy to "space out" or daydream about irrelevant issues. This happens to almost everyone from time to time. If you find that you have lost focus, don't become worried or judgmental toward yourself, just gently bring yourself back to the track of the fantasy.

Don't assume that all imagery has to be visual. Some people do not visualize well but are very good at body imaging. They can imagine bodily feelings, posture, and movement, and they can imagine their body in different shapes. This is called kinesthetic imagery, and people are capable of interesting and profound internal experiences through this modality. (I am one of those people, and consequently this book contains a number of guided fantasies which are primarily kinesthetic.) A few people even use mainly auditory imagery. So if you have trouble visualizing, don't despair; notice what internal imagery you are producing on other channels.

Sit or lie in a completely relaxed, comfortable position, one that you can maintain in stillness for as long as the fantasy lasts, sometimes up to 40 minutes. I recommend lying down unless you are likely to fall asleep. If you discover that you tend to fall asleep during guided fantasies, then it may be best to maintain an upright sitting position without head support. This is also recommended at times when you are unusually tired or have just eaten a big meal. This position tends to keep people awake while still allowing a state of deep relaxation. You will discover in time which position works best for you.

Movement

In some of the exercises we use body movement or dance as a way of exploring and expressing ourselves in a physical way. Some people have difficulty with this because of its public nature. They may feel self-conscious about how they look while dancing, inhibiting themselves from moving freely. If this happens to you, remember that we only care how the movement *feels* to you, not how it appears to others. The other group members will probably not even be looking at you; they will be involved with their own experience. Feel free to start out with small movements if that is more comfortable. Moving freely will become easier over time as you gain more experience with it.

Sharing in the Group

After each exercise, set aside time to share with the group what you experienced. This gives you a chance to deepen and elaborate the meaning of your experience, and to get feedback from the leader and other group members. However, if the experience feels too private or if you are still too immersed in it to want to talk, feel free to pass. Also, if you are new to the group and don't yet feel safe enough to share with the whole group, it is OK to wait until you are more comfortable.

When someone else is sharing, feel free to comment on their experience. However, please emphasize feeling reactions, rather than insights or advice. Be careful not to get into discussions of abstract issues, and not to take the focus away from the person who is sharing.

Dealing with Difficulties

Occasionally you may get part way into an exercise and not be able to complete it. This could happen for a number of reasons:

1. You simply may not be ready to go further in this direction in your growth at this time.

2. You may be blocked from taking the further emotional steps that the exercise asks.

3. An exercise may stimulate images or memories that are so compelling or have such a charge of emotion that they must be dealt with first.

In cases 2 and 3 you may want to explore the experience further in order to alleviate any discomfort and to learn as much as possible about what emerged. Many examples throughout the book illustrate how this can be done. Not completing an exercise should not be viewed as a negative outcome. Important material has come up, and you are in a perfect position to gain a valuable insight or work through a critical issue. This may turn out to be more useful than if you had completed the exercise.

If the group is being led by an experienced professional, ask them to help you explore the material. Otherwise seek help from the people in your peer group or from your partner. If you are working alone you can explore the issue by writing in your journal or by talking to a trusted friend some time later. Often just giving the matter some extra time will allow you to work through the issue. If this does not happen sufficiently and you are left in pain, I recommend consulting a professional psychotherapist.

Speaking from the Text

All the exercises involve a leader who guides the rest of the group through the experience and (with a few exceptions) does not participate. The material to be spoken by the leader is written so that it can be used verbatim, but it will be most effective if you make it your own rather than reading it exactly as written. There are a couple of ways to do this:

1. If you're willing to go to the extra work, write out a new version of the exercise using your own words and phrases.

2. Use the book directly but improvise as you go, rephrasing, adding, and embellishing according to your own style.

If you are new to leading group exercises, I recommend starting with the first option and moving to the second later on. A very important caution when you are reading from a text: *Do not simply read it word for word.* It will very likely sound dull or stilted to the participants. Instead, as you are leading the exercise, read each sentence or phrase silently to yourself first, then speak it aloud with feeling. Always speak to the group, not to the piece of paper. This will help to give the words the life necessary to evoke the right experience for the participants.

The expressiveness of your voice is very important to the impact of the exercises. Different parts of an exercise call for different voices. The inductions should be spoken in a slow, dreamy, hypnotic voice. The explanatory parts should be matter-of-fact. Those parts which are meant to evoke a particular feeling or experience in the participants (loving, celebratory, sad, sacred) should be spoken with that quality of voice. The best way to achieve this is to put yourself into the state intended for the participants, and let your voice come naturally from there.

Three dots in the text ". . ." indicate a pause. These are often around ten seconds, though this can vary considerably. Pauses of half a minute or longer are explicitly indicated. Don't feel bound by these instructions. Use your discretion about how long each pause should be according to how much time seems to be needed to process the directions preceding the pause. You can often get an idea of this by observing the facial expressions and other nonverbal reactions of the group members, or by imagining how long it would take you.

Feel free to insert additional pauses as they seem warranted. However, do not insert pauses randomly just to slow down the instructions. When you are giving a series of explanatory statements which need to be finished before the participants can continue the fantasy, don't pause between sentences. This would leave people hanging or creating premature images that they might have to discard after hearing the rest of the instructions.

The exercises are written as if there were just one leader. If you decide to use two, the co-leading can be handled in the following ways:

1. Take turns leading different sections of an exercise. The appropriate place to switch is often when the music changes.

2. One person speaks the major content of the exercise and the other adds words or phrases which elaborate on and embellish what the first person says. This is similar to a hypnotic double induction.

Music

Recorded music is used in all the exercises. I have found it enjoyable and exciting to select just the right music to evoke the appropriate mood for each portion of each exercise. Music helps to induce trance, to elicit certain feeling states, and generally to increase the potency and effectiveness of the exercises. The exercises can be done without music, but they would be weakened. Most of the music used in this book is New Age music. It can be obtained at spiritual or New Age or metaphysical bookstores, through catalogs,[1] and, increasingly, at your local record shop.

With a few exceptions, you don't have to use exactly the piece of music which I specify, only one which creates the same mood. Therefore, for each piece of music I have indicated the mood it tends to evoke. (The best situation would be to have a skilled musician backing up the leader and improvising to follow the flow of the exercise. This can only be approximated by recorded music.)

Sometimes the piece of music is to be played through to completion. In this case if you substitute a different piece, take into account the length of the selection as well as its tone. In other cases, the music is played as long as needed and then faded out. This is indicated by the words "as much as needed." Sometimes the piece needs to be played more than once to fit the timing of the exercise. Then you will need to record the piece back-to-back so there are no significant pauses to break the flow of the exercise.

It is very important not to distract the participants during an exercise. They are deep in trance and are experiencing an entirely different world from the ordinary reality of the leader and the tape recorder. Any unnecessary pauses or sounds of clicking will remind them of this other reality and take away from the trance experience. Therefore how you handle switching from one piece of music to another is important. I have done this in two ways:

1. I prefer to use stereo equipment with two tape decks so that the next piece of music can be in the second deck ready to go. When one piece finishes, the second is immediately activated.

---

[1] *Heartbeats* catalog, Backroads Distributors, 41 Tamal Plaza, Corte Madera, CA 94925, (800) 825-4848.

Switching cassettes can then be done while the music is playing, when the noise from this is not so distracting.

2. Occasionally I have recorded all the pieces for one exercise together on a single tape. This eliminates any distractions while switching music, but it introduces a problem. You must then be concerned about timing each section of the exercise to the music you have already recorded. This decreases your spontaneity and introduces an extra worry.

For those who don't want to go to this trouble, I have included with each exercise a simplified music schema where just one piece of music is used.

I use some categories of music (evoking particular moods) frequently. I list these here along with various pieces of music which evoke that mood. Any of these may be used when the directions call for that category.

Heart Music

1. "Pachelbel's *Canon*," extended version, from *Timeless Motion* by Daniel Kobialka

2. "Seapeace" from *Seapeace* by Georgia Kelly

3. "The Way Home" (especially the first section) from *Perelandra* by Kevin Braheny

4. "Abraham's Theme" from *Chariots of Fire* by Vangelis

5. "Neranzoula" from *Odes* by Irene Papas and Vangelis

Celebratory Music

1. "Eric's Theme" from *Chariots of Fire* by Vangelis

2. "Silk Road" from *Silk Road* by Kitaro

3. "Pachelbel's *Canon*"

4. Next to last piece on side one of *Heaven and Hell* by Vangelis

5. Credits from *Starman* soundtrack by Jack Nitzsche

Sad Music

1. "Home" from *Country* soundtrack by Charles Gross
2. "Rêve" from *Opera Sauvage* by Vangelis
3. Adagio by Albinoni

Inductions

Most of the exercises use an induction to take the participants into a deep, receptive place for the exercise. The major part of each induction is written out as part of the exercise description. In most exercises, this is to be preceded by some simple relaxation instructions. I present two variations here; feel free to make up your own.

The following should be spoken in a slow, hypnotic voice. They can be shortened or lengthened depending on your sense of the group's needs.

Induction—Variation I

Close your eyes and begin to turn your attention inward. . . . Pay attention to the physical sensations where your body is being supported by the floor or the pillow or the chair. Just let yourself feel the sensation of touch and support. . . . As you do this you may find yourself becoming more relaxed and quieter inside. . . .

Now bring your attention to your breathing. Notice the sensation of your breath as it passes in and out of your nostrils as you inhale and exhale. . . . Just keep your awareness focused in that place and on those sensations. If you find your mind wandering, gently bring it back to the physical sensations. . . . Now feel the air as it passes down behind your throat and down your windpipe. . . . You are moving deeper inside yourself, becoming still inside. . . .

Now feel the movement of your chest and belly, in and out as you inhale and exhale. . . . Settling down gently, letting go. . . . Now feel the beating of your heart from the inside. The soft, regular rhythm of the blood moving through your body. . . .

Induction—Variation II

Close your eyes and turn your attention to the sensations of your body. . . . Feel your body resting on the floor (pillows, chair, etc.), and know that you can relax and let go as much as feels appropriate right now, relax into resting on that surface. . . . You are completely and gently supported by the floor. Feel yourself sinking into the floor as if it were a soft surface that caringly supports you, rocks you, massages you, taking you deeper inside. . . . Letting go into that soft sense of support, being caressed, feeling very comfortable and safe. . . . Becoming quiet inside. . . .

Trance Suggestions

It helps if you sprinkle trance suggestions throughout the induction and at other appropriate places in each exercise. I have included some of these in the text, but I suggest that you add more as it seems appropriate. The following are examples:

Coming to those still places of safety and rest . . .

Finding that you can let go even more . . .

Becoming grounded, centered in yourself . . .

Deeper and deeper into your inner world . . .

Finding yourself going deeper into the psyche, to those places where the unconscious is more available to you . . .

Bringing People out of Trance

When an exercise is over and it is time to bring people out of trance, suggest that they gradually reorient to the room and current physical reality, bringing back with them whatever they have gained from the exercise. This need not be elaborate. The following is an example:

> Now gradually begin to come back from the place where you have been, bringing with you all that you have gained from this experience, . . . beginning to come back to this room, feeling the floor or pillows under you, hearing sounds in the room, . . . taking your own time, . . . slowly coming more toward ordinary waking consciousness, . . . beginning to move around a little, to stretch, . . . opening your eyes, becoming alert and awake, feeling refreshed.

Other Suggestions

I prefer to limit the size of groups I'm leading to ten participants, and in writing this book I have assumed a group of that size. However, it is possible to do this work successfully with larger or smaller groups. (Jean Houston works with groups in the hundreds. I once led a very successful workshop with four people.) Most of the exercises can be done with a group of any size. In a few exercises the group interacts as a whole, and for these, larger groups may have to break down. They will also need to break down into small groups of ten or less for the sharing after each exercise, with participants returning to the same group during an entire workshop. This provides continuity and encourages the development of intimacy and group cohesion, which are so important to this work.

Ideally the room where the exercises are held should have a place where you can sit comfortably in a circle for sharing, room to lie down for guided fantasies, and enough room for everyone to dance freely. A rug and pillows, or couches and soft relaxing chairs are preferable. The room should be free from distractions.

Especially during the guided fantasies, arrangements should be made so that there are no phone calls, visitors, children, or pets, and outside sounds, especially sudden noises, should be minimized.

Ritual and movement may be unfamiliar to some people and may even lead to discomfort and embarrassment because of the public nature of these activities. If you suspect this may be a problem in a group you are leading, you can eliminate or modify the sensitive parts of an exercise, or you can introduce it in such a way as to minimize difficulties. You can do this by acknowledging that the modality may be strange and unfamiliar, explaining its value, and asking the participants to try it in a spirit of experimentation.

This work uses some spiritual concepts and language that may be unfamiliar to some people and may bring up negative associations for others. This can cause them to resist the work if it is not handled carefully. I believe that most, if not all, of the concepts presented in this book can be understood and accepted (at least on an experimental basis) by everyone if presented sensitively. Avoid language that may be offensive to people or that is obviously incompatible with their worldview and values.

Allow plenty of time after each exercise for people to share their experiences with the group. Participants gain a broader perspective by getting feedback on their own experiences and hearing about others'. Group intimacy and bonding are also strengthened.

In addition if you, as leader, are planning to do individual work with people, this is the perfect time for it. While each person is sharing, notice if they were unable to complete the exercise as intended or if important material was brought up that needs to be processed. You can invite them to do the individual work right then in front of the group. This enables the whole group to participate in that person's intense work, thereby getting to know him or her at an entirely different level.

After some particularly deep and moving exercises, you may want to allow an extra five or ten minutes for people to be with themselves in silence so they can fully absorb the experience before beginning the sharing. Use your intuition in deciding when this is called for.

See chapter 21 for additional discussion of how to design and structure a workshop or group.

SECTION ONE

Developing a Relationship with Yourself

Introduction

DO YOU LONG FOR a close, intimate relationship? Consider for a moment the quality of intimacy you have with yourself. Imagine looking forward to being alone with yourself late at night to think over the day, to explore your hopes and fears, to confide in yourself about recent troubles. Imagine really enjoying your own company; imagine having a best friend deep inside yourself.

Developing a solid, caring, loving relationship with yourself is one of the most important steps in your overall growth. If your self-relationship is not solid, you may depend too much on love relationships to meet your needs. When you are without a love relationship, you may feel lonely or depressed, and you may find it hard to progress in other areas of your life. You may be driven to become involved with someone who is not appropriate for you.

Once you are in a relationship, you may discover one of the following problems: You may alienate your partner by smothering them with your needs. You may give up your needs altogether in order to please your partner. You may avoid challenging an unsatisfactory relationship for fear of losing it.

In the normal course of growing up, to the extent that they receive adequate parenting, children come to feel good about themselves and others. In addition, as they mature, they internalize the functions the parents served so that they are able to give themselves more and more of the support that they originally received from their parents.

However, our parents had their own problems and life struggles, and were not always able to give us what we needed. So in most of us, this process is not fully complete. Developing a relationship with yourself means fully internalizing the parenting functions: learning how to support yourself, nurture yourself, guide yourself, and protect yourself—on many levels. It also involves internalizing some of the functions of other relationships, such as friend, lover, or teacher. This means befriending yourself, confiding in yourself, loving yourself, valuing yourself.

When you develop a solid relationship with yourself, you have an invaluable foundation of self-support. You have a bedrock of solidity inside that can carry you through pain and disappointment. You know you can always turn to yourself and receive comfort and acceptance. What a wonderful feeling of security! You also have access to more of your own richness—your capacity for inner direction, for insight, discipline, creativity, and fun. You are no longer driven by a need for other people to fill your emptiness, because inside you feel full of yourself in the most positive sense. You can choose to be alone if necessary, or you can reach out to others from a place of wholeness.

In this culture we are unconsciously trained to avoid relating to ourselves. Women are usually trained to depend on their relationships with others for all of the care and love they need, to give to others what they need themselves, hoping to get it back in that way. Men are frequently trained to bury their needs altogether or to transform them into strivings for sex or success.

Many of us have internalized a tendency to judge ourselves harshly about almost everything we do, so that developing a loving, accepting relationship with ourselves becomes very difficult. Most of us are taught that being alone is not something to be enjoyed, unless we are being entertained by an outside source.

Our culture doesn't recognize that the quality of our self-relationship is extremely important to our well-being.

My Experience

I have used both the male and female ways of avoiding a relationship with myself. In my early years, I was closed to my feelings and needs and I emphasized intellectual and athletic pursuits and achievement. As I discovered psychotherapy and the personal growth movement, I opened up to my feelings and interior life. In addition to all the benefits of this, I uncovered a great need for love and affection, and I focused this need exclusively on the woman I was involved with, causing difficulties in the relationship.

Then a decade later, after the ending of a different relationship, I realized that in both relationships there were difficulties having to do with my not fully supporting myself, and I became determined to change this. Shortly thereafter I was introduced to the concept of having a relationship with myself during a ritual[1] in one of Jean Houston's workshops. This was revolutionary for me. I realized that it was possible to direct toward myself some of the longing I had always directed at women. As I first felt that yearning for a connection with myself, I experienced a powerful sense of coming home! I was reconnecting with something incredibly valuable in myself that I had been ignoring for so long.

I spent the next two years learning to support myself, being present with myself when alone, valuing my inner thoughts and feelings, and generally deepening my relationship with myself. This has made an enormous difference. I have felt much more

---

[1] Jean Houston, "The Ritual of the Beloved of the Soul," in *The Search for the Beloved,* p. 143.

solid when I've been on my own, and I have been able to find and nourish a relationship which is really working for me.

• • •

This section contains the following exercises in which you learn to befriend yourself and to relate to different parts of yourself:

The Child and the Higher Self
Befriending Yourself
Reowning the Shadow

The following exercises in other sections also deal with the self-relationship:

Opening the Heart
Nurturing Touch
Acceptance
The Flight of Empowerment
The Expanded Body

1

The Child and the Higher Self

ONCE YOU START exploring the inner workings of your psyche, you will discover that you are not just one person, but many. We are all made up of many different parts or subpersonalities, and each of them is almost like a separate little person inside. In this exercise, you become acquainted with some of the most important ones. Getting to know your various parts, or selves, provides insight into how you really operate and creates opportunities for healing. You gain access to the positive qualities of each part, and you can resolve and strengthen the relationships among the parts.

Your child self is the part of you that is still a child, living in the past and functioning with child-like attitudes. Eric Berne has described the child in detail in Transactional Analysis.[1] We all have internal models of ourselves and others, which are developed largely during childhood. Painful situations from the past tend to twist these models in a negative direction. For instance, many of us have an internal child who is needy—for touch, for nurturing, for understanding, for love—because we weren't given enough when we were children. Others of us have a child who is

---

[1] Eric Berne, *Games People Play* (New York: Grove, 1964).

rageful because of ways that we were controlled or intruded on as children.

If you try to ignore and deny your child self, your needy or angry side, it won't go away. It will just go underground, and without realizing, you will act it out with people when you least expect or desire to. You will find yourself driving away potential mates because of the subtle ways they feel smothered by your needs. Or you will alienate friends and colleagues when your anger leaks out.

To work through this you must call up your inner child, recreate a painful situation from the past, and give that child whatever it needed back then. Then healing can occur which begins to correct this distortion and build a more positive model. If your needy child is acknowledged and given caring and nourishment, it will begin to feel loved, and your neediness will gradually be replaced by strength and self-support. If your rageful child is allowed expression and given support for its autonomy and integrity, it will begin to feel safe in the world, and the anger will subside.

This process happens most effectively when you fully open yourself to re-experiencing the pain of not getting what you originally needed. This loosens the internal model and makes it more accessible to modification. Then when your child self is given what he or she needed, this can readily penetrate and take hold. In this exercise your child is nurtured by an adult version of you; that is, you parent yourself. This makes the experience even more powerful because you are internalizing the parenting function; you are learning to give yourself the support you need. When this is fully internalized you will have a reassuring solidity and self-support.

The child self is also a reservoir of many vital qualities of youth, such as spontaneity and playfulness, which may have been lost to the responsibilities and conformities of adulthood. Through contacting your inner child these can be accessed for enthusiasm and joy in your current life.

The Higher Self

The higher self is that part of you that is the source of the higher human faculties such as love, wisdom, and purpose. You might think of it as the part of you that is fully evolved or perfect, the part that is the intersection between your ordinary self and the spiritual realm, the part of you that is divine. The higher self has been given many names: transpersonal self, Self, extended being,[2] soul, deep self. Psychosynthesis sees the transpersonal self as a living entity of pure being at the core of the superconscious (the spiritual realm of the psyche).[3] The Indian sages of the Upanishads identified the individual Self with the cosmic Self, believing "that God stands in the same relationship to the universe as Self stands to the body and personality."[4]

The higher self isn't just an interesting idea or something you may someday discover. It has been experienced in various forms by myriads of people of all traditions throughout the centuries, and it exists in each of us, whether or not we have accessed it. Sometimes it makes itself known as an inner voice of wisdom which can answer profound questions and help to direct your life. Sometimes it appears as a mythic figure such as a wise old man, or a divine source of love, or an object of devotion. And sometimes it is experienced as a state of being in which you are wise and powerful and loving. This last is the form it takes in this exercise.

The higher self doesn't have to be created or developed. We usually think of these higher functions as taking a lifetime to develop in ourselves. While it may take a long time to develop the ability to *live from* your higher self, it is not that difficult to access. Finding your higher self gives you a taste of your potential and helps to bring those higher qualities into the fabric of your everyday life.

---

[2] Jean Houston, *The Possible Human*, p. 93.
[3] Piero Ferrucci, *What We May Be* (Los Angeles: J.P. Tarcher, 1982).
[4] Ralph Metzner, *Opening to Inner Light* (Los Angeles: J.P. Tarcher, 1986), p. 86.

I have experienced my higher self in many ways: sitting alone in a forest, sinking into the silence and peace, feeling profoundly connected to the natural world; emerging from an exercise in a Jean Houston workshop feeling a deep passion and purpose to serve the world; standing back from a difficult interpersonal situation, letting go of resentment and defense, feeling compassion and love for the people involved.

Subpersonalities

You will experience three different parts of yourself in this exercise: the child, the higher self, and the adult self. Transactional Analysis (TA), one of the most popular systems for explaining our different sub-selves, also identifies three parts: the Parent, Adult, and Child. TA does not recognize the higher self. In this exercise, I have combined the TA Parent and Adult into what I call the adult self. This is not because I think the distinction between the two is unimportant, but simply that it is not salient to the purposes of this exercise.

Research into multiple personality sheds some interesting light on these issues. People with Multiple Personality Disorder seem to have more clearly delineated versions of the subpersonalities that we all have. Because of extreme physical and sexual abuse as children, they have split off certain of their selves so as to not be overwhelmed by the pain. These selves become full separate personalities over time and experience themselves as different people in the same body. By exhibiting the structure of their psyches in exaggerated form, they provide us with information about how all of us are made.

The "host" personality is the one who has an identity in the world and copes with everyday reality. This corresponds to the adult self. Most people with multiple personalities also have one or more child personalities whose development is arrested at a certain age and who literally function and experience life as children. Most interestingly, many of them also have a personality called an "inter-self helper," who is wise and caring and helps to understand and coordinate the other personalities and sometimes helps to guide a therapist in working with the person. These inter-self helpers also frequently seem to have many of the spiritual qualities associated with the higher self.[5]

Circumstances

This exercise can be used as an overall introduction to Inner Journeys work. It's suitable for inexperienced people because the first part of the guided fantasy is easy for a beginner to follow. The range of the exercise is such that it can be used as a complete short workshop in itself. It contains both psychological and spiritual sections and both guided fantasy and personal contact.

Working Alone. When doing the exercise alone, skip the last part, or do it by imagining that you are looking into the eyes of someone you are close to.

Working with a Partner. When working with a partner, take turns leading each other through the guided fantasy first. Then do the last part together as follows: one person can speak each paragraph of the directions, then put down the book and make eye contact to carry them out, then speak the next paragraph, and so on.

Time: 40 minutes.

---

[5] John O. Beahrs, *Unity and Multiplicity* (New York: Brunner/Mazel, 1982), p. 109.

The Exercise[6]

[People arrange themselves for a guided fantasy, and the leader begins with an induction.]

♪   "Home" (from *Country* soundtrack by Charles Gross, twice, as much as needed; or other sad music)

Now imagine that you are on a beach at the seashore alone. Notice the waves breaking on the shore, the seagulls. Feel the sun on your body, the sand under your feet. Smell the salt water. See the clear blue sky and perhaps some rocks along the shore. . . . And as you look around, you notice that there are hills behind the beach and a path winding its way up to higher ground. Walk away from the ocean now and follow this path. Notice what it feels like to walk on the path, how it feels on your feet. Notice the vegetation growing around the path on the hill. . . .

At the top of the hill you come to a flat grassy area, and the path winds around to the side and leads back out toward a cliff overlooking the ocean. As you approach the cliff from a distance, you can make out a single tree growing there, and underneath the tree is a small figure. As you move closer, it seems that it might be a child crying. And as you get closer still, you see or sense that it is you when you were a child, and that the child is crying. It is you as a child at a time in your life when you were having trouble or difficulty, when you were experiencing pain or sadness or fear.

Walk up to the child who is you, and ask it what the problem is. Let the child pour out to you all the pain, all the feelings and just be there with it, to hear and to comfort. [Allow a minute.]

♪   "Starla's Eyes" (from *Piano Means Soft* by Charley Thweatt; bright, childlike tone)

---

[6] Based on Jean Houston, "Recalling the Child," *The Possible Human*, p. 91.

Now you can't change what happened, but you can give yourself-as-child something now that will help to heal the hurt. Sense what the child needs right now. Sense what it is that was not given back when the original hurt happened. It might be love or respect or acceptance or nurturing that is needed. The child might need to be seen clearly and appreciated, or might need advice or encouragement or help or teaching about life. Between the need you sense as child and the understanding you have as adult, get in touch with what the child needs, and then give it.

You can do this by holding or stroking the child or having it lay its head on your lap or any other way of touching that feels right. Or you can tell the child what it needs to hear. You might say things such as:

"I accept you just as you are."

"You are very special to me."

"I love you and I care about you."

"You have so much to offer to people."

You will have a couple of minutes now to give your child self exactly what it needs. [Allow 2 minutes.]

Now take a moment, if you haven't already, to become yourself-as-child and to deeply take in what you are getting from yourself. Become the child, take a deep breath, and let the caring permeate you, let yourself feel those good feelings that come up in you as you are receiving from the adult. Take as much time as you need with it. Enjoy it and let it warm you. [Allow until the end of the music, about 2 minutes.]

Now gradually let go of the child, and come to a quiet place inside yourself. You will be connecting with the child again later in the exercise.

♪ "Pachelbel's Canon" (twice; uplifting, loving tone)

Now you are going to get in touch with a third part of you—a deep and powerful part. Begin to breathe deeply through your mouth, and with each breath imagine yourself growing, developing, expanding. Imagine yourself, with each breath, becoming more and more of what you have the potential to be. Feel yourself becoming wiser, stronger, deeper, brimming over with life. Keep breathing and imagining this process happening with each breath. Find yourself becoming fuller and wiser and more developed. . . .

As you do this you are getting in touch with what is sometimes called the higher self, or the deep self, or the transpersonal self. It has many names. This is the part of you that is in touch with inner wisdom. If you had 1,000 years to grow and develop and actualize all of your potential, this is what you would become—and it is in you now! It is there already, even if you can't live from it every moment. This is the part of you that is fully developed spiritually, that is in tune with all of creation.

In this place you are so powerful and grounded and open that you are no longer afraid or insecure, no longer competitive or tense, no longer worried about many of the day-to-day problems that your adult self needs to be concerned about. In this place you are able to see the essence in people and to love fully and unconditionally. In this place you are full of joy and deeply at peace. . . . Continue breathing now, and continue expanding with each breath and developing with each breath, and with each breath becoming more and more in touch with this part of yourself, more and more becoming your higher self. [Allow a minute.]

Expanding, connecting, deepening, being, loving, open, powerful, wiser, grounded, connected, peaceful. . . .

And now take a moment to get in touch with what your current adult self needs from your higher self. Do you need direction, insight, inspiration, healing, love? Whatever it is, be the higher self and use your wisdom, your strength, your deep sense of being to give the current self what it needs to help it along its path. This may happen in words or in images or in a bodily or spiritual sensing, in any way that feels right. You will have a few minutes now to give to your adult self from your higher self. [Allow 2 minutes.]

And now bring all three parts of you together—the child, the adult, and the higher self—and let them relate to each other. Let each give to the others the special gifts that it has to offer. The child brings deep feeling, desire, pure energy, openness, vulnerability, simplicity. The adult brings caring, intelligence, responsibility, the ability to act in the world. And the higher self brings wisdom, depth, purpose, inspiration, love, peace. Let all these qualities come together in you now as each of these beings gives of their best, and as all three parts relate to each other in whatever ways feel right. [Allow 2 minutes.]

Rejoice now in these relationships you have within you. The nurturing, caring connection between your adult and child selves, and your deepened connection with your higher self. If you have been looking only outside yourself for many of these things, you now know that they are inside as well. The love and the wisdom are within you. . . .

You will be able to reconnect with your child or your higher self whenever you need to after this. And in the weeks and months to come, continue these relationships, strengthen the connections, deepen the intimacy within you. In this you find some of your richness and complexity. For you have many parts with many stories. These are only three. You have many selves, each with something unique to offer to you and to others. Let yourself sense this abundance of possibilities within you, appreciate it and let it support you in whatever you do. . . . [Music ends.]

Now gradually begin to come back from where you have been, retaining as much as possible of the expanded state you are now in, and bringing with you that sense of the three parts of yourself.

[Bring people out of trance. Then ask them to pair up and sit facing their partners.]

Sit and make eye contact with your partner. Just take a moment to look into their eyes, even if it seems strange. Take a moment to tune into this person you're with. This is an opportunity to be with and appreciate them in a way that we rarely do with each other. . . .

♪   "The Way Home" (first movement, from *Perelandra* by Kevin Braheny, twice, as much as needed; or other heart music)

Now become your child self—your open, vulnerable, deep-feeling child self—and honor your partner from that place. Appreciate your partner as a child might. See the strength and caring behind those eyes. Imagine how good it might feel to be taken care of and comforted by this person, even if you don't know them very well. . . . From that open place you're in, see into the deep part of your partner where they have reserves of affection, nurturance, protectiveness, caring. And honor them for that. [Allow half a minute.]

Now become your adult self and honor the child in your partner. Look into a different part of their being now, and see the young, open, soft qualities that this person has. Let yourself see into parts of them that they may not know much about. Behind those eyes are needs and vulnerabilities and the capacity for deep feeling. Let yourself see that and honor them for it, appreciate it in them. As the adult, seeing this in them, feel your appreciation and your caring. . . .

Also see that this child is capable of much more as well. The child can be playful, fun-loving, enthusiastic. See the part of this person, however well it may be hidden, which is lively and energetic, perhaps even mischievous at times. Imagine what fun it would be to play together. . . . Feel your deep recognition and appreciation of the whole child self of your partner. . . .

And now, once again become your higher self, and honor and empower your partner from that place. Be in touch with your deepest wisdom and love and strength. From that place let yourself see and affirm the uniqueness of your partner. See beneath the surface to their deep essence. See all the essential beauty, the lovableness. See the complexity, the many levels, many parts, many stories. Honor and celebrate your partner from your highest and most loving self. From that place, let the unconditional love pour out. . . . And know that you are deeply honored in return. Sense the connection, the deep connection beyond personality, beyond words. . . . [People take a few minutes to share with their partners.]

♪ Simplified music: Use "Pachelbel's Canon" as described above and also for the last part.

Experiences[7]

Deserving the Higher Self

I will describe in detail the experience of Sherry, a 40-year-old schoolteacher. She spent most of her life feeling vaguely childlike, inadequate, and powerless. Even though she was warm and caring and easily able to connect with people, she didn't value herself as a person. In recent years, through both group and family psychotherapy, this had begun to change as she started to assert herself and to like herself, but the old tendency toward self-judgment remained strong.

Sherry was drawn to Inner Journeys work because she wanted to know herself in an inward way that went beyond problem-solving. She was very pleased with what she had gained from therapy, but sensed that there was more to her than what she had discovered so far.

She is able to image clearly and easily, so as the exercise started she immediately felt herself at the beach. The child she

------

[7] In this exercise and throughout the book, in order to protect the identity of participants, I have changed names and other identifying characteristics, and in many cases I have even used aspects or experiences of two different people in creating one person's story for this book.

saw crying under the tree was about seven years old. When she approached and asked her child self why she was crying, the child at first turned away in hurt. Sherry realized that the child was upset because her parents didn't seem to understand her or care about her. She felt alone and unwanted. Sherry gently reached out to the child and stroked her back, and gradually the child relaxed and began to trust her.

She told the child that she understood how hard things were for her, and that it wasn't her fault. She took the child in her arms and held her, telling her how special she was and how much she cared for her. It was very satisfying for her to be giving her child self what she so desperately needed. It was more difficult for her as the child to take this in fully. She kept not being sure if she deserved it. But her adult self persisted and eventually the child opened up and let herself be filled and warmed by the love. This brought her close to crying. "It touched me really deeply."

Since Sherry hadn't done this kind of work before, the concept of the higher self was new to her, and she had some difficulty with it. Afterwards we had the following conversation:

Sherry: "I had a lot of problems with the third part. I felt I wasn't doing it right. I had to continually say, 'No, remember, don't judge yourself. You're OK.' But I felt like I wasn't giving my partner enough strength and I didn't have that part of it together enough."

Jay: "How much were you able to tune into your higher self during the guided fantasy?"

Sherry: "I felt like I was doing that somewhat, but maybe I could have done a lot more."

Jay: "That wasn't the intention of my question. Talk about what you *did* get of the higher self, not what you didn't get."

Sherry: "Well, I knew that part of me was there, that it existed, and that it needs to be developed more. I found myself slipping back into the adult all the time. I would think about what's currently going on in my life, and then it would go away.

I would breathe in and I'd feel it, and I'd breathe out and I couldn't have it."

Jay: "So breathe in and feel it, and describe what it feels like, right now."

Sherry: "It's hard to describe. It feels very peaceful and not judging at all. [pauses] It makes me want to cry. [crying] I don't know why. [pauses] It just seems like things are very sad. Things aren't as they should be at all."

Jay: "Being the higher self is the way they should be?" (Sherry: "Yeah") "And that gets you in touch with how much . . . " (Sherry: " . . . they're not there.")

Sherry: "I guess I feel sad that I'm not in touch with this part of me as much as I could be. It's like I can't transcend all the things my head keeps saying."

Jay: "So take a moment and go back again. Take another breath and let yourself be in that higher self place again."

Sherry: [pause] "I'm not getting there."

Jay: "What's happening?"

Sherry: "Somehow I think I shouldn't be there. I don't have the right to be there."

Jay: "You don't have the right to be your higher self?"

Sherry: "I feel like I haven't earned it, which I don't agree with. I mean there's this fight going on in my mind. [pauses] Just then I got this feeling that I'm very, very good, and it's OK for me to be there. In fact [very softly] I ought to be there."

Jay: "Good."

In this way Sherry took an important step toward feeling worthwhile and deserving of good things, and made a beginning in opening to her divine side. Notice that she was actually quite successful in contacting her higher self, even though she thought she wasn't. Her self-judgment came from low self-esteem, not from an accurate perception of how she was doing. When people do not feel good enough about themselves, it may be hard for them to accept the very positive self-image associated with being the higher self. They often manifest this problem by judging themselves negatively on their performance of the exercise.

You may also have noticed that I could have taken Sherry farther with the work; specifically I could have persisted in asking her to become the higher self and stay with it for a while, which she never allowed herself to do. This might have been valuable, but it also might have been more than she was ready for at the time. I decided that working through the issue of her deserving the higher self was enough for then.

During the eye contact part of the exercise, when she was not being asked to be her higher self, Sherry allowed herself to be fully present with her partner. Afterwards she described it to her partner: "I saw us sitting in a sandbox, and it made me feel this big bubble of [makes playful sound] really silly, and I felt almost embarrassed at how exuberant I felt. I saw tears in your eyes and I didn't know if you were getting that from me or I was getting it from you, but I felt it going back and forth, sharing the emotion."

A Related Experience

The issue of deserving to be powerful came up for Sherry in another exercise later in that same workshop. In the Expansive Movement exercise (chapter 15) people imagined being various animals and experimented with feeling their personal power through movement. When she was being a lion and also as an eagle, Sherry felt quite strong, though it felt strange and unfamiliar. Then she experienced a series of powerful images, feeling herself as the Sphinx; as a tall tree swaying; as Joan of Arc, riding on a horse, running through the woods, talking to voices. Each one of these was potent but embarrassing to her because of the personal power and self-worth inherent in the image.

Finally, she had an image of herself as the Blessed Mother, standing very straight and tall and strong, letting grace come through her open hands. This was a very clear higher self image, and the most powerful and difficult one for her. To imagine herself with such divine power and goodness was almost overwhelming, yet she took some steps toward believing that this is truly a part of her.

Notice that her superconscious was unrelenting. It kept presenting her with image after image of power and worth despite the protests of her ordinary self which had been programmed for self-deprecation. She came away from the workshop buzzing with a new sense of her inner depth and how much she might have to offer to the world, and feeling puzzled about whether to trust this. She continued to work on these issues in the Inner Journeys group, and she sought out other growth experiences which also confirmed and expanded her new sense of self. As a result she began taking more power in her relationship with her husband, and she started to explore how to use her talents more creatively in her work life. We will follow Sherry's development further as the book progresses.

Other Higher Selves

After opening to their child self and experiencing the contact between adult and child, most people are ready for the higher self.

One woman reported, "When I got to the higher power place, inside me was a wonderful fountain of energy moving up and energy moving down, at the same time and in equal parts." She had been exhausted that day, "and then on the inside this fountain took over, and it provided incredible energy. It felt like it was tuned to a higher source."

Another participant, John, described his experience of his higher self as follows: "As I got larger, I started to become more transparent and experienced breaking down into filaments of light that eventually merged with everything. I felt it go down into the earth, out into the atmosphere, through people. I felt this tremendous release and relief, like a lot of weight had been lifted off me, freed."

Even people who have done this kind of work before often encounter surprising and delightful images. Melissa reported, "When I got to the higher self, I got an unexpected set of images. There was a fire where her face should have been, a fountain of fire. The sparks flew up and up, and when they fell they were water. Now I realize that it is like a painting I've done of my version of the holy grail, which is a bowl of fire that's dripping water at the same time. It's my idea of abundance, which is what my higher self had to offer. What that higher self represents to me is all the energy in the universe, all the time, and it's absolutely trustworthy. I was watching the face fountain erupt like a volcano and then turn into wonderful water until I started dancing and splashing in the water as a child, and then I noticed that the water wasn't water, it was the Milky Way. I'm dancing on the Milky Way. [laughs delightedly] It was totally unexpected. I did not get any of the things I would normally have anticipated."

The Parts Come Together

The following experience illustrates how it can be important for the child, adult, and higher self to come together. Linda is a woman who was quite experienced with growth and spiritual work. She had already had experiences of contacting both her child and her higher self. She needed to strengthen the connections between them.

In this exercise, she saw her child as a 13-year-old sitting at the piano, experiencing the music "as a beam coming in from the source, coming down through me, through my heart and out of my hands." Then she felt herself at 13, choosing to cut off that flow at her wrists. She remembered getting messages from her parents that she didn't deserve to be alive, which she translated as not deserving to have things flow so easily. So in order to try to please her parents, she had cut off her creative flow and spent her time working and struggling to feel worthwhile.

"My bigger self was a tree. It was wonderful. I expanded and expanded. I felt my whole innards getting bigger. At the end I became a tree with a child in the heart and a mid-sized adult in there, too. That was real powerful, that last one." This was a healing of the experience she had at age 13 when she cut off her connection with her higher self.

Eye Contact

The eye contact part of the exercise gives people a chance to extend and deepen their experiences from the guided fantasy and to bring them into the interpersonal realm. They experience their different selves in connection with another person and see the other person's corresponding selves. It encourages people to open their hearts to a virtual stranger in a way that is very unusual in this society, and therefore expands people's sense of what is possible. The connections people make with each other are often deeply moving.

One man reported: "It was like I was an artist, and every time I would look at her face I would paint that face different because it had a different meaning, one time sensuality and love, another time she was dressed as if on a Greek island. I guess the theme that went through the whole exercise was love, loving myself, loving others. From that inner love that I have, being able to give something to other people."

John to his partner: "When I as a child looked at you as an adult, I felt no fear, just real open to you. I perceived a lot of goodness and warmth. When I looked at the child in you I saw a boy who had probably been the first friend in my whole life. I felt that sense of first reaching out to a friend. [As the higher self] looking at your eyes, your face, it was like a real oneness after a while. The sense of self stayed, but with the filaments dissolving into other filaments, it really was a sense of how everything's connected."

Melissa: "I realized, as we were working together, that Lena and I picked each other clearly the moment I walked in the door. She had all the qualities I wanted in a mother. She had a wonderful sense of fun and play, so most of my sharing with her was recognizing her mischief and her wickedness and liking it a lot." (Lena: "I'm going to adopt you.") "Fine. I accept." (group laughter)

Linda to her partner: "I've been sitting here feeling really connected to you, and I'm aware that whenever I've done an exercise like this, it creates this bond. My heart can feel you right here, and I could've been paired with anyone in the room, and I would feel that. Lately I've been asking myself—meditating on—how I hold love out of my heart and how I let it in. It's magical—something got opened in this exercise that probably won't go away."

2

Befriending Yourself

DURING THE TWO YEARS that I worked on developing a relationship with myself, one of the most important choices I made was to treat myself as if I were a close friend. There were many activities that previously I would not have chosen to do alone—going for a long hike in the forest or sitting up late at night going over important life issues. When I had done them alone I devalued the experiences, feeling they were poor substitutes for what I really wanted. During this time, however, I purposely chose to engage in these activities with myself, being a companion for myself, paying close attention to and valuing my experiences. Some of these times were very pleasant and some were rough, but through them all, I came to know myself as a friend.

When I felt bad I would sometimes turn to myself for comfort rather than to another person. I would hold myself and rock myself; I would imagine myself as a baby whom I was comforting and loving. When meditating, I would sometimes go into a very quiet space where I could sense myself as a presence in the silence, a presence that I could relate to. One Christmas Eve when I found myself alone, I designed and performed a ritual which affirmed my relationship with myself and also celebrated part of our Christmas tradition from my childhood.

After a while I found myself reacting differently to disappointment or rejection. When something happened to make me

sad, such as a rejection, my experience of the sadness was different. It felt less heavy, less bad. I no longer compounded the
sadness by feeling bad about myself for being the kind of person
who would be rejected. I felt only the sadness, and that was much
easier. Without fully realizing it, I was now supporting myself
through painful feelings.

In this exercise, you encounter yourself as a friend and
discover the potentials of this relationship.

Circumstances

This is the best single exercise for introducing the concept of a
relationship with yourself.

Time: 15 minutes.

The Exercise[1] ─────────────────────

[People arrange themselves for a guided fantasy. The leader starts
with an induction.]

Imagine that you are in your bedroom. Look around and see
how many of the details you can make out. . . . What feel do
you get from the room? . . . Walk over and look out the window.
How does the view affect you? . . .

Now walk into your kitchen, notice all the details, the
colors, the shapes, how things are organized. . . . What do you
smell? . . .

───────────

[1] The beginning part of this exercise is inspired by Joanna Macy's exercise
"Learning to See Each Other," *Despair and Personal Power in the Nuclear Age*,
p. 158. Her exercise is done in pairs and involves connecting deeply with a
stranger. I have adapted it here in connecting with oneself.

Now go into the bathroom and notice it in a similar way. . . . What feel do you get in that room? . . .

And now go into the living room and examine it also. . . . How comfortable is it? How pleasing is it to you visually? . . .

♪   "Rêve" (from *Opera Sauvage* by Vangelis, as much as needed; or other sad music)

Now imagine that you are expecting a visit from an old friend. You hear a knock on the door, and you get up and open it to let them in. The person who appears at the door is you. You may see yourself visually or sense your presence or hear your voice. . . . Invite this visitor who is you to sit down and you sit across from them. . . .

Let yourself feel friendly and caring, the way you would when meeting an old friend, and take in this person from that place. What do you notice about them? . . . Looking from a larger perspective, who is this person really? What is unique and special about them? . . .

Now as you look at this person, let yourself remember the pain they have experienced in their life, and open yourself to that. Feel your compassion for them, your empathy, just like you might with a friend in pain. . . . Hurts and sorrows are there, accumulated over a lifetime. Feel with this person in their disappointments and difficulties, their griefs and fears. This person has pains that they may never have shared with another person. Open yourself to them now, from your most caring place. . . . And become aware of your desire that this person be free from sorrow, and free from pain, and free from the causes of suffering. . . .

♪   "Neranzoula" (from *Odes* by Irene Papas and Vangelis, as much as needed; or other heart music)

Now become aware of the strengths and abilities and talents this person has. Appreciate them just the way you might appreciate a good friend. . . . Let yourself see and appreciate the gifts which they have already realized in their life, and also appreciate those hidden potentials that they may only be dimly aware of. . . . Deep inside this person may be reserves of ingenuity, wisdom, wit, endurance, loving. Open yourself to all of these, and feel your joy for them. . . .

Consider this person's potential, who they can become. Consider what this person might do, and be, and accomplish in the future, . . . and also consider how good it might feel to work together with them toward a common goal, to collaborate on a project, acting boldly and trusting each other, supporting each other through difficulties, inspiring each other. . . .

♪   "Seapeace" (from *Seapeace* by Georgia Kelly, as much as needed; or other heart music)

Do you need a special friend? Do you need someone to love, to confide in, to be intimate with? You have one deep inside you whom you may not have noticed. Your friend is there and has been there all along. You may not have been looking in the right place, in the right way. Feel the possibility of having that special friend, feel your desire for that connection, open yourself to the yearning for that unique bond, deep inside. . . .

Now once again imagine that you are sitting with yourself. Make eye contact, feel the other presence, take in this person who could be this special friend. . . . They've been with you a long time; they know you well. You've been through a lot together. They know your deepest fears and greatest hopes. They've shared a lifetime with you. They've criticized you and cared for you, fought you and loved you. Feel that deep connection. . . .

Spend some time talking with this special friend, especially talking with them about your relationship. Tell them how you are feeling toward them right now, . . . and how you usually feel toward them. . . . Talk about what your relationship has been like in the past. Have you paid much attention to it? Has it been rocky? Has it been close? . . . What has changed over time? . . . What do you want for the relationship in the future? What are your hopes and fears? . . . Are there any requests you want to make? Any limits you want to set? [Allow a minute.]

Remember that this special friend will always be with you to confide in, to spend time with, to care for you in bad times, to share joys, to help figure out difficulties. No failure, no rejection, no abandonment can ever part you. You will never be alone. . . .

Open your heart to this person now. Feel the love beyond reason, beyond deserving. Feel the deep connection with yourself that can never be broken. . . . From this place of strength you can love others more freely, from this place of peace you can risk more easily. Feel this place of deep self-connection and know yourself whole. . . .

Now let something emerge from your unconscious which represents this loving relationship with yourself. It could be an image, or a phrase, or a physical sensation, or all three. . . . Hold this in your heart as an anchor, as a way of remembering this connection you have now. In the months ahead, if you are out of touch with yourself, use it to bring back the bond, to renew this experience of love and connection with yourself that you are now feeling. [Allow half a minute. Then bring them out of trance.]

♪   Simplified music: Use "Seapeace" all the way through.

Experiences

The Plant That Grows Back

Sandra is a 45-year-old optician whose major personal issue revolves around strength and weakness. She has been a timid, fearful person who, though very open and talented, has had trouble realizing her potential because of her fear of stepping out in the world and her tendency to collapse under pressure. She joined the Inner Journeys group to work on developing her strength and self-confidence, and also to discover a deeper sense of purpose and a way to express her creativity.

She described her experience in the exercise as follows: "When I first looked at her on the couch across from me, I realized that [crying] I didn't consider myself worth having as a friend. But then when you asked me to appreciate her, I could see how strong she was and the good qualities she had. And I really wanted to look deeply into her eyes. It was even more powerful than when I did it before with [a group member] because now it was like looking into this person who was who I am.

"I really wanted to have her as a friend. I'm doing some new and risky things right now, and I asked her to support me through them, and maybe even to appreciate me for what I'm doing. She was quite willing to do that. I imagined that whatever I tried, I would be taking this friend with me, and that was a comfort. Whatever situation I found myself in, we'd be able to check in with each other to see if it felt right.

"The symbol of this friendship that came to me was a plant that was growing right up out of my body and flowering, with the roots going down through me into the center of the earth. It felt like it was a plant that was so strong [deeply moved] that even if you broke off the top it would keep on growing." [crying]

Jay: "Can you feel that strength in yourself now?"

Sandra: "It's like I can feel the strength, but I still have a shadowy fear that I will become this very frightened person. I have a feeling of strength, but it can slip away from me in an instant. I hate feeling that I can't depend on that strength and courage."

Jay: "But it also can come back in an instant."

Sandra: "Yes. It's like this continual back and forth. I guess I'm more familiar with the fright than the strength. If I could just balance them some. I feel like I'm not asking too much." [crying helplessly]

Jay: "Certainly in here I've seen your strong side coming out more and more. Is that happening in your life?"

Sandra: "I feel like it is."

Jay: "You're focusing now on your fear of falling into the scared part, and even though that happens, I want you to focus instead on the fact that the strong part is growing. And that even though you fall into the scared part, you also come back to the strong part. Instead of desperately trying to hold on to the strong for fear of losing it, just be with it lightly and trust yourself."

Sandra: "That's right. I've experienced that in other ways, that if I stop fighting the fear, it does go away. [She gives an example from a dream.] It was the fighting that caused the difficulty."

Jay: "You know that wonderful plant image you had, let yourself come back to that now. Go into that image and feel it."

Sandra: [pauses] "I can see it now, the way it branches out. It has orange flowers on it."

Jay: "Even if the top got cut off, it would have the strength to regrow. [Sandra: 'Yes.'] OK, so even if you fall into the scared part, which is like having the top cut off, [Sandra: 'Oh, yeah!'] the strength is still there. So, feel that in yourself."

Sandra: "Right now it's like the plant is here [indicating her torso and legs] and the tops have been broken off, but it's definitely all through my center."

Jay: "Right, good. Just stay with that, and know that you can always come back to it. Even if the tops are broken off, even if you're scared and weak, the plant is still there, and it will grow again."

Sandra: "Yes, I can see that I can grow back quickly. It's almost like teasing. If it's not safe . . . " She imitates the teasing. The group laughs.

Jay: "The plant's teasing you?"

Sandra: "The plant's teasing . . . the world."

Jay: "Oh, the world. OK, tease us some."

Sandra: Nonverbally acts like a plant playing hide and
seek, in a shy, seductive way, full of life. The group loves it.

Jay: "Wonderful!"

So Sandra made some real progress in developing a relationship with herself and coming to appreciate her resiliency. We
will meet Sandra in later chapters as she works further on this
issue and also begins to discover her sense of life purpose.

Notice the potency of imaging a symbol for her self-relationship. It can be used not only to refer back to the experience later,
but also as a medium for working through difficulties.

A Fun-loving Friend

Judy is a 35-year-old nurse practitioner who was in the process of
ending her marriage. She had never really felt seen or understood
by her parents, and spent many years looking for this in relationships with men. She found in her husband someone who appreciated her for the first time in her life, and though this acknowledg-
ment was healing, it also encouraged her to become dependent on
him. When he decided to end the marriage, she was devastated.
During the exercise, she realized that she had always been afraid
to be alone in the world, had negated herself as a best friend, and
had looked to her husband and others to fill those needs.

She had also learned early in her life that it was important
to please her parents by being a "good girl." Her need for the
approval of others carried over into her adult life, and she became
staid and proper, a "nice lady" whose inhibitions made her appear
older than her years. In the exercise, she found herself relating
to a much younger (teenage) version of herself, who was fresh
and full of fun, who was rebellious and defiant and didn't care
what other people thought of her. They kidded and laughed and
spent time just hanging out together. Judy envisioned taking the
younger self along with her to work and other places as a charm-
ing, vital playmate.

In this way, Judy made progress on two issues at once. She began to provide for herself the care and companionship she had always needed from others, and she opened up the aliveness and spontaneity that had been suppressed all her life. We will follow these themes further with Judy in later chapters.

Working Through Difficulties

Those people who don't manage to connect well with themselves during the exercise are able to pinpoint exactly where they had trouble, thus facilitating later work. For example, Barbara had trouble during the compassion part of the exercise. At one point she was experiencing herself as the one who was receiving the compassion: "I had this compassionate, warm, loving, accepting friend, which I understand and need, but she looks like this blob." Barbara had been a dancer all her life, but when she stopped she put on a great deal of weight. She realized that she associated compassion with being heavy (because of her mother), and this contributed to her difficulty in losing the weight. In her individual work she became the thin dancer self and danced her compassion for herself.

3

Reowning the Shadow

W E ALL HAVE PARTS of ourselves that we feel bad about without even knowing it. The shadow is a Jungian concept that refers to those parts of ourselves which we have disowned because we have been taught to feel that they are unacceptable or "bad."[1] Our shadow sides actually contain what are potentially positive characteristics, but we have been trained to feel ashamed or guilty about them, so we deny them in ourselves. As a result they become represented in the unconscious in a distorted, perverted form, so that when the shadow comes up in a dream or guided fantasy, it may appear evil or repulsive. For example:

1. Disowned assertiveness might appear as violence or exaggerated macho behavior.

2. Disowned sadness might appear as self-pity.

3. Disowned sexuality might appear as sexual promiscuity or perversion.

4. A disowned need for intimacy might appear as "clingy-ness" and dependency.

---

[1] June Singer, *Boundaries of the Soul* (New York: Anchor, 1973), p. 215–227.

My Experience

The inspiration for this exercise came out of my own explorations of shadow. One of my significant disowned qualities was aggression, a kind of raw, earthy, bodily power. I am one of those men who is repulsed by the perversion of aggressive masculine energy that pervades our society in the form of macho attitudes, militarism, violence, excessive competition, and other forces that are threatening to destroy the planet. I have spent many years developing my softer, feminine side and have been well rewarded for my efforts, but in the process I also disowned the healthy side of my aggression.

I had been noticing for months that violent images were emerging from my unconscious. In dreams and guided fantasies I frequently encountered ravening beasts, devils, and other horrible images. For a while I avoided dealing with them. I didn't want to acknowledge that these creatures were roaming around in my head, but I finally realized that they weren't going to go away. I had to deal with them. I believe that (like everyone) at the core I am a loving, life-affirming person, and if I go exploring inside I will eventually reach that positive core. So I knew I needed to act on that belief and face those horrible images.

One weekend I rented a cabin in the forest in order to spend some time in nature alone. On Saturday afternoon I went hiking and found a lovely spot where I could sit quietly on the bank of a river. As I sat there I gradually slowed down and went deep inside myself. I wasn't surprised when one of those horrible images arose—a sea serpent with a huge mouth, gigantic teeth, and a wicked, murderous look on his face. I decided to face it this time, so I stayed with the image and let a fantasy unfold. I somehow entered the serpent's mouth and proceeded to take a trip down his throat, which was inexplicably lined with red velvet. I seemed to go down and down forever, as I went deeper into trance.

When I reached the bottom, I emerged from the throat into a wilderness area. There I was confronted by a large, angry bear.

He roared at me and whacked me around a little, although I was not hurt. He was angry because I had been ignoring him, and his roaring and attacking was to get my attention and to let me know that he was an important part of me. I accepted the message and was able to consciously own the aggressive part of me that he represented.

When I left the river to hike back to my cabin, I had an uphill climb through wild country, and I reveled in the physical exertion of it. I felt myself as the bear, striding powerfully, running, leaping, feeling the strength of my body in a new and exciting way. I was reowning my shadow physically as well as psychologically. The whole experience was so meaningful to me that I based this exercise on it.

Good and Evil

Exploring the shadow brings up the whole question of the intrinsic moral qualities of human beings. Are we basically amoral, overly sexual, aggressive, selfish beings who must be socialized in order to curb our wild, anti-social nature? This is the philosophy of orthodox Freudians, fundamentalists, and many political conservatives. Or are we basically good—loving, cooperative, caring—as long as our family and social environments nurture us and support our growth? This is the point of view of humanistic psychologists, political progressives, and many others.

Clearly I hold the second point of view. I believe that when we see evil in ourselves, it is either an illusion of shadow or the residue of painful life experiences. That is, it may derive from a distortion of our naturally good tendencies, a distortion caused by inadequate parenting or destructive life situations. Thus whenever you find something in yourself that seems bad or destructive, I believe you can trust yourself to explore it deeply. When you get to the bottom of it, the evil will vanish. You may find that the only problem is that you were taught to feel bad about that part of yourself. At worst you will find that your destructive behavior comes from a twisting of healthy impulses and intentions, which can be straightened out again by working through what originally caused the distortion.

Projection

When we disown our shadow sides, we may feel tempted to project them unconsciously onto others; that is, to attribute to others those things that we want to deny in ourselves. For example, if someone is needy but is unconsciously denying their neediness, they will be especially attuned to any sign of need in others and quick to condemn it. They will certainly exaggerate the amount of neediness they see, and they may even see it when it isn't there.

Until recently, projection of shadow has assumed its most dangerous form in international superpower politics. The United States and the Soviet Union have tended to deny their own shadow qualities (exploitation and repression of their people, domination of other countries, warlike tendencies) and to paint themselves as the embodiment of good and right in the world, while attributing all manner of evil to the other. Of course, in both cases there are real evils to see in the other, but the projection has prevented us from seeing the things we need to clean up at home, and also has kept us in a dangerous arms race. With the current changes in the Soviet Union and the ending of the Cold War, this projection is disappearing. Let's hope we don't pick a new national enemy to project onto.

Circumstances

This is a very powerful exercise. Since it takes you into parts of yourself that you feel bad about, you need to approach it with great care. It should be used only when there is sufficient trust and support in the group and enough time afterward for you to work through difficulties that arise. When using this exercise with people who may have serious personal problems, the group should be led by a psychotherapist (or someone with comparable skills) who can help them process the material that may emerge. If you are not working with a professional, make sure you have made some arrangements for dealing with whatever may come up. See "Dealing with Difficulties" on page xxxvi.

Time: 25 minutes.

The Exercise ─────────────────────────

It is not necessary for you to figure out what your particular shadow is beforehand; that will emerge from your unconscious during the exercise. If the exercise feels threatening, remember that your shadow side really contains positive characteristics and that these will emerge as the exercise unfolds if you stay with it.

[People arrange themselves for a guided fantasy. The leader starts out with an induction.]

Now you will be going down a deep cavity of some sort. It might be a well, or an elevator, or a staircase, or a mine shaft, or the throat of a whale or sea monster, or a hole in the ocean floor. You may climb down, or fall, or float down, or be carried down, or move down in some other way. Let this happen now. . . .

Feel the sensation of moving down the cavity. . . . Observe the walls; what material are they made of? Reach out and touch them. . . . You begin to notice that scenes appear at intervals in the walls as you move down. You see an image of an animal or bird. . . . As you continue to move down, you move on past that scene. Now you see a beautiful natural landscape. . . . You move on down below that scene as you continue to descend through the cavity, moving deeper into your psyche as you go.

[Continue describing scenes and mentioning the downward movement in both cavity and psyche. The entire sequence of scenes[2] is as follows:

an animal or bird,

a beautiful natural landscape,

a scene from your present life,

a scene from your life of about 10 years ago,

a scene from your high school years,

a childhood scene,

an event that has made world headlines recently,

a world event of 10 years ago,

a world event of 100 years ago, and

a scene from ancient times.]

Now you see that you are nearing the bottom of the cavity. . . . You finally reach the bottom, landing without difficulty. Notice what it is like there. . . . There is a door in the wall or floor of the cavity. Open it and move through. You are now entering shadow country. . . .

♪   *Ignacio* (second movement by Vangelis; eerie, dark tone, gradually moving to a sweet, uplifting tone; slow, spiritual quality)

Look around shadow country. Get a feel for the place. What is it like down there? . . . As you are taking in your surroundings, you hear a noise behind you. You turn around and see a figure who represents your shadow. It could be a person, an animal, a mythological creature, god, devil, etc. Envision it or sense it.

---

[2] The form of this induction is taken from exercises by Jean Houston.

What does it look like, how does it feel to you, what is it doing? . . . It now begins to interact with you according to its nature and according to the message that is has for you. The interaction could be verbal or physical; it could be friendly or unfriendly. Let this happen now. [Allow about a minute.]

Finish the interaction. . . . Now you are going to become the shadow figure. Feel what it is like to be in that body, to see out of those eyes, to experience the world that way. . . . Begin to explore the shadow country and to do things as the shadow figure. What is it that you want or need? Who or what do you encounter? What happens? How do you feel? It is essential that you do this with total acceptance and even enjoyment of who you are. Let go of all judgment, all doubt, no matter how strange or awful your actions might seem to you normally. You are fully the shadow figure; you want to do all these things and you understand why. You are invested in what you are doing and you feel OK about yourself. [Allow about a minute.]

You now begin to notice that your actions and feelings as shadow are changing, being transformed. Continue exploring shadow country, letting your activity begin to exhibit the true life-affirming nature of the shadow that was hidden before. Having dropped judgment and fully experienced yourself as shadow, you are now being transformed. That part of you that might have seemed evil before is now clearly revealed to have a healthy, positive side. As you continue to explore the country, you are more and more in touch with the strengths and positive qualities which you had previously disowned. [Allow about a minute.]

And now, having reowned these discounted parts of yourself and experienced the positive side of your shadow, take some time to explicitly recognize these strengths. Be fully in touch with these positive qualities in yourself and affirm them. Say 'I recognize my assertiveness' or gentleness, or sexiness, or whatever your positive qualities are. Affirm your newly discovered strengths. Feel your wholeness. [Allow until the end of the music, another minute or so.]

You now return to the place where you entered shadow
country and begin to go back up the way you came down, . . .
passing scenes from the world, . . . scenes from your life, . . .
scenes from the natural world, . . . and finally coming out the
top of the cavity. [Then bring them out of trance, and have them
very gradually stand up.]

You will have an opportunity now to explore your shadow
even further through free-form movement. You will be moving
as the transformed shadow, or if you have not yet fully made the
transformation, you may begin the movement as the original
shadow, and let the transformation complete itself as you go. If
you have not gotten far enough with your shadow to be ready for
movement work at this time, it is perfectly OK to sit out this part
of the exercise.

♪   "Fata Morgana" (from *Tunhuang* by Kitaro; danceable, neutral
      tone)

Close your eyes. Get in touch with your transformed or original
shadow. Take a position which reflects your shadow figure—
standing, sitting, crouching, etc. As the music begins, start exploring the room as if it were shadow country. Let your sense of
the shadow come fully into your body. Feel those shadow qualities, those newly-owned strengths as you move. [Allow a couple
of minutes.] And now if it feels appropriate, interact with others
in the room from this place. [Allow until the end of the music,
another couple of minutes.]

♪   *Heaven and Hell* (next to last cut on first side, by Vangelis; or
      other celebratory music)

And now as the music changes, let your movement become a
dance, a dance of celebration of your transformed shadow, a
celebration of those qualities that you are discovering in yourself.
Ground them deeply in your body, in your movement, and feel
the expansion of who you know yourself to be! [Allow until the
music ends, about 4 minutes.]

♪ Simplified music: Use the *Ignacio* cut as above. This piece is
   important for the power of this exercise; use it if at all possible.

Experiences

This exercise evokes powerful and deep responses in many people.
Reowning and transforming one's shadow is not an easy task; it
takes courage and ongoing work. Not everyone will be able to
complete this exercise the first time. Those who do are usually
deeply moved and changed by the experience. Some of those who
don't are left in pain, so it is very important to allow sufficient
time afterward for individual work. Usually when a person gets
into difficulty during the exercise, the symbols and feelings are so
potent that a great deal can be accomplished afterwards.

Part of the power of the exercise comes from the particular
music that is used. The evil, haunting tone of the beginning is
a powerful evocation of shadow, and the transformation happens
in a complex and gradual way in the music just as it must in the
psyche. I recommend experimenting with the coordination of the
instructions and the changes in the music. I found that I needed
more time with the dark part of the theme, so I taped a version
with the first couple of minutes of the piece repeated.

Sometimes a person meets a shadow figure that they can
intuitively understand or whose meaning readily unfolds during
the exercise. This makes it fairly easy for the person to have the
courage to identify with the shadow and trust that something
positive will emerge. This was true for me in my experience with
the bear, and also in the following examples.

The Wrestler

We met Sandra in the last chapter, with her image of the plant
that grows back. She is a petite woman struggling to develop her
inner strength. In this exercise, she found that her shadow figure

was a huge, powerful, mean professional wrestler. When she became the wrestler, she felt so powerful that she was not afraid of anything. This is a perfect illustration of how her disowned strength showed itself in a negative form in her psyche. As the transformation happened, she was pleased to find that because of her lack of fear she no longer felt any need to be violent. During the movement part of the exercise, she enhanced the experience of her strength by feeling it in her chest and arms and in her legs as she danced.

The Street Tough

Bill is a 38-year-old teacher who was drawn to Inner Journeys work because of his fears about nuclear war and his desire to do something about it. Despite his strong feelings about the issue, he had not found an organization to become involved with or a project that he could follow through on. As our work progressed it became clear that these difficulties were because of his lack of self-confidence and a tendency to sabotage himself.

Bill's shadow figure also dealt with power and violence. His was a death figure who engaged in various forms of mayhem—stabbing, bombing, car crashes. After he became the figure, it transformed into an angry tough guy who knew how to get things to happen. What Bill had disowned was not his anger or aggression, but his ability to accomplish things. His transformed shadow figure was able to use his aggression in the service of accomplishment. After the exercise, he took his work a step further by risking showing the group his transformed shadow. He acted out the street tough for us, with characteristic voice and gestures: "Hey man, I know exactly what I'm gonna do, and nobody gets in my way or you'll be sorry." We'll follow Bill throughout the book as he works through his personal issues and becomes empowered to take action on the nuclear threat.

The Engulfing Slime

Sometimes a shadow figure emerges that has no apparent meaning for the person, or is so negative that they balk at identifying with it. Then it takes extraordinary courage, or help from the leader, to complete the exercise successfully. Judy is the woman from the last chapter who made friends with a teenage version of herself. Her shadow figure was a kind of slime or gooey sludge. She wasn't really able to identify with it in the exercise, but in working with her individually afterward, I was able to help her reown and then transform it.

As she became the slime, she realized that she wanted to move all over and surround people or objects. To explore this she began to slime all over a pillow. At first all she could focus on was how bad she was for not caring about the pillow, but then as the transformation happened, she realized that she desperately wanted physical contact, that she was very needy. The uncaring, engulfing slime was the shadow representation of her disowned needs for touch and comfort.

As she went further into the neediness, she felt like a baby in her crib, crying out for physical contact and not getting it. At this point the shadow was transformed and she felt completely OK about having those needs. After she fully experienced the pain of the baby, I encouraged her to imagine getting the touch she needed, thus providing a healing counterpart to her original deprivation. In this way Judy took another step in working through her dependency. It comes up in a different form in chapter 5.

The Princess and the Tornado

Sherry is the woman from the first exercise who had trouble feeling that she deserved to be her higher self. The following individual work occurred after another exercise. I have placed it here because it is a beautiful example of the unknown shadow. In that exercise, people made a journey to the top of a tower where they met an archetypal figure who gave them their inheritance—an ability connected with their life purpose. (The fantasy involved imagining a huge spiral.)

Sherry had had trouble with part of the instructions which involved doing three or four things at once. When she couldn't do it exactly right, she became confused. I said it was OK not to do the exercise exactly as instructed. She responded, "But my problem is I keep trying to be perfect, and if I'm not doing it right, then I make myself crazy." She then described her journey up the tower.

Sherry: "At the top of the tower was a beautiful, sun-filled castle room with a big bay window. Sitting in the window seat was a children's-story fairy princess with the pointed hat and the gauzy dress and the blonde hair and blue eyes. As I approached her she said, 'This is how you think I am. You have this fantasy that if you were perfect, this is how you would be. You would be a blonde, blue-eyed princess with an hour-glass figure. She took off the pointy hat and said, 'No, that's not who I am, and it's not who you are. And that's OK, because you are a princess anyway but that's not how princesses really look.' That was very comforting.

"We looked out of the bay window over this beautiful landscape—the realm, and my inheritance was appreciation, that I could see things and appreciate them as they are. I could really see things, not just look at them, but see, see the beauty in things, see the good in things. But the vortex thing was very hard for me because I kept seeing a tornado. It was more like a sucking, destructive whirlwind than the reaching thing. It was hidden, untapped power that was barely contained and could be destructive."

Jay: "And that was part of your inheritance, too?"

Sherry: "Maybe. I didn't give it much thought at the time."

Jay: "Certainly untapped power that can be destructive, can also be creative. If you're interested let's try something."

Sherry: "Sure."

Jay: "Put yourself back in the tower room, looking out the window and getting a sense of your inheritance of appreciation and ability to see, to see deeply into things. . . . Let me know when you're there."

Sherry: "Mm hm. I'm there."

Jay: "Keep looking out the window, and now you're going to see the tornado, the vortex. Use your ability to see and appreciate to look at the tornado and to see deeply into it."

Sherry: "I see that it's very, very powerful. It's swirling, and there's things caught up in it—houses and trees and animals and people and broken things all swirling around in it. It's on the horizon."

Jay: "Keep looking, keep using your inheritance of appreciation and ability to see past the surface of things."

Sherry: "How can I appreciate something that's so destructive, that's threatening the realm? There's this beautiful, peaceful kingdom, and on the horizon is a threatening tornado capable of destroying villages and people and everything in its path. It's pretty hard to appreciate something like that. It's going to hurt people, it's going to hurt the earth. It's not beautiful, it's ugly! It's dark, it's destructive, [crying] and it is also me."

Jay: "How is it you?"

Sherry: "'Cause I am like a tornado. I tear through things and break things and destroy things and push through things and hurt people [still crying.] It's looming on the horizon and I'm running away. I don't want to be that thing; I want to be the fairy princess [general laughter]."

Jay: "Do you remember the shadow exercise we did? This didn't come up in your shadow exercise, but this tornado is an aspect of your shadow. I want to propose something. Like we did in the shadow exercise, you would become the tornado and

identify with it. You would revel in its power and whatever else
you experience as a tornado, including the destructiveness if
that's what happens. And through that you would transform your
shadow into its positive aspects that have been hidden because
you didn't accept them. So if you're interested I'd like you to try
it."

Sherry: "All right."

Jay: "So be the tornado, and really feel yourself as a tornado. Drop all of your judgments, any idea that there's something
evil or bad or wrong about this, and allow yourself to be whatever
you are as a tornado. You might be whipping around or picking
up houses or playing with your power or your wind or whatever
else. Be fully there, being it and enjoying it, just letting yourself
go, with no judgment at all. Describe what that feels like as you
do it."

Sherry: "I'm just whirling around and moving forward. I'm
at the top of it so I can see where I'm going. When I bump into
things, instead of hurting me, I just knock them down. And
anything that gets in my way just gets tossed aside."

Jay: "Good. Keep going and enjoy it; get into it! Feel it.
Be with that power, knocking things aside."

Sherry: "Just break things. I don't care what they're worth;
I just break them. Houses become like little sticks. I just pull
things up, and I don't care if they break. I don't have to be
careful. [pouting] I'm tired of being careful! [some anger]."

Jay: "Good, go with that."

Sherry: "I don't have to be careful. I don't care about any
of these things. [more anger] They're not mine. I can break
them. Let somebody else pick up the pieces. Take that! [general
laughter] Boom!" [flinging her arms around]

Jay: "Good, good. Do that some more. Keep going."

Sherry: "Boom! There goes an apple tree! [gleeful] Who
cares if I pull it out by the roots." [still flinging her arms around]

Jay: "Good, enjoy that power, and the abandon."

Sherry: "And there goes a window!" She pauses.

Jay: "And now start talking about the positive aspects you got in touch with in yourself."

Sherry: [laughs] "I can't be hurt. I hurt other . . . not that I hurt other things, but that other things can't hurt me. I'm bigger than they are. I'm more powerful than the things that would want to hurt me. I have great speed and force to move forward. I can move in any direction I want. Nothing can get in the way."

Jay: "And there's an abandon, there's a freedom," [Sherry: "Freedom."] "a lack of constraint, a lack of worrying and holding yourself back. There's a liveliness."

Sherry: "Yeah. Space, spaciousness, of having tremendous room. Everybody makes room for me:"

Jay: "It's the opposite of trying to be perfect, isn't it?" [general laughter]

Sherry: "If I can't be perfect, the hell with it! I'll be a tornado." [more laughter]

Jay: "There's a freedom from worrying what other people think, and what's going to happen. There's a kind of looseness."

Sherry: "Not worrying what other people think. The realm was very peaceful, but it was also very . . . it was like stick figures, little wooden farms that you'd find in a toy store. It needed to be shaken up."

In this work Sherry is learning to own her personal power and assertiveness, as well as her freedom and spontaneity. Many women are taught to feel that their power is somehow bad and destructive, and so they deny it and it appears in the deep psyche in forms such as the tornado. Men, of course, have the opposite dilemma; they are taught to disown their soft, gentle sides. Ideally, rather than becoming one-sided according to our gender conditioning, we all need to integrate our strength with our caring.

Later that day during another exercise, Sherry saw the tornado become small. It was drawn up the tower stairs and into the hand of the princess, so that they could work together. She would guide its power with her love. In this lovely way Sherry took an important step toward integrating these two sides of her psyche. As a result, she became less afraid of her own power and more willing to take risks that involved possible conflict or confrontation.

The Monk and the Priest

As I mentioned before, the term shadow is often applied indiscriminately to any dark or negative side of the self. Indeed, these other sides sometimes emerge during this exercise, despite the most careful definition of shadow at the beginning. Some people encounter shadow figures that represent not disowned positive aspects of themselves, but actual destructive or self-destructive parts. These shadow figures are often internalized versions of people who have hurt the person.

When this happens, the transformation cannot happen exactly as it is designed to in the exercise, because there isn't a disowned positive part hidden in the shadow image. The shadow must be transformed into the opposite or healing version of the original shadow. This is illustrated by the following example, which also comes from Sherry:

The shadow country was medieval catacombs, and Sherry's shadow figure was a dark, rigid, faceless monk, who was writing down everything she had done wrong in her entire life. He was coldly keeping track of all her sins so he could pass judgment on her when she died. This represented her internalized image of a part of the Catholic Church. She was deeply upset by her fear that she couldn't rely on her own sense of right and wrong, but would burn in hell if she disobeyed the church. Here we can begin to get a sense of why Sherry had trouble feeling worthwhile.

However, she managed to find within her depths a healing version of the monk, a spiritual figure who symbolized her ability to trust her own internal sense of morality. This was a priest who was marching with the farmworkers, singing a resistance song. He knew in his heart what was right and what was wrong without relying on external rules, and he acted on this knowledge. He cared about the poor and disenfranchised, and he devoted his life to helping them. As she contacted this active, loving part of herself, she felt free again and reinvigorated.

This completed the shadow exercise for Sherry at that moment, but later in the day, while doing a different exercise, her unconscious took it a step further, and she encountered a positive side of the original monk. He was sitting at a desk in an academic setting—reading, writing, studying. He was lighter, no longer cold or rigid. He represented the search for knowledge and the desire to make knowledge available to all people. He represented the teacher and networker in her, providing information and opportunities for people to advance themselves.

Looked at more closely, the distinction I have been making between disowned positive parts and truly negative parts begins to blur. I believe that all of our negative parts contain at least a kernel of positive intent, and that the best way to change them is to begin by accepting them (see chapter 6). Perhaps the most significant aspect of this exercise is the self-acceptance that comes through harvesting the positive part of the shadow.

For example, for one woman, Marcy, her shadow represented such a deeply hated part of her, that she was unable to reown any of it during the exercise or even to tell us what it was. But she did consider the possibility that it might actually have a positive side, and even this much was deeply moving to her. In this way she took a first step toward loving herself.

SECTION TWO

Opening the Heart

Introduction

LOVING AND BEING LOVED—isn't that what we all really want out of life? Yet it can be so difficult to achieve.

We are all born with an open heart, but for it to stay open we need high quality care. We need to be loved for who we are and supported in developing our own sense of separateness. We also need to feel that our love is received, that it is OK for us as children to love our parents. When we don't receive this kind of parenting we must defend ourselves against the pain, and so we close our hearts.

If we are not loved enough or if the love we are given is conditional, we eventually have to defend ourselves from the hurt and the unfulfilled longing. This also shields us from our own love feelings. If we are rejected or judged, made to feel guilty or inadequate, we also close our hearts to protect against these feelings. If we are intruded on or smothered, we may harden ourselves in order to protect our autonomy and integrity. In all these ways we can lose our open-heartedness.

Of course with all the complexities of adult life, providing ideal nurturing is a tall order for our parents, who are only human after all, so all of us have had to close our hearts to a certain extent. As we grow and struggle to open our hearts again, we may have to deal with the vulnerability that this brings, the fear of rejection or criticism. Old pain and grief may resurface along with dependency needs. We may have to work through the fear of being used or smothered, the danger of giving away our power.

Men are especially likely to have difficulty with this because we have been conditioned to devalue softness and vulnerability and our need for relatedness and to value independence and toughness. A man may feel that it is OK to love someone who is dependent on him, such as a child, because that leaves him in control and able to defend against his own vulnerable feelings. But letting go and opening up his needs and softness can be experienced as shameful and threatening.

As a young adult my heart was pretty closed. Through my background and conditioning as an American WASP male and a scientist, I developed a mechanical approach to life and a strong need for control. Even though I was married for five years during my twenties and quite attached to my wife, I wasn't capable of really loving her. In therapy I worked through many of the personal issues that had caused me to close down, and I also worked on releasing the tension and chronic holding in my body, which literally had constricted my heart. On more than one occasion as my heart was opening, I could feel small sharp pains in the physical organ as the long-term constriction was melting away. Gradually my heart began to open, and I found a softness and a hitherto unknown access to my depths. However, along with this I had to deal with dependency issues that emerged.

Because of the vulnerable, needy feelings that arise as you open your heart, you may close back down again in order to regain your strength. Men are especially prone to this attitude because we have been taught that our self-esteem depends on always being strong and in control. Again and again I have felt like I had to choose between being open and needy or closed and strong. However, opening your heart is not weakness although it can reveal a weakness that was already there. On the contrary, it takes great strength and courage to open yourself and to meet the world with love and vulnerability.

Slowly, as I worked through my neediness and became more self-supporting, I became less afraid of rejection. I found it easier to be loving, especially in a primary relationship. This has been tremendously rewarding. In my current relationship I have been able to love fully from my core without much fear of rejection or danger of losing myself. And my love has been returned in full, allowing a deep intimacy to develop.

The Meaning of Love

Love is a tremendous source of strength; giving love is perhaps even more nourishing than receiving it. To open your heart fully and experience the wonderful reservoir of love inside is not only a great pleasure, but a potent reminder of your essential goodness and power.

Perhaps the most profound and meaningful experiences of my life have involved opening my heart. Those times when I have felt closest to experiencing what life is all about have come when I felt suffused with love. I remember especially a time when I was vacationing in the woods. As a result of some consciousness exercises my heart opened to an unusual extent. It was bursting forth with love for myself, my partner, my friends, and everything around me. I felt a soft, sweet melting that was truly ecstatic. I walked outside the cabin into the forest and found myself literally in love with the trees! This experience has remained with me as an inspiration and a reminder of what is truly possible.

Opening the heart involves a loosening of boundaries between yourself and those that you love. It means opening yourself to others' experience of life, empathizing with them, seeing deeply who they really are. It means caring about them, placing their welfare on a par with yours. In love you let go of that rigid sense of self-protection and personal striving. You feel yourself united with your beloved, and this brings joy and a freedom from the narrow confines of the ordinary self.

Many philosophies and spiritual traditions see love as the basic meaning of life or perhaps even the very ground of existence, as exemplified by the saying from the Course in Miracles, "Teach only love, for that is what you are." The central goal of many spiritual traditions is to love God or spirit, and through this to bring your love to all of the world around you. In mystical states, people have loosened their boundaries to such an extent that they have felt united in love with all of humanity, even all of creation. From these experiences have come profound and lasting personality changes which have led many people to lives of inspiration and extraordinary service to the world.

In studies of near-death experiences,[1] which seem to provide an unbiased glimpse of the spiritual realm, people frequently encountered a being or presence who radiated unconditional love of a purity and intensity far surpassing anything they had previously experienced. When some of them were led to review their lives to see what they had accomplished of their life purpose, the criterion invariably used was how much they had loved.

The lack of love in the world generally at this time is one of the major contributing factors to the crisis we are facing. As individuals, groups, and nations, we tend to relate not with love, but with competition, domination, dependence, or mechanical indifference. These attitudes breed hatred and fear, paranoia and manipulation. The healthy society we need to create must be built on love, in all of its varieties.

This doesn't mean that the solution is as simple as "love everyone." Our unloving, destructive attitudes are woven into our cultural values and our institutions, into the very fabric of our society, and changing them will require more than just learning to love. But love is an essential ingredient in that change.

---

[1] Kenneth Ring, *Heading toward Omega* (New York: Quill, 1984).

Love is not just interpersonal; it has many forms. There is love of your community, your ethnic or religious group, love of humanity. There is love of your home, your land, love of the earth and its creatures, love of God or spirit. Love has many different meanings and covers a wide variety of feelings, attitudes, and behaviors—from romantic love to altruistic love, from erotic love to spiritual love, from parental love to brotherly love. The first exercise in this section deals with love in all its forms; the others are more specific. The exercises in this section are as follows:

Opening the Heart
Nurturing Touch
Acceptance

The following exercises also deal with opening the heart:

The Child and the Higher Self
Befriending Yourself
Planetary Compassion
Envisioning a Healthy Society
The Naming Ritual
The Expanded Body
Surrendering the Heart

4

Opening the Heart

THIS EXERCISE ENCOURAGES you to open your heart in order to experience the full extent and variety of your loving. You have an opportunity to experience how your loving is not limited to any particular person or object, leading to a deep affirmation of yourself as a source of love.

Circumstances

In most cases, this exercise leaves people in a wonderful, warm, loving state, but occasionally painful feelings may also arise. Love is not the only feeling which resides in the heart, so in opening the heart, we must be prepared for whatever feelings are strongest at the moment, including sadness, grief, or longing. Working through these can be very beneficial, so it is important to do the exercise in a situation where people can be helped and supported through deep feelings that may emerge.

Included is a variation for use in social transformation workshops, and one for use in workshops on developing a relationship with yourself.

Working Alone. This exercise can be done alone without using a tape recorder. The directions are short enough that you can read each part to yourself, then close your eyes and do that part of the fantasy. For the last parts involving a partner and the group, you will need to imagine the partner and the group.

Working with a Partner. When working with a partner, one of you can read the directions while you both follow them.

Time: 40 minutes.

The Exercise

This is a guided fantasy which will be done in pairs. You will be sharing with your partner the images that arise for you throughout the exercise, even as you go into trance together.

Pair up, and sit or lie down in relaxed positions for a guided fantasy, with partners placing your heads close enough together that you can talk to each other comfortably. A recommended position is lying down ear to ear with feet pointing in opposite directions. Since you will be talking to your partner as you are going into trance, it is important to do the sharing in such a way that you do not pull yourself out of the altered state. Please place your heads close enough together that you can hear each other without raising your voices or turning your heads, and please make your descriptions brief and avoid getting into conversations about your images.

I will start counting from one, and with each count I will ask you to imagine something and then share it with your partner. One: Imagine a landscape or natural setting, such as a sunset or forest scene. . . . Two: Imagine another landscape setting. . . . [Continue with these through five.] Six: Imagine a sensory experience, such as eating ice cream or petting a cat. . . .

[Continue with sensory experiences through ten, and then move to the next category. Periodically suggest that they are going deeper into trance. The complete scheme[1] is as follows:

  1–5: A landscape or natural setting, such as a sunset or forest scene

  6–10: A sensory experience, such as eating ice cream or petting a cat

11–15: A person whom you have been close to at some time in your life, even briefly

16–19: A pleasant memory

20–23: A character or scene from mythology or fiction (from a novel, movie, play, or story)]

♪ "Pachelbel's Canon" (extended version, from *Timeless Motion* by Daniel Kobialka, as much as needed; or any other heart music)

  24: Feel the beating of your heart from the inside. . . .

  25: Imagine your heart as a flower partially open and partially closed. . . .

  26: See and feel the flower gradually opening. . . .

  27: Imagine rays of light or energy radiating out from the petals of the flower. . . .

  28: Begin to think about all the things you love about your life and about the world. For example, you might think about the way your partner's or child's hair falls on their face while they're sleeping; a shaft of sunlight falling on a fern in a redwood forest; the feelings engendered in you by a great piece of music or a great work of art; the courage and caring people sometimes show to each other in emergencies.

Each time an image arises, share it with your partner. You don't have to take turns. You will have plenty of time for this. [Allow about ten minutes.]

---

[1] The counting up to 23 is adapted from Jean Houston's "60 levels down" trance.

Now bring this to a close, and very gradually sit up and face your partner, taking time to do it slowly so that you don't take yourself out of the state you're in. . . .

Take your partner's right hand in your left hand, and place it on your heart and hold it there. . . .[2] Now with your heart open and connected to your partner in this way, honor them for what you have just seen of their loving nature. . . . Silently and through your touch, honor them for the parts of their story you have heard, for their openness, for their ability to love and for their lovableness. . . . Feel into their essence, their deep nature, where they are deeply loving and fully open. . . . And feel the love and the honoring being returned to you in full. . . .

Now gradually form a circle with the entire group, holding hands. (You will have a chance to share verbally with your partner after the exercise is over.) . . . Just sit and make eye contact with the other people in the circle. . . . Let your loving expand to include all these people, even if some of them are strangers. . . . Reach out with your heart and include the whole group. See each person's loving nature and their essential beauty. . . . Feel the power of this circle of love we have created. . . .

Now close your eyes and go deep into yourself. . . . Feel yourself bathed in love. Imagine that love is not just an emotion, but a substance that fills the room, that fills you and emanates from you and supports you. . . . Imagine that love is a way of being and living, the ground of reality from which we emerge. Feel yourself immersed in it and supported by it as an integral part of the whole. . . .

[Bring people out of trance, and then allow them to return to their partners to share their experiences.]

---

[2] The position for this heart embrace comes from an exercise by Jean Houston, "The Lamp and the Knife" from Psyche and Eros, *The Search for the Beloved*, p. 171.

Variations

The last paragraph can be varied according to the type of workshop or group in which the exercise is being used. In a social transformation workshop, it could be as follows:

> Now close your eyes and go deep inside yourself. . . . Let this circle be a sign to you of all the things you thought of today that you love about life, things that are precious to you, that you don't want to lose. In the weeks and months to come, let it be a reminder to you of why you are working to heal our planet. When you become distracted or sidetracked, when you need some inspiration, remember this exercise, this circle, these precious things that you love. Let them rekindle your passion for a peaceful world where these things are no longer in danger.

• • •

In a workshop on developing a relationship with yourself, the following paragraph could be used:

> Now close your eyes, go deep inside, and feel your heart again. You may notice how open it is, how open you are, the deep sense of loving you feel. . . . As you feel this, know that it is yours. No one other person is required for this love to emerge. You did not need to be loved first. . . . All that good, warm loving is just there in you, waiting for opportunities to show itself. The love you may need is there deep inside you. The goodness, the life, the treasure is right there inside you. You don't have to look for it in anyone else. . . . Take this awareness into the deepest part of you and know yourself. Feel the peace and the wholeness that come from this. Know yourself complete.

The preceding three ending paragraphs can be combined in any way that seems appropriate.

Experiences

A Celebration of Feeling

I will describe in detail the experience of Don, a 42-year-old college professor. Don had always cared about other people and about the planetary crisis, but this came primarily from an intellectual perspective. He had recently begun to feel that there was something barren about his exclusive emphasis on reason and intelligence. He came to Inner Journeys work out of a need to feel more deeply for other people and to discover and ignite his passion about changing the world situation.

He reported on his experience in the exercise as follows: "When you asked us to see our hearts as flowers, I didn't get anything very distinct. I don't visualize well anyway. But the physical experience was incredible; my whole chest was melting and going out. My heart really opened, as it rarely ever has."

He was moved to the point of tears while describing the things he loved, especially in remembering special times with his children. "It was pretty wonderful for me, such a contrast to my mundane day today. My work is not touch oriented or spiritual in any way, so it was great to come here and be close to someone and tell them wonderful things! I censored very little. I tend to lose sight of all the good things in my life, and it felt like a celebration to sit there and feel my heart and think of people I admire and places I've been. I tend to be pretty hard on myself, running around every day, and this just felt like a birthday party."

Don to his partner: "When we did the honoring, it was so easy to honor you. I had just heard what you loved about life, so I knew immediately that you're a loving, wonderful person. I didn't have to work at that at all. See into your essence? Of course, I just had."

At the end of the evening Don was soft and glowing, very different than when he arrived. As Don continued with Inner

Journeys work, he also joined a therapy group where he worked on how he related to the others in the group. Between the two he made considerable strides in developing his ability to contact his feelings and connect with others from the heart. This showed up especially in his relationship with his wife and children. In later chapters we will follow Don's exploration of his concern for social change.

A Close-knit Group

The following comments on this exercise were made by a group of people who knew each other quite well and were experienced in doing this kind of work.

Grace described her flower image as follows: "A cross between a sea anemone, a water lotus, and a third flower with millions of little petals and a round yellow center. It opened all the way out, and the petals went all the way over and touched [stretching her arms wide and behind her back.] It was like an incredible heartbeat going out from here and all the way back [joyous and excited]. It was wonderful! So often when I work with heart energy it's directed only toward what I'm facing, and I sometimes have a feeling of something sinister coming from behind. So it was very important to have the energy open in all directions."

Stella had done the exercise with Grace and Janet as a triad. She described the honoring part as follows: "I had an image of you (Grace) on your horse in the pyramids, and an image of you (Janet) as an eight-year-old in a long yellow dress with a big grin."

Grace: "For me it felt like our three essences were the same; your voices were my voice and we were saying the same thing. I didn't even feel like I was honoring Stella, Grace, Janet; it was like all-of-us. And oh, the relief of tapping into that, the joy of reconnecting with 'We are one.' "

Connecting with the group as a whole at the end of the exercise broadens the experience to include the element of community. Afterwards Janet was beaming, absolutely radiating love. With tears in her eyes, she told the group what special people they were and how much she appreciated having them in her life. We will hear more from this group in chapter 12.

5

Nurturing Touch

HOW OFTEN HAVE YOU YEARNED to be held and deeply nurtured as if you were a child again? It is a profound need in all of us, no matter how old we get.

To the extent that we receive good nurturing as children, we develop a sense of basic trust in ourselves and the world.[1] We are able to live from a place of knowing that deep inside we are good, we are lovable, our impulses and feelings can be trusted. We experience the world as a relatively safe place, where we can get what we need. We feel confident that we belong, we can make our way, we can find love and respect.

In the early years, this nurturing is conveyed primarily through touch, being held, rocked, stroked, etc. So, touch becomes a central factor in the development of that early sense of trust and belonging.[2] Touch is also an essential ingredient in the healthy growth of an infant. Adequate tactile stimulation is essential for proper brain development and for a well-functioning immune system. Studies have shown that children who are severely deprived of touch (in an orphanage, for example) will actually die for lack of it even if they are adequately cared for in other ways.

All of us have had times during childhood when we were not given as much caretaking and nurturing as we needed, or

---

[1] Erik Erickson, *Childhood and Society* (New York: Norton, 1963).
[2] Ashley Montagu, *Touching* (New York: Harper & Row, 1971).

when the way it was given was problematical. This is especially true for those of us in the baby boom generation who were raised when the prevailing child-rearing practices encouraged bottle feeding on a schedule and discouraged picking up and holding children lest they be spoiled.

These deprivations can cause us fears and inhibitions which affect bodily freedom, capacity for intimacy, self-esteem, and much else. We may have difficulty asking for what we need from others or taking in what is given. We may feel awkward or timid when it comes to reaching out for touch, or tense and afraid when others reach out to us. We may also feel insecure about our ability to give to others who are in need.

Deprived of touch and nurturing as a child, your needs as an adult can become so strong as to drive others away. Or you may cut yourself off from those needs so thoroughly that it is hard to let anyone near. This can lead to alienation from your body so that it becomes stiff and tight. Rather than being a natural source of pleasure, you may experience your body as machine-like or you may be afraid of losing control. All of these things can affect your ability to support yourself and feel good about yourself.

This urgent need for touching which many of us feel is compounded by the fact that in this culture touching is only allowed in love relationships and parent-child relationships. In most other situations it is restricted to brief handshakes and hugs or structured touching such as massage. Any other touching becomes sexualized and therefore fraught with danger and misinterpretation. So in order to satisfy their need for touch, many people become preoccupied with finding a love relationship, sometimes to the exclusion of more important growth issues.

Let's hope that as we heal our deprivations of childhood and become free and comfortable with touch as adults, we can loosen some of our social restrictions on touching and begin to create a society that truly nurtures all of its people.

In this exercise you uncover your childhood need to be nurtured, and then you have an opportunity to be cared for in the way you needed, through the sense of touch. It is an experience of giving and receiving parental or nurturing love, which helps to deepen your sense of basic trust. The exercise also will help to increase your comfort with touch and to enhance and validate your ability to nurture another person.

Circumstances

Working with a Partner. This exercise cannot be done alone. When working with a partner, the one who is doing the nurturing can double as the leader, reading aloud all the directions for the one being nurtured, and reading silently their own directions.

Time: 45 minutes.

The Exercise[3] ——————————————————————

In this exercise you will pair up and take turns nurturing each other physically. So find a partner and decide who will go first in receiving nurturing. After the first person has gone through the entire exercise being nurtured by their partner, you will switch roles and go through it again for the other person.

The person who will be receiving should lie comfortably on the floor or pillows in a fetal position. [Begin with an induction.]

♪   "Home" (from *Country* soundtrack by Charles Gross; or other sad music)

Imagine that you are floating down a lazy river on a raft in the warm sunshine. Feel the gentle sway of the raft on the water,

——————
[3] Adapted from an exercise designed by my colleague Eva Brown.

relaxing you even further. Feel the sun on your body, warming
you nicely, but not making you too hot. . . . Floating down the
river, enjoying the sun, hearing the birds in the distance, seeing
the banks of the river moving past as you float along, letting go
even further, going deeper inside yourself, just floating down the
river. . . .

This is the river of your life, and you are floating backward
in time, one year back, two years back, remembering scenes from
those times as you float along back through your life, having
scenes just flash by, three years ago, floating down the river, . . .
five years ago, continuing to float, going backward, . . . ten years
ago, finding yourself growing younger as the years slip by, . . .
fifteen years, remembering what it was like, . . . if you haven't
already gotten there, coming to your early twenties, . . . floating
back further, to your teenage years, noticing the changes in you,
how different you feel at this age, floating back, . . . coming to
your childhood, feeling what that feels like, scenes flashing by,
floating back. . . .

Finding yourself as a young child or a baby, feeling in need.
You are feeling a strong need to be nurtured, held, cared for,
stroked, or cuddled. You may feel bad or lonely or sad or scared,
or perhaps you just need nurturing because you are a child. In
any case you need someone to be there for you, to make it better.
Feel that longing, let yourself really experience that feeling, that
yearning for nurturing. . . .

Let yourself feel it in your body. Get a sense from your body
of how it needs to be touched. Don't think it out, just feel from
the inside what your body needs. Trust your body to tell you what
it needs; it remembers. Do you need to have your back supported,
your hair stroked, do you need to put your head in someone's lap,
do you need to be held in someone's arms? Whatever it is, let
yourself feel that need in a very physical way. . . .

♪   *Awake and Dreaming* (by Alex Jones and Doug Cutler, as much
     as needed; sweet, loving, childlike tone)

Now as you feel ready, let your partner know what you need, how you'd like to be touched. You can do this nonverbally by moving toward them and connecting with them with your body, or you can tell them how you would like to be touched, ask them for what you need. If it feels too threatening to ask for exactly what you want, then ask for as much as you are ready for at this time. Don't be deterred by the fact that you're not as small as a baby. We can approximate just about anything you need. Partners, ask me for help if necessary. . . . Take your time, feel yourself, feel your need, and move toward it whenever you are ready. . . .

Partners, open yourself to your most loving and caring place. Let your heart go out to this child who needs you, and relax into giving them the touch and nurturing they need. Make sure that you are in a comfortable position, too. Move around or do whatever you have to do to become comfortable and relaxed. Make sure that you are enjoying the experience, too. Otherwise your tension will be communicated to your partner. If your partner asks for anything that you don't feel comfortable with, feel free to tell them what your limits are, and if necessary, the two of you work out together something that feels good to both of you. . . .

People receiving the nurturing, just let yourself surrender to the comfort and the pleasure. Open yourself, take in the caring, take in the love. Know that you deserve this, that you deserve to be loved and cared for. . . . Know that the open, warm, vulnerable, needy part of you is special and lovable, that you are lovable, that you are valuable, that it is a pleasure to touch you and to nurture you. . . .

Feel free to move around to get more comfortable or to assume a different position, to be touched in a different way. You can ask your partner for something different if you like, or you can ask them to do what they are doing in a slightly different way. You can change what you want as many times as you like. Shift your weight around as much as you like, or stay completely still. Do whatever you need to do to get really comfortable. This is for you. . . .

Relax and sink even deeper into the warmth and fulfillment of this moment, of this connection. Bask in it, let it fill you, let it complete you. . . .

Partners, feel free to nurture in whatever way your body wants to from the place you're in. Don't be limited to what your partner asked for. And don't forget to shift position if you need to; make sure you're comfortable, too. Take care of yourself while you're nurturing. And babies, if your partner touches you in any way that doesn't feel right to you, feel free to let them know that it's not something you want. . . .

Just keep taking it in, relaxing into it. The care and the nurturing, it's your birthright. Just breathe deeply and let yourself go into it. This is all for you. It's OK to get exactly what you need. [Allow another 4 or 5 minutes.]

Now very slowly separate, slowly move apart from each other. People who have been receiving, take with you the feelings of warmth and wholeness and all the goodness that you have been receiving. As you separate from your partner, take that with you. Slowly disengage until you are lying on the floor by yourself in a comfortable position, still feeling loved and cared for, still feeling deserving, still feeling filled and complete. . . .

Lie relaxed on the floor by yourself. Spend a few minutes in this place having those feelings by yourself. Feeling whole, feeling loved, feeling special, feeling deserving, and feeling all that inside yourself. Feeling that the wholeness is in you. Knowing that even though you may have gotten there today by receiving from another person, that place of fullness is yours. It's a place that you can be in when you're receiving from another person, and it's also a place you can be in when you're alone.

Take a few minutes now to be in that place by yourself, feeling the warmth inside, feeling the completeness, feeling the relaxation. [Allow a minute.]

[Bring them out of trance. Make sure that the people receiving the nurturing have enough time after that to come back from the deep place where they've been. Then have partners switch roles and go through the whole exercise again, shortening the explanations where appropriate. After that, partners take some time to share their experiences with each other.]

♪ Simplified music: Use *Awake and Dreaming* as above.

Experiences

Being Nurtured

Sandra is the woman who has been working on developing her strength. She reported, "I always saw myself as more of a nurturer, but I really liked being nurtured. I felt a longing—for touch and nurturing from my father—that I didn't even know I had. I also remembered a game my sister and I used to play in bed tracing each other's faces.

"The visualization helped in getting a clearer fix on what I needed at certain times. It felt really good to be able to ask for those things. It was a little easier to ask when I remembered that it's a valuable thing to allow another person to give. When she was nurturing me, her very strong hands on me gave me a feeling of my own strength. I was amazed that her strength didn't make me weak, it helped me to know my own strength more. I ended up with a golden glow and felt, maybe for the first time, that I could voluntarily recapture that." This experience added another strand to Sandra's growing sense of inner strength and wholeness.

The Ideal Mother

Sometimes old feelings emerge during the exercise that prevent a person from taking in the nurturing. The following individual work illustrates how this can be resolved. It involves Judy, the woman with the inner teenage friend and the engulfing slime as her shadow.

Judy: "As we came close to my turn, I felt like a little kid in a classroom who wanted to escape. It was really bad. In the exercise we did before, I got in touch with some tender feelings going back, really sad feelings [crying], and I didn't want to go through that again.

"I know where it's coming from. [feeling deeply] I'm afraid if I let go, I'll be coming from such a needy place that I'll fall apart, and I don't want to let that happen. If I allowed myself to feel that nurturing, there wouldn't be much of me left. I've always been very conscious of how much I needed from my mother and never got, so it was very scary to let myself go and fantasize this coming from her. That's when I got in touch with those really sad feelings. When I was imagining that I was getting the nurturing from my mother, I wanted to stop it, like it was counterfeit or something. I could never go back and get the real thing, and this wouldn't work."

Jay: "Do you want to try going further with that now? I have some ideas. [She nods.] I'll have you do something different than imagining you're getting your needs met by your mother. But to start with, go back and really feel what you needed from her." After a pause, she nods, visibly upset.

"OK, I'd like you to imagine that you grew up in a different family, that you grew up in a family where you had an ideal mother, who could give you exactly what you needed in terms of this kind of nurturing and touch and caring. I want you to imagine that you're with her now. Let yourself visualize what she looks like, this ideal mother, who loves you and cares for you deeply and is able to tune in to what you need. Feel that sense of being with her. [pause] What's happening?"

Judy: "I can't find a face, or a body."

Jay: "That's OK, can you feel her presence or hear her voice?"

Judy: "I keep seeing my mother."

Jay: "Mmm, it seems you don't want to take it from someone else. Let's do this as a first step toward imagining it with your
mother, OK? Given the difficulty you have with her, that needs
to come later. Imagine yourself with an ideal mother who can
give you exactly what you need."

Judy: "I still can't find a face or a body, but I have a voice,
and I'm remembering a typical scene where we would visit my
grandmother in the car. I would see these kids I would be afraid
of, and I would slide down to the bottom of the floor board and
hide. My mother never noticed it, or if she did, she never helped
me through it.

"So I hear this comforting voice saying, 'It's OK, Judy.
What's wrong? Why are you upset? I see what you're doing. Are
you OK?' " [sobbing]

Jay: "Good. Keep going. Let yourself respond to her."

Judy: "I told her that I wasn't OK, that I was scared, and
then she held me."

Jay: "Good. So really be with that. Feel the holding. Feel
it in your body. Feel her warmth, her touch. Experience how
that makes you feel. [breathing deeply, relieved, satisfied] Mmm,
good. Just take some time to be with that, and really take it in.

[After a long pause] "If you're willing to take this even
further, I'd like you to be able to actually get some of that
physically here. Do you want to do that?"

Judy (after some hesitation): "Yeah, I'll go for it."

Jay: "My idea is to have you curl up in the middle of the
floor, and have anybody who wants to come around and touch
you. Let me know if you'd like to do it differently."

Judy: "I'd like to sit up."

She sat in the center of the group, and people moved in and
touched her in various ways. One person held her for a while.
Everyone was involved. Judy was able to open herself to the
attention and love she received and to allow herself to drink
deeply. People felt wonderfully relieved and satisfied to be able
to give to her.

Notice that Judy thought she was supposed to imagine being nurtured by her mother in the exercise, even though I never mentioned that. She clearly wanted to be able to imagine that, but was too conflicted to do it. When I directed her to imagine an ideal mother, that removed the conflict and allowed her to take this step in being healed. At some time in the future, she may want to imagine being nurtured by her actual mother, and that would be a further step in the healing process.

About a year after this, Judy did a related exercise which dealt with nurturing as a child. She reported being hesitant to go into it, fearing what might happen. "But this time was beautiful!" She felt grounded both giving love to herself and receiving it. In addition she had grown much more self-supporting in her outside life. She completed the divorce from her husband and worked through the grief over that loss. She developed a strong support system of friends, and is now working with vigor and determination toward achieving financial stability.

Feeling Nurtured by Yourself

The last part of the exercise helps people to internalize the nurturing function. The exercise takes them into a place of feeling warm and cared for, and then they are encouraged to associate this with being alone. Thus they take a step toward being able to nurture themselves.

One man reported: "When you said to keep the energy with us as the partner leaves, I actually visualized a ball of energy that was holding me. I was really struck with, 'This is for you, and it's OK to feel it.' Just being by myself made it concrete. I got something significant that I didn't have when I started. It felt very important to be self-sufficient."

A woman said, "It was a very intimate thing to be held that way. And it was important to know that separations do come and the feeling can endure. You don't have to hold on to the person to have the feeling; you contain the feeling. It was freeing. The strength was definitely still there."

6

Acceptance

ONE OF THE GREATEST gifts you can give or receive from another person is that of being seen deeply, accepted fully, and appreciated and honored for who you are. The word "naming" comes up in a variety of places to describe this kind of loving. Jean Houston has a ritual (see chapter 15) which is based on the concept of naming from *The Wind in the Door* by Madelaine L'Engle.[1] In that exercise, naming means honoring and empowering a person.

Naming also appears in The Riddlemaster Trilogy by Patricia McKillip.[2] Here the emphasis is on seeing the person clearly for who they are and accepting them. I have been deeply moved by that story and the love relationship between its two main characters, Morgon and Raederle. In order to illustrate the concept of naming from this book, I will quote two passages. In the first one, Raederle had for the first time fully exercised the great magic powers she was born with, and almost come to grief, breaking a flagstone on the floor of the throneroom. Her brothers were startled and bewildered by her power, and she felt like a stranger in their eyes.

---

[1] Madelaine L'Engle, *The Wind in the Door* (New York: Dell, 1973).
[2] Patricia McKillip. The trilogy consists of: *The Riddlemaster of Hed*, 1976; *Heir of Sea and Fire*, 1977; *Harpist in the Wind*, 1979. Published by Atheneum Publishers, an imprint of Macmillan Publishing Company, New York.

She turned. [Morgan] stood at the threshold . . . he was watching her; she knew from the expression in his eyes, how much he had seen. As she gazed at him helplessly, he said softly, "Raederle." It was no warning, no judgment, simply her name, and she could have wept at the recognition in it.[3]

Later in the story, Morgon was feeling amazed at how much Raederle had stood by him despite his not treating her very well. When he asked her why, she replied:

"I don't know. I wonder sometimes, too. Then you touch my face with your scarred hand and read my mind. Your eyes know me. . . . You have spoken my name in a way that no other man in the realm will speak it, and I will listen for that until I die."[4]

I have yet to be able to read this passage aloud without tears welling up. I am deeply moved by it because it seems to describe the essence of the love I want and the love I cherish. I have longed to be named the way Raederle was by Morgon, and when I have felt acknowledged in that way, I have become deeply bonded to the person naming me, just as she did.

This sense of being named is a crucial part of what every human being needs, especially as a child. It is an important basis for a healthy sense of self-esteem. It is one of the attitudes that Carl Rogers identified many years ago as necessary for successful psychotherapy.[5] And it is part of that ideal of loving central to many spiritual traditions. The ability to give this acceptance to

---

[3] From *Heir of Sea and Fire*, © 1977 Patricia A. McKillip. Reprinted with permission of Atheneum Publishers, an imprint of Macmillan Publishing Company.

[4] From *Harpist in the Wind*, © 1979 Patricia A. McKillip. Reprinted with permission of Atheneum Publishers, an imprint of Macmillan Publishing Company, p.166.

[5] Carl Rogers, *Client Centered Therapy* (Boston: Houghton Mifflin, 1951).

yourself is also crucial for the deep self-bonding and self-support that will allow so much else to grow in you.

The Meaning of Acceptance

"Acceptance" as I'm using it here doesn't mean blanket approval. If I accept someone, it doesn't mean that I agree with everything they do, or that there is nothing about them that needs to be changed. It means that I see the person fully and clearly, including those aspects that may be self-destructive or harmful to others, and I love them anyway. I might want to see them change some things, but my attitude toward them is still one of caring and love, not judgment or disdain.

This same distinction applies to self-acceptance. Many people do not understand the very important relationship between self-acceptance and change. Self-acceptance helps to promote positive change and self-judgment helps to prevent it. Many people think that if they judge themselves harshly for destructive behavior, they are more likely to change the behavior, and that if they accept themselves with that behavior, they will never change it.

The reverse is actually true. Self-judgment promotes guilt, despair, and feelings of inadequacy. You are likely to avoid honestly looking at yourself if you tend to be harsh with yourself. Positive change is not nurtured in such a climate. Self-acceptance, on the other hand, promotes good feelings, flexibility, and the courage to take risks. It is not so dangerous to see your weaknesses clearly if you will not punish yourself for them. Self-acceptance and the desire to change go hand in hand.

Of course, it is possible to accept yourself and avoid the need to change, but then the problem is not the self-acceptance, but the avoidance. Self-judgment rarely helps in any positive way. What is needed instead is a kind of healthy self-challenge that does not diminish your acceptance of yourself.

Circumstances

Working Alone. When working by yourself, the last part must be done by imagining looking into the eyes of someone you know.

Working with a Partner. When working with a partner, each person should be led through the first two parts by the other. Then for the third part, one person can lead both of you through it together, putting down the book after reading each paragraph in order to make eye contact and participate in the exercise.

Time: 25 minutes.

The Exercise ─────────────────────

[People arrange themselves for a guided fantasy. The leader starts out with an induction.[6]]

Remember one of your favorite foods as a child, and imagine that you are eating it now. Taste it. Savor it. . . .

Remember a place your family went for vacations or outings when you were a child that you particularly liked. Be there as vividly as you can. Enjoy all the sights and sounds, remember the activities. . . .

Remember a friend from high school or college or your early twenties. Visualize what they look like. Remember what it was like to be with them. . . .

Remember a favorite teacher or mentor from any time in your life. Imagine yourself talking with them and learning from them. . . .

─────────

[6] This extended induction is adapted from "Priming the Memory Bank," from Jean Houston's *The Possible Human*, p. 88.

Remember a time when you were in love, how you felt about that person, how you felt about yourself. . . .

Think about the person who is now your closest friend. Remember what it is like to be around them. What are your feelings toward them right now? . . .

♪ "Seapeace" (from *Seapeace* by Georgia Kelly, as much as needed; or other heart music)

And now remember a time from any point in your life when you were named by someone, when you were seen fully in all your parts and accepted, when you were recognized for who you are and loved. You may remember a person who generally treated you this way, or you may remember a specific time when someone did this. If you don't remember a time when you were *fully* named, pick a time that comes close to it. Take a moment now to let this memory surface. [Allow half a minute.]

Now if you have thought of a person who generally accepted you, think of a specific time with that person that stands out, or imagine one, imagine how it would have happened with that person. . . . Now everyone evoke your memory of being named in all its richness. How old were you? What was happening in your life? What was the physical setting, the sights, the sounds, the smells? . . . And how did this person show you the recognition? What did they say? What was the look on their face? Did they touch you in a certain way? . . .

Remember how you felt inside. Take time to luxuriate in those feelings. You may have felt secure, warm, accepted, loved. It may have made you feel good about yourself, appreciative, relaxed, peaceful. Whatever the feelings, let yourself feel them now. Take all the time you need to be with those feelings. Bask in those feelings, letting them fill you and complete you. You deserve it! [Allow a minute.]

♪ "Seapeace" (again)

Now take a moment to get in touch with a situation in which you named someone, perhaps in a way that is similar to the way you just remembered being named. A situation in which you felt accepting and loving toward someone. It may have been someone who came to you for understanding and help in a difficult situation. It may have been a child or even an animal. It may have been someone you were very close to or a virtual stranger. It may even have been a character in a story or movie. . . .

Remember what it was like to be with this person when you were in that open, accepting place. Feel it as if it were happening now. . . . Especially feel how it feels inside you to be in that place. . . .

Now let go of the particular situation, but remain in that internal place you have found where you can see deeply into people and accept them. Imagine that you are with a different person, and that person is yourself. Imagine yourself as a separate person sitting across from you, and look deeply into yourself from that place of unconditional acceptance and love, seeing everything about you from that place. . . .

See your strengths and talents and special unique qualities, and affirm these. . . . See your flaws, your weaknesses, and accept these in yourself with an open heart. . . . See all your difficulties and all your triumphs, all your delights and all your pain, all your idiosyncrasies and all your ordinariness, all your loves and all your hates. . . . Take in all of you from this loving place, and name yourself with full acceptance. [Allow a minute.]

Now be the part of you being named, the part receiving this deep acceptance. Open yourself to it; take it in deeply. Enjoy it; savor it; bask in it; let it support you. [Allow a minute.]

• • •

[Bring people back out of trance. Then pair up, and allow about five minutes for partners to share their experiences. Make sure that they know each other's first names before starting the next part. Begin that by sitting face to face.]

♪ "Seapeace" (again)

Now make eye contact with your partner. . . . While you're doing that, take a moment to return to that open, caring, loving place that you've been exploring during this exercise. That place where you can see deeply into others and name them. Take a moment to find that place inside yourself. . . .

From that place, take in your partner. Take in this person whom you may not know very well, whom you may have just met. Take them in with your eyes. Take in as much of them as you can—the things they have shared with you in the last few minutes, possibly things you might already know about them, and most importantly whatever you see in their eyes. . . . Take in all of these things from that place of unconditional acceptance and naming. . . .

Let yourself accept all of your partner, all their flaws and all their strengths. . . . Take in this entire person sitting before you, with their own unique and deeply felt life history, even if you don't know what it is, with their own special hopes and dreams. . . . Take them in and name them deeply inside yourself. . . .

Then when you are ready, express this by simply saying their name aloud. When you have been named by your partner, open yourself to it. Give yourself time to fully take it in before you move on to naming them in return. [Allow a minute, then give partners time to share this experience with each other.]

Experiences

Our friend Sherry described her experience as follows: "It was a very beautiful exercise, and so personally rich. It brought me back to my college days in the darkest moment of my life, when there was a shining star. Really wonderful. I had been very depressed, spending long periods of time not talking to anyone. My room-mate, whom I really admired, was caring and accepting and drew me out, so that I gradually began to feel better about myself. It was very important."

When asked to name herself, Sherry had difficulty getting past the things she didn't like about herself. She realized that she had seen herself almost exclusively in negative terms and needed to focus instead on her positive qualities. Eventually she was able to name herself. "That was really helpful for me. The relaxation helped to quiet down my head so I could listen to my heart. I named myself 'Emily,' from a Paul Simon song. Emily's word is 'namaste'—I see the good in you." Naming herself in this way recalled the soft, gentle, peaceful, loving side of her.

Another person reported that during the first part of the exercise she thought of a time in her life when "I felt a great deal of acceptance and a wonderful sense that all of my unexpectedness and unusual qualities were joyously cherished. I believed I would be able to do anything." She really identified with Raederle in the story. "I was feeling how scary it is when you finally awaken to your power and wait to see how people are going to react to you. I liked being able to name myself; it made other people's reactions less important. I have also been getting in touch lately with the namer in myself, so it was a pleasure to name someone else, to recognize another person's essence."

A Sensuous Naming

When people are asked to name themselves, some people are painfully confronted with their feelings of low self-esteem and tendency to judge themselves. Sometimes they are able to work this through during the exercise, and in other cases the exercise prepares the way for individual work afterwards.

Sally did the exercise during a particularly rough time in her life when she was feeling very self-judgmental, so it was difficult for her to feel anything positive about herself. "What I could feel was the longing to be seen." Afterwards I asked her to formulate how she would like to be named and then took her on a guided fantasy to meet a higher part of herself who would name her in that way. She walked through a meadow and then into a forest, where she met a woman "in her late twenties with long flowing hair and a wreath of flowers and one of those wonderful ethereal, very light gowns. She has placed me in a large pool of water with water lilies, and my clothes have disappeared. She is pouring healing oil or milk and honey (I can't decide which) over me. It's exquisitely sensuous, wonderful." This was her symbolic expression of being recognized and loved by a higher aspect of herself. It's a feminine version of the kind of self-naming that happens in the Flight of Empowerment (chapter 14).

Sally was paired with Sarah, whom she knew well. After the exercise they shared their experiences in naming one another. Sarah: "I was just sitting here feeling very contented and pleased, basically just enjoying you. The things that are difficult for you are also difficult for me in some ways, and it's easier to accept them in you than it is in me."

Sally: "I was appreciating how tolerant we are of each other. I was appreciating a quality of yours that I sometimes call 'slow,' seeing it as a part of your gentleness. There's something very lovely in that, and I remembered enjoying your dancing last year, seeing how beautifully you move. So much of what you do feels like a dance. I was just feeling a lot of love for you. And also pride at watching you begin to take your own stride in your work, watching your hidden strength come out and go public."

Accepting One's Appearance

Sandra is the woman working on developing her inner strength, who had the image of the plant that grows back. She couldn't reach a place of self-acceptance during this exercise. Sitting across from herself, she saw her head as blank, representing her difficulty in accepting her physical appearance. (She is actually quite attractive.) Then she saw a dark tunnel with a big "No" of non-acceptance rising up to blow her head off her body. This was a very upsetting and graphic depiction of the violence of her self-judgment.

In working with her on this individually afterwards, I had her place all the negative messages she tells herself (e.g., "You're ugly") in a ball. She then pounded on it in rage, telling the messages to go away. This helped her to own some of the aggression and to feel her power. She then took the ball to an open window and threw it out while the group supported her by blowing the messages away on the wind. At this point she was feeling strong and open and much better about herself.

I decided to take it a step further. I had her stand in front of a mirror and look at herself, suggesting that she see past the surface appearance into her essence of power and light and love. After a while she was able to do this to such an extent that her heart opened to herself in a very moving way. With tears in her eyes, she said to her image in the mirror "Sandra, I love you."

SECTION THREE

Social Transformation

Introduction

WE ARE IN THE MIDST of a planetary crisis of dangerous proportions. Even when we lull ourselves into thinking that life as we know it can go on indefinitely, most of us now realize that we are on a collision course with disaster. If we don't make some fundamental changes, we risk destroying ourselves and much of the planet through nuclear war[1] or environmental collapse.[2]

In the early 1980's, a nuclear war was a serious and immediate threat because of the aggressive posturing and planning of the Reagan administration. Since then, there have been major steps toward a reduction in the nuclear threat because of the positive changes happening in the Soviet Union and the greatly improved relations between the superpowers. However, there is now another very serious threat which could cause as much destruction as nuclear war—global climate change because of the greenhouse effect. There is compelling evidence that if we don't make substantial changes in energy use, deforestation, and other activities that are causing the greenhouse effect, the resulting global warm-

---

[1] Robert J. Lifton and Richard Falk, *Indefensible Weapons* (New York: Basic, 1982).
[2] William R. Catton, Jr., *Overshoot* (Chicago: University of Illinois Press, 1980).

ing might cause massive ecological destruction, loss of human life, and possibly even the collapse of our entire civilization.[3]

However, there are some signs that our society may be in the process of making the fundamental changes which would allow us to solve this problem.[4] In fact, I believe we are undergoing a major historical transformation,[5] during which we will greatly alter our worldview, values, social structures, institutions, and political system—our entire way of life.

For 300–500 years we have been living in what is called the industrial era, with its emphasis on materialism, science, industry, and reason. Our lives have been structured in terms of domination, competition, and bureaucracy. Our society has looked at everything mechanistically—the universe, the earth, the human being, the psyche. We have seen them as objects to be analyzed, understood, controlled, or dominated. This has brought us great advances in our ability to protect and nourish ourselves and free ourselves from drudgery.

However, it has outlived its usefulness. The immense success of this worldview has brought about a new historical situation which it cannot comprehend. Our need to control and remake the natural world is threatening to destroy our ecological life support system. Our tendency to compete with and exploit each other has generated tremendous fear and resentment, and consequently we are frequently on the edge of war.

In most cities it is no longer safe to walk the streets at night. Drug abuse, violence, and crime are all on the rise. People feel alienated from each other and distrustful of their elected officials.

---

[3] Robert Gilman, "What's Wrong with the Climate" In Context, No. 22, Summer, 1989.

[4] Willis Harman, An Incomplete Guide to the Future (New York: Norton, 1979); and Alvin Toffler, The Third Wave (New York: Bantam, 1980).

[5] Lewis Mumford, Transformations of Man (Gloucester, MA: Peter Smith, 1956).

There is an increase in diseases related to the immune system, probably because of the toxicity of our daily environment.

Over the past 25 years, there have been many signs of the emergence of a new worldview and value system. In the '60s, middle class youth revolted against the values of their own culture and produced many lasting changes in mainstream society. For the first time in modern history, women are rising to take their equal place in the governance of the world.

Interest in consciousness and spirituality is on the rise, as evidenced by the popularity of Shirley Maclaine's *Out on a Limb* and other "new age" happenings. Ecological awareness is developing, and more people are moving to rural areas in search of a quiet, unhurried life close to nature. Even science is increasingly adopting a holistic systems approach in all areas of study, from holistic health to the new physics.[6] Through modern advances in communication and transportation, an interdependent world society is emerging.

Historically these times of transition from one major era to another have invariably involved great upheaval, when the old culture no longer works and a new one has not yet taken hold. This time, however, there is a difference. We have the technical knowledge and the awesome physical power to destroy ourselves in the process. The breakdown of industrial society is causing tremendous stresses, psychologically and politically. Though it seems that a new era is coming, we don't know if it will arrive soon enough, if we will change rapidly and smoothly enough, to avoid serious trouble.

Society is not a static object that we must change, it is a process that is collapsing and undergoing a transformation. We need to guide and facilitate this transition to avoid disaster and to bring on the cooperative, ecological, loving society which is trying to be born.

---

[6] Fritjof Capra, *The Turning Point* (New York: Simon & Schuster, 1982).

My Personal History

My own personal history reflects both the difficulties of the old order and the emergence of the new. I grew up as a typical successful product of this society—a white male WASP, bright, highly educated, top of my class. I went into computer science, earned a Ph.D., and excelled at basic academic research, teaching at the University of California at Berkeley and developing a national reputation in my sub-specialty. I had an adequate social life, married while in graduate school, and seemed headed for the American dream.

That was on the surface. Underneath I was pretty rigid, emotionally closed, and incapable of loving. My body was tight and controlled, and I couldn't let go into pleasure. I had become in some ways like the machines I worked with. I was easily moved to anger and was often condescending toward others. My wife and I had periods of being unable to get along that were baffling to us. I wasn't unhappy, but my horizons and capacities were severely limited—to intellectual and athletic pursuits and professional success. The realms of relationship, body, nature, art, and spirit were all foreign to me. I had been channelled into the narrow confines of the late industrial era.

I was saved by my own natural curiosity, Berkeley, and the '60s. I moved to Berkeley in the summer of 1968 and explored the best of the cultural movements of the '60s and '70s. My vistas expanded tremendously. I came alive and gained a breadth and depth of living that made me a more humane and loving person. Things were not always easy, however. I switched careers, ended my marriage, gave up on some of my counter-culture experiments, and worked through a lot of pain in my own therapy. I learned from both the difficulties and the joys.

In the '80s this led to involvements with political activism and spirituality that have enriched my life further. Overall I gained flexibility of body and psyche, openness, freedom, an ability to connect deeply with other people and the natural world, an understanding of my inner life, and a passion for social transformation. In twenty years I have gone from total immersion in the old culture to being in the center of the emerging one.

Many of you have tales to tell which are every bit as rich and relevant. Some of you probably have never fit into the old culture, because of your gender, race, or social class, or because your personality from the beginning was attuned more to the emerging one. Some of you have suffered the pains of the dying culture more than I have. We each have something unique to offer in this time of transition. My understanding comes from knowing personally the limitations of even the best of the old order, and choosing to transform my life in the new direction. I still have many changes to make, but I am firmly on the way.

Your Personal Response

You may find it difficult and frightening to face the planetary crisis squarely, to let in the emotional impact of the dangers we face. It is doubly hard because most of us feel so powerless to change things. However, facing this issue is an essential part of your personal and spiritual growth and can be extremely rewarding.[7] Confronting your worst fears and feeling compassion for people everywhere, envisioning a new society, connecting with others who care deeply about the planet, developing a sense of your particular strengths and contributions to social change. This process engenders courage, depth of being, and a sense of commitment and purpose. By viewing yourself and world problems in proper perspective, you can discover that you have much more power to contribute to meaningful change than you realized.

In thinking about what you can do to help, don't be restricted to the traditional avenues for political action. Many people think only in terms of electoral politics or the protests and civil disobedi-

---

[7] Joanna Macy, *Despair and Personal Power in the Nuclear Age*, chapters 1, 2.

ence of radical politics. There are many other possibilities for effecting positive political change ranging from nuclear comedy to ecological research. In addition, the larger social transformation involves many dimensions other than political change, from personal growth to institutional innovation.

Our task is not to take an established, entrenched social order and make massive changes in it by brute force. We are in the midst of a major transition; the industrial society no longer works. Many forces and movements are gathering momentum right now—political movements, social innovation, new role structures, alternative worldviews—and though not all of them are positive, this is a time of ferment, possibility, and hope.

The way we are living our lives right now is contributing partly to the dying social order and partly to the emerging one. The way we buy and consume, the way we eat, our relationships, our living situations, and many other aspects of our lives are all relevant to social change. By becoming aware of this we become more powerful. We can appreciate and expand on those aspects of our lives that are enhancing the emergence of a new, healthy society. Our personal growth not only benefits ourselves but also contributes to social transformation.

We also have vast opportunities to influence other people— not just their politics, but their values, their worldview, their way of being. We can affect the institutions that we support or participate in. We can try to change our work situations or seek employment that is life enhancing. We can create community with like-minded people so we exert a collective influence and begin to create new social customs and mores. We also need to change those aspects of our political and economic structure that are contributing to the crisis.

This is a time of opportunity as well as danger, a time for creativity and innovation. As the rigidities of our old social and psychological structures fall away, we have the chance to create new ones which will truly promote love, self-realization, and harmony with the earth and other people. We have the fascinating task of growing new psyches and a new society. What an exciting time to be alive!

About This Section

The exercises in this section and the next are designed to facilitate your facing the planetary crisis, exploring your emotional, moral, and spiritual responses to it, and becoming empowered to find your unique contribution to creating a new social order. These exercises were designed for use in workshops dealing specifically with these social issues.

With some modification, the exercises can also be used in workshops and groups with the more usual focus on personal and spiritual growth. The two areas are not all that separate. Especially when dealing with the issue of life purpose, the social and the personal/spiritual go hand in hand.

When I have designed an exercise for a social transformation workshop and then used it in a regular workshop (or vice versa), I have used slightly different phrasing or other modifications. Therefore, some of the exercises in the book are written in two variations. See the Circumstances part of these exercises for further information about variations.

The exercises in this section are:

Planetary Compassion
Envisioning a Healthy Society

The exercises outside this section that are designed for social transformation workshops or have socially oriented variations are as follows:

Opening the Heart
all Life Purpose exercises
Manifesting Your Intention
The Naming Ritual
Affirmations

7

Planetary Compassion

OUR DAILY NEWSCASTS show an unprecedented amount of pain and suffering in the world—starvation, torture, war, untreated disease, homelessness, despair, and destruction of the biosphere. Most of us would rather avoid seeing this suffering and feeling the pain of it. This is natural and understandable. It seems so overwhelming that we feel we'd be putting ourselves through anguish for no good reason.

Nevertheless, there is enormous value in letting ourselves feel our compassion for the pain of the world. We are naturally compassionate beings; we spontaneously respond to and care about others—other people, animals, and the earth. This is a sign of our humanity, our interconnectedness, and our love. You can open yourself to this pain without being overwhelmed if you are grounded and if you do not absorb or hold on to the pain. It can become a deepening experience, one that teaches courage through facing the worst and emerging stronger, one that brings maturity through opening your heart to what is, no matter how terrible.

From this experience comes the motivation to act, the commitment to dedicate ourselves to the higher purpose of relieving suffering. Also from this comes a sense of connection, of oneness with those who are suffering and with other compassionate souls.

Service in the world and the alleviation of suffering are emphasized in all the great spiritual traditions. As you develop spiritually and grow in awareness, compassion, wisdom, and love you naturally reach out to the suffering that you encounter. In ancient times, this meant serving those in your village who were in need or those you encountered in your wanderings.

Now, however, we live in a global village, and all people are our brothers and sisters. Through the media and through travel we have the opportunity of knowing about people all over the world and discovering the extent of their suffering. In addition, we all are endangered; everyone is threatened by nuclear war and ecological collapse. It is no longer enough to be caring with those we meet face to face. We must be aware and compassionate on a planetary level as well. But we can grow into this difficult task, we can learn the largeness of soul that is required. This exercise will help with this.

Feeling Part of the Larger Movement

Feeling our connection with others who are concerned about the world is an important part of empowerment for social transformation. It is all too easy to think that you have to solve all the problems yourself, which leaves you feeling overwhelmed and helpless before the immensity of the world situation. The truth is that we are part of a large movement of people from all around the world who are attempting to solve these problems, yet we sometimes think only in terms of the effect of our individual actions.

As a reflection of our cultural emphasis on individuality, we tend to see ourselves as isolated persons rather than as parts of a larger whole. In evaluating the impact of your efforts in the service of social transformation, it is empowering to focus on the impact of the groups and larger movements you are part of, not just on your personal impact. If you work with battered women, you are part of a movement of women who are doing the same, and all of you are part of the larger women's movement. If you are working to bring spiritual values to the company you work for, you are part of a larger movement such as described in *The Aquarian Conspiracy*,[1] and you are part of the still larger spiritual renaissance of our time.

As you contribute your small amount to the workings of these groups and movements, let yourself feel your impact in terms of the accomplishments of these larger wholes. At this writing, it seems likely that the U.S. and the Soviet Union will sign the first treaty to reduce stockpiles of nuclear weapons. I am feeling a personal sense of pride in this because I see it as an outgrowth of the massive efforts of the peace movement during the 1980s. Even though I can't say that anything I personally did had any significant impact, I contributed my part to this success, and it feels very satisfying. This exercise will help you to reconceptualize your thinking along these lines.

Circumstances

Working Alone. When working alone you will need to skip the sharing of images in the group, and you will need to imagine someone you know for the eye contact part of the exercise.

Working with a Partner. One person can lead both of you through the first part of the exercise, including sharing images with each other. Then take turns leading each other through the rest of the exercise. During the last part, the one who is leading should be available for eye contact.

Time: 25 minutes.

---

[1] Marilyn Ferguson, *The Aquarian Conspiracy* (Los Angeles: J.P. Tarcher, 1980).

The Exercise[2] —————————————————————————

[People sit in a circle in relaxed positions appropriate for a guided
fantasy. Sitting in a circle is necessary because during part of the
fantasy you will be speaking to the group. The leader begins with
an induction.]

♪   "Adagio" (by Albinoni, three times, as much as needed; or other
      sad music)

Let yourself tune in to what's happening in the world now in this
time of social breakdown. There is much pain and suffering and
great danger for the future. Gradually open yourself to this. What
aspects of this suffering move you the most—not your own suffering, but that of people you know, or know of, or have read about.
Recall images you have seen in the media, situations you have
witnessed in your travels, or heard about from talking to friends.
Let these images and thoughts and sensings about pain in the
world arise for you. [Allow about 4 minutes.]
      Now whenever someone feels ready, share with us one of
your images or sensings. Evoke it for us, so we can sense it too.
And allow a moment of silence after each sharing so that we can
take it in before going on to the next. [Allow about 10 minutes.]

♪   "Rêve" (from *Opera Sauvage* by Vangelis, as much as needed; or
      other sad music)

Now start tuning into your breath, pay attention to the breath,
feel it moving in through your nose, down your windpipe, into
your lungs. . . . Now imagine that it passes out through your
lungs and into your heart. And then out through your heart and
chest and back into the world. Imagine your breath as a loop

—————————
[2] This exercise is derived from Joanna Macy's exercises "The Well," pg. 123,
"Breathing Through," pg. 155, and "Learning to See Each Other," pg. 158,
from her book *Despair and Personal Power in the Nuclear Age.*

passing down through your heart and out, connecting you with the world. . . .

At the same time put your awareness into the bottom of your spine, where you're sitting. Feel your connection with the floor or the chair or the pillow you are sitting on. Ground yourself through your root chakra, ground yourself into the earth. Imagine yourself, your energy extending downward from the tip of your spine down into the earth. Feel yourself deepening, connecting to the ground. . . .

Feel that groundedness while you also feel the loop of your breath, passing your breath down through your heart and back out connecting you to the world again, and then back in and through your heart. So you are feeling both the breath and the groundedness. . . .

Now begin to take in some of the images you have seen or heard during the last few minutes. Take them in with your breath and let them pass through your heart. As you do that, make sure you don't hang onto them; let them pass through your heart and then back out into the world, into the larger resources of the world. . . . As you are doing that, stay in touch with your connection to the ground. . . .

Let yourself be enriched and enlarged by this experience, as painful as it is. As it develops your compassion and your strength, know that your heart is large enough and open enough to contain this pain, and then let it go. Let each image pass through your heart, let it be warmed, maybe even transformed by your heart, let yourself open to it, and then let it pass through and let it go.

Remember, if you have any difficulties, if the pain threatens to be too much or to be overwhelming, bring your attention back to your grounding, back to your seat on the earth, your connection to the planet. Feel the strength and solidity of that connection. [Allow 2 minutes.]

Now become aware that just as you are open to the pain in the world and connected in this way, you are also open to and supported by the strength and goodness in the world. Just as there is great danger and suffering in this time, there are also great resources to be tapped. You do not have to solve these problems alone.

♪   "Neranzoula" (from *Odes* by Irene Papas and Vangelis, as much as needed; or other heart music)

Now gradually open your eyes, staying in the open place you're in. . . . Look around the room and take in the other people in the group, these people who also care deeply about what is happening in the world. Let your eyes move from one to another and feel your connection with them. . . .

Now pair up with someone sitting near you and sit facing each other. . . . Look into this person's eyes and take a moment to get to know this person silently. . . . Know that this person also cares about the suffering in the world, that their heart is open just as yours is, that they are also moved by compassion. . . . Now acknowledge your partner with a touch or the squeeze of a hand, and move on to another person. . . .

Sit facing this person and look into their eyes. . . . Let yourself become aware of the potential this person has to contribute to the healing of our world. . . . Let yourself see in them the strengths and abilities that this person has been given. You may see things they are not even aware of. Behind those eyes may be reserves of creativity, or wisdom, or determination, or ingenuity. Rejoice in the powers and talents you see. . . . Now touch this person in some way as an ending, and close your eyes. . . .

Realize that you could be sitting in such a circle with any of the millions of other people around the world who care about our predicament and are attempting to do something about it. Imagine yourself now sitting in this expanded circle, perhaps with people from your support group or organization, or people with whom you have networked, people you may meet briefly at a rally or a meeting, people who have touched you at a workshop. Or perhaps people you have never met who are doing work similar to yours. Or even people in other lands with different concerns, who nonetheless are working to heal our world. . . .

Know that you are part of a vast network of people working for a better world, and that even though the problems are great, so are the resources. Your contribution, however small it may be in your eyes, is an integral part of the work of this great movement. You are part of something much larger. Feel this now. Open yourself to it, and feel yourself deepened and expanded. . . .

♪   Simplified music: "Adagio" as above.

Experiences

Images of Suffering

Tears are common during this part of the exercise. Evoking images for each other helps people to open up even more to their feelings and provides mutual support through this difficult experience. The following are examples of images evoked:

"My nephews at 3 and 8 already becoming identified with Rambo and He-Man and military things."

"The dumping of chemical wastes into water, the poisoning in the name of progress."

"So many people defeated, feeling that they're not able to find the American dream, turning to drugs or falling into mental illness."

"The mothers, wives, and sisters in El Salvador who have organized to find their men who have been brutally murdered and tortured."

"Peasants in Nicaragua waiting for the bombers to fly over."

"The black people in my neighborhood walking around feeling like they are inferior because their skin is brown."

"The child whose mother threatens to take a switch from the tree to hit him."

"People who are consumed with rage and hate, who are always looking for somebody to blame or hurt."

"The hole that's been created in the ozone layer, and the continued destruction of our beautiful planet."

"Pregnant teenagers not knowing where to go or what to do."

"The clearing of the rain forests; the incredibly beautiful, lush, alive rain forests being bulldozed, and all of the species that are being destroyed."

"The MX taking off and leaving a corkscrew trail across the Pacific sky after we tried everything we could think of to stop it."

"A 15-year-old boy who called me to ask if the siren he heard meant that the bomb was going to fall."

"The people of Africa holding on, as a matter of life and death, to their old traditions, to their cattle, even though these are contributing to their starvation."

The Passion of the Heart

Don is the intellectual man we met earlier who was working on opening his heart. During the first part of the exercise, he found images of suffering coming easily and quickly to him but without the corresponding feelings. When other people in the group shared their images and he heard the emotion in their voices, his barriers started to melt. Compassion and sadness began to well up in him. While breathing through the heart, this became stronger and he began to feel the stirrings of a real passion for helping people in need.

"I've been trying to do my work from a place of service rather than self-gratification. I'm moving in the right direction, but it's been hard, because I've been coming from my head. In this exercise, that all just vanished. After feeling that compassion, there was a sense of higher connection so that the desire to serve just happened, just came from my heart. It was wonderful!

"I felt caught up in and dedicated to something larger than myself, something more important than my own welfare—not just intellectually, but all through me. It was very powerful. I felt connected to the people in the room and to other people I've never met. I felt transported to a whole other level. I would love to be able to live from there!"

After this experience and some other similar ones, including the one in chapter 10, Don experienced a renewed energy and vigor in his determination to apply some of his academic work to social issues. His excitement led him to work much more effectively. Ideas came to him at all hours of the day and night; his creativity was tapped in a way that had been missing for years.

Breathing Through the Heart

Beverly is an experienced political activist who had felt overwhelmed by the pain of the world before, and she was afraid to do the exercises. We arranged to have her sitting next to me so she could reach out to hold hands when she needed during the exercise. She experienced deep grief during the first part of the exercise and made good use of the physical support. At the end of the exercise she was left feeling strong and solid. The permission to let go of the images was very important; it provided a freedom she hadn't had before.

During the last part of the exercises she reported, "It felt very comforting as soon as I saw the beauty of all of you and your sensitivity to the world's pain. I felt the support that is there, and the awareness and the desire to help that is there. The pain and distress of it all felt much lighter."

Our friend Sandra reported, "The image I had that stuck with me was that of a small frightened child in the middle of the street crying with buildings blowing up all around. When the child came through my heart, it was transformed into a shiny laughing child. I noticed that happening with angry people as well. As they went through the heart, they were filled with a positive sense of what they could do instead of being angry. It happened with all the images [crying]. The hopeless people were renewed in some way. I was just amazed that it happened with every one. And so my feeling was [deeply moved] that I could also pass myself through my heart and be renewed." In this way she took another step toward self-acceptance and self-support, the cornerstone of the inner strength she is building.

Grounding

Being grounded in your body and connected to the earth provides a stability and strength that is crucial to being able to tolerate the pain in this exercise without being overwhelmed. The following individual work illustrates this:

Barbara is the woman who danced her compassion for herself in chapter 2. In this exercise, she felt depleted by passing all the images through her heart. She felt overwhelmed by the number of situations because of her need to fix them all immediately. This led to an awareness that she was not grounded enough, and she asked me to help her with this by guiding her in a fantasy of becoming a tree, as Morgon had done in the Riddlemaster Trilogy.

Jay: "Imagine yourself walking into the forest and finding a particular tree that draws you, one that seems particularly grounded. Stand next to it, and watch it, and be with it. To start with, just observe and feel what that tree is like, the depth of the roots, the strength of its trunk, the patience, the ability it has just to be and not have to take care of things, not have to fix things, that rootedness in nature, in the cycles of nature, that deep connection to the ground, to the physical earth, to the dirt.

"And when you're ready, begin to let those qualities flow into you—all the qualities of the tree, the groundedness, the patience, the earthiness. . . . Get in touch with those qualities in you, as you take them into yourself. As this happens more and more, find yourself becoming a tree—your torso becoming the trunk, your blood becoming the sap, your feet becoming the roots, perhaps your arms becoming the branches, maybe your fingers becoming the leaves. . . . Feel yourself slowing and deepening—life still moving through you, but in a different way. . . . Without losing your sense of being a tree, describe what you're experiencing."

Barbara: "Very solid, . . . sturdy, . . . an enormous corona of leaves. But what I feel most is the roots, thick roots going deep, meandering, seeking all kinds of nourishment from the earth, water. The roots keep on spreading deeper."

Jay: "And now from that place, breathe in some of the images from the previous exercise, some of the images of pain and suffering. Know from the tree place that you don't have to fix them right away, that you bring your patience and your grounding and your compassion to those images. Let them flow in and flow through you and be warmed by your love, and know that you're so deep and so grounded and so solid that you can contain any of these images and all of them, and that your sturdiness remains. Let the images pass through you. The suffering is real, your compassion is real, then they pass out, and you remain solid."

Barbara: [pause] "Thank you. . . . That's a piece I forget." She described her experience: "The roots kept on growing, and more and more earth was surrounding them as they extended further into the ground. There was energy coming up through me from my connection with those depths, so that I didn't feel the exhaustion I get in my heart when I'm needing the other person to reciprocate. It was a physical feeling. The more I root, the more I ground in what sustains me, the more I can tolerate. The tree is a dynamic thing. If something is going on up here so I need nourishment, it will root more and more."

8

Envisioning a Healthy Society

ALLEVIATING SUFFERING isn't our only social task. We also need to help build the kind of society in which suffering is not as likely to happen, the kind of society that promotes health, love, creativity, peace. Since we are in the midst of a major societal transformation, we have the opportunity to influence the new social order, to contribute to the new worldview that is being born. Like few other generations, we have the chance to create a new world.

If you could have your heart's desire, what kind of world would you like to live in? My motivation for social transformation work comes primarily from my own visions of a healthy society and my longing for it. I find myself deeply moved by Utopian novels which explore models of ideal societies.[1] I have always yearned to live in a world in which people can be healthy and safe, connected with a community and fulfilled as individuals. And I am intrigued by the difficult question of which societal structures and values might best promote this.

Many political activists are motivated by compassion for the suffering of others or by fear that a holocaust is threatening. However, you can also be motivated by the hope of creating

---

[1] Ursula LeGuin, *The Dispossessed* (New York: Harper & Row, 1974); Ernest Callenbach, *Ecotopia* (New York: Bantam, 1975); Ernest Callenbach, *Ecotopia Emerging* (Berkeley: Banyan Tree, 1981).

something new and better, by the sense of future possibilities. Envisioning a positive future is very empowering. Imagining a healthy world and how we might get there empowers you to act with clarity and direction. Being moved emotionally by your vision enables you to act with passion and force.

Having a positive social vision also allows you to work for specific alternatives that will be healing and life-affirming. In the 1960s many of us first became aware of the destructive, life-denying trends of our society and focused our energy on stopping them. Now we are older, more experienced, and hopefully wiser. While we must still work against the evils of the world, it is now time to implement positive new social structures and ways of being to take the place of those which no longer nurture us.

Of course we will never have a perfect society, so one could call the exercise unrealistic and impractical. However, holding a magnificent goal in your heart is a powerful way to be moved to creative action. The goal can be gradually approached even if it is not completely attainable.

Much of our sense of what is possible for society comes from our memories of the best that has happened in our own lives and our sense of what is possible for us personally. This exercise builds on that.

Circumstances

A variation is included that is appropriate for workshops that are personally oriented but whose members are open to concerns about social transformation.

Working Alone. When working by yourself, the exercise can be done as is except that you must skip the parts which involve group interaction.

Working with a Partner. When working with a partner, each person in turn should lead the other through the guided fantasy part, with the one being led saying their visions aloud at the point where the group is asked to do so. Then one of the partners should lead both together through the movement part at the end.

Time: 30 minutes.

The Exercise

[People sit in a circle in relaxed positions appropriate for a guided fantasy. You need to be sitting up because you will be speaking to the group later in the fantasy. The leader begins with an induction.]

Remember a place in nature that means a lot to you. See the colors and shapes, smell the smells, feel the air, be there as vividly as possible. . . .

Now remember a time when you felt particularly alive and vital. Let yourself be fully present in the memory. Feel what that experience was like. . . .

Remember a person who means a lot to you or meant a lot to you at some time in your life. Imagine yourself being with that person right now. Feel what that's like. . . .

♪ "Pachelbel's Canon" (extended version from *Timeless Motion* by Daniel Kobialka, as much as needed; or other heart music)

Now think of a time in your life when you were very loving or in love. It could have been with a lover, a child, a family member, a close friend. Remember it as vividly as possible. Really put yourself back there. Feel what it was like. . . . Now imagine that your life is structured in such a way that you are loving like this much of the time. And imagine that the people you are close to are also able to be loving much of the time so that you are part of a loving community of friends and family. . . . Now imagine that society is changed in such a way that everyone is able to be loving much of the time.

See what images come to you about what it would be like for people to live in this kind of society. . . .

Now remember a time when you were engaged in work that was very meaningful for you and tapped your creativity. This can be either a job or an avocation. Let yourself remember this time as vividly as possible. . . . Now imagine that your life is structured in such a way that your life work is very meaningful and creative for you. And imagine that this is also true for the people around you, especially the people you work with so that you are part of a community of creative people, engaged in work that is important to you. . . . Now imagine that society is changed in such a way that this kind of work is possible for everyone. Let images come to you of what life in that kind of society would be like. . . .

Now remember a time when you were in a place of great beauty and peace, either in a building of some sort, or in nature. Be there as vividly as possible. . . . Imagine that your life is structured in such a way that you are able to live in, work in, and easily get to places of beauty and peace. Perhaps not the extraordinary kind of beauty you just remembered, but still places that satisfy and enrich you. . . . And now imagine that society is changed in such a way that everyone is able to live in places that are beautiful and satisfying to them. What images come to you?. . .

Now remember a time when you were having an argument or a power struggle with someone, and the two of you were able to resolve the conflict in a very constructive way. Maybe you were able to resolve it in such a way that each of your feelings were taken care of, or that each of you got much of what you really needed in the situation. You ended up feeling good about each other. Think of a situation like that and remember it as vividly as possible. . . . Now imagine that your life is structured in such a way that you are able to resolve your conflicts in this kind of creative way, and that's also true for the people around you, the people you're close to and work with and interact with. So your world is a peaceful, cooperative world. . . .

Now imagine that society is changed in such a way that every-one is able to resolve personal conflicts like this much of the time. And imagine that society is structured such that conflicts and power struggles between groups in society are also handled this well. Imag-ine that conflicts in businesses and schools and other institutions are resolved constructively, that conflicts between institutions, be-tween racial, religious, and ethnic groups, and especially between nations are also handled well. . . . What would it be like to live in this kind of a world? . . .

Now whenever someone feels ready, share with us one of your images of a healthy society. Evoke it for us, so that we may share in your excitement. Allow a moment of silence after each sharing so that we can all take it in before moving on to the next. [Allow about 10 minutes.]

Now imagine that you live in a society made up of the best of your visions and others that you have heard today. Take a moment and feel what it would be like to live in that kind of world. What would your day-to-day life be like? . . . Place these images and feelings in your heart. Open to this vision and let yourself feel any yearning that is rising in you, any longing you may have to be part of such a world. . . . Let this vision and this longing be a hope, a promise of what is possible, of what you are working toward. . . . Keep it in your heart as a reminder, when things get difficult, when you get discouraged, when you wonder if it's worth bothering, re-member this vision of what is possible for the human race. Let it inspire you to greater commitment, greater risk, and greater passion in your work for social transformation. . . .

[Bring people back out of trance, and then have them gradu-ally come to a standing position.]

♪   "Bindu Devas" from (*Lotussongs II* by Ojas; light, happy, danceable music)

Stay in tune with your vision of that possible world and your life in that world. As you imagine this, let your body begin to move with the music and the vision. Staying with that same vision, but now from a livelier place. Imagining what a day in your life might be in this world. [Allow a minute.]

Continuing your fantasy, let your movements become larger. Begin to turn them into a dance, a dance of celebration of your life in this new healthy society. Act out this new life symbolically. [Allow a minute.] If it's appropriate for the way this new world would be, let your dance begin to involve you with other people. Connect with other people or with the whole group in your movement, just as you would in your life in this ideal society. [If people are hesitant to initiate this, the leader may need to start. Allow until the music ends, 2 or 3 minutes.]

Variations

This exercise can be changed by adding or substituting sections on (1) learning, growth, and education, or (2) handling loss or misfortune well. These would follow the same pattern as the above sections. I have also shortened it by deleting the section on beauty and the environment.

This exercise can be used in a setting other than a socially-oriented workshop. In this case, the last paragraph of the guided fantasy needs to be changed because it assumes that people have already made a commitment to work for social transformation. The second half could be reworded as follows:

Keep it in your heart as a reminder of what is possible for the human race. Let it inspire you to greater interest and involvement in work for social transformation. . . .

Experiences

The primary value of the exercise is not so much in the content of people's visions, but rather in the inspiration and yearning, the hope and commitment that are engendered by the visions. People are simultaneously reminded of the problems of our current society and inspired by the possibilities of something better. It is more of an emotional outcome than a cognitive one. It would be useful to follow this exercise with a brainstorming session so as to build on the emotional flow of the exercise with a cognitive mapping of a new society.

The Visions

People tend to have visions that run the gamut from the personal through the social to the political. The following is what one group shared with each other during the exercise:

"I see people living in close touch with nature. I see houses spread out through the forest connected with paths, so that people wake up and move and work in a real connection with the natural world."

"I see families having access to nature and cultural opportunities that enrich their lives. I see parents getting some relief from the burdens of caring for children, so that they have the room to love and value their children. And the children growing up without needing to start the cycle of violence and hurt over again."

"I have a picture of a kaleidoscope of all kinds of people. Each has their own idea of what's fulfilling work for them, and they all fit together into a pattern. The very differences in the colors add to the kaleidoscope feeling, and the overall pattern moves. There is a place for each one. I see people looking each other in the eyes, taking responsibility for what's going on between them, knowing that it's possible to work things out so that one doesn't have to lose and the other to win. The joy and the pain shared."

"I see a society in which everyone has enough. Everyone has enough love, enough work to do, enough play, enough space, enough happiness, enough beauty, enough access to power, enough food. There are sufficient resources for everyone, so there is no need to feel at a disadvantage. There is a dynamic sense of give and take, of sharing and creating. Barriers between people are removed."

"I see a classroom in this world for young children, a classroom filled with light, with grown-ups who feel OK about themselves. The children in each stage as they grow up also feel OK about themselves. They are happy and busy as they work or talk, without fear or competition, knowing that they're loved within their families and within the school. The school is simply an extension of the neighborhood and the home."

"I see the different countries knowing that they are all actually one. I see the diplomats gathering and shaking hands and reaching agreement in an open manner with a sense of trust, with a feeling of cooperation."

Yearning for a New World

Bill is the man we met earlier who was concerned about nuclear war and whose shadow was a street tough. During this exercise he was moved deeply, remembering times when he was first in love with his wife and when he felt connected and creative with the children he was teaching.

He had a vision of a world totally free of nuclear weapons, in which he and others could plan to raise children knowing that their future would not be threatened. He also saw a loving society where people could live close to the earth. "As I heard other people's visions, it all coalesced into one blur. I can't remember what was said except that I had an image of self-esteem running rampant. It just seemed that everyone ought to be able to live in a society like that. I felt tremendous yearning for that world and that way of life."

Bill continued, "The movement part was great fun and very energizing. I loved dancing and playing with people and acting out what that healthy society might be like. I got a sense that maybe we can really do something to get there. I feel really excited right now; let's go out and do it!" [group laughter and agreement] Here the excitement and positive visioning help to break through Bill's blocks against action. He explores his social concerns further in the next chapter.

SECTION FOUR

Life Purpose

Introduction

THIS SECTION DEALS with the issue of life purpose. It asks: What gives your life meaning? What is your life really all about? Is there more than the pursuit of pleasure and security? What are the larger concerns that might impel you to action? What is your particular gift to the world?

These are crucial questions for us all. Even if you've never thought about it, you operate out of some understanding of the meaning of your life. If you are approaching mid-life or if you're in a time of crisis and transition, this issue may be just emerging into your consciousness. If you have reached the point in your development where you are no longer dealing primarily with old pain and unmet needs, you may find it becoming an important priority. [1]

I define life purpose as a person's contribution to the world that gives their life meaning through dedication to something larger than themselves. It might be working for social transformation; rendering service to people who are in need; living from an attitude of love; unleashing your creativity, or developing your highest spiritual potential.

---

[1] Abraham Maslow, *The Further Reaches of Human Nature* (New York: Viking, 1971).

I believe everyone has a life purpose to be created or discovered. At a certain level of psychological development people need to identify and manifest their purpose. Being blocked in this area can lead to apathy, depression, despair, and a variety of other psychological symptoms. It can even lead to physical symptoms.[2] On the other hand, finding and fulfilling your life purpose can lead to pleasure and satisfaction of a depth that is unmatched by more self-oriented pursuits.

This issue is also a central aspect of spiritual development. True seekers desire union with the divine not for their own gratification, but in order to bring back the wisdom and riches they have gained for the good of humanity. The goal is not simply to know God, but to live in the world from that knowing, to bring the divine into form. People speak of feeling "called" to a certain spiritual vocation; they speak of obeying the will of God in loving and serving others. "There is no solution to the problem of meaning except to transcend the motivations of the [ordinary] self. The path to that transcendence is service."[3]

Finding Your Life Purpose

Your higher self is the part of you that understands your life purpose. It lives in the larger flow of your life, the deeper meaning underlying the particular events. You may sense this purpose when you are able to be quiet and alone and go deeply inside yourself. You may get a hint of it when you are unexpectedly moved to strong emotion by a scene in a movie or something in the news. A project or an ideal may stir your passion deeply and draw you in; you may find yourself devoting long hours to it

---

[2] Brugh Joy, *Joy's Way* (Los Angeles: J.P. Tarcher, 1979).
[3] Arthur Deikman, *The Observing Self: Mysticism and Psychotherapy* (Boston: Beacon, 1982), p. 114.

doggedly or joyfully. You may be surprised to find yourself passionately espousing a point of view at a social gathering.

For some of you, once you have sensed your life purpose, you will begin to express it naturally in your life. Others may have a long, hard road to follow before they actually manifest their purpose in the world. This process often involves much experimenting, personal growth, overcoming blocks, developing skills and contacts, etc. Gradually you hone in on more and more satisfying and influential ways to contribute. It can be especially difficult to make your career an expression of your life purpose, as most of us want. This may require much perseverance and creativity throughout the process. Keep in mind that engaging in this process itself is part of the expression of your life purpose.

One of the problems with our current social order is that it allows only a small minority of people to have life work that is simultaneously meaningful, creative, and financially rewarding. Yet everyone should have this opportunity. The good news is that more people are searching for this kind of work, and this is putting pressure on corporations and other institutions to provide these possibilities. Companies are slowly becoming more flexible and allowing employees more participation, autonomy, and responsibility. There is also a great upsurge in small businesses which have started in recent years, as people opt out of the corporate world in order to pursue their own visions. So in your search for a career that is not only personally satisfying but also manifests your life purpose, you may also be participating in the transformation of our social institutions.

Life purpose is not only found through career. It may involve serving the world in other ways—through volunteer work, artistic endeavors, loving your children, or the seemingly little acts that can be so important. You may sense that your life purpose has primarily to do with a certain way of being in the world which would permeate everything you do—being caring for those in need, being courageous in the face of hardship, being true to yourself, living simply, daring to speak your mind.

The following exercises in this section are designed to help you sense your life purpose:

The Dedication Ritual
Gaia
Finding Your Contribution

The following exercises in the next section deal with empowerment toward manifesting this purpose in the world:

Manifesting Your Intention
The Naming Ritual
Expansive Movement

The following exercises also deal with life purpose:

The Flight of Empowerment
The Expanded Body

9

The Dedication Ritual

WHAT CONCERNS MOVE YOU to a sense of higher purpose? What do you care about deeply enough to dedicate your life to? This exercise deals with the source or motivating principle behind your life purpose. You'll be looking not so much at what you might *do* to fulfill your life purpose, but rather at the deeper reasons behind your wanting to do it. We can view life purpose as having three aspects:

1. *Action*—what you actually do in the world—is the most obvious aspect.

2. *Being*—refers to the kind of presence you manifest in the world—loving or angry, courageous or timid.

3. *Source*—refers to the larger reasons that inspire your life purpose, the "why" behind your action or being.

For instance, the action part of my life purpose involves leading groups and workshops, writing, and doing theoretical work in psychology. For the being part, I am working at being loving, creative, and letting go of my needs for self-importance. The source level for me comes from my conviction that at this time in human history we are faced with a planetary crisis that will result in either a brighter future or an unprecedented disaster. I am dedicated to avoiding that disaster and helping the human race continue in its evolution. I am also dedicated to helping create a healthy society, one based on love and reverence for the earth, where everyone is free and has access to the good things in life. My choices for my actions spring from these sources.

The following are examples of the source level. People have been dedicated to:

> living things and the earth
> the future of the human race
> the children of the world
> people who are dying (or some other group of people in need)
> the liberation of blacks (or some other oppressed group)
> god or spirit (however conceptualized)
> the creation of beauty
> the freeing of the human body
> love

The source level involves a dedication to something larger than yourself, a concern that goes beyond your daily struggle to achieve happiness and security. It lifts you out of the usual self-centered mode into a realm where you are part of larger and more meaningful concerns. You feel deeper, more open, more real. You touch on the essence of life.

Even though the source of your life purpose will be something larger than yourself, it may grow out of some of your own most intense personal concerns. You may be dedicated to ending child abuse because of the way you were abused as a child. You may care deeply about social justice because of your own disadvantaged background. You may want to end the nuclear threat because your own child is having nuclear nightmares. Your personal life crises and trials can provide the juice and passion behind your life purpose.

People who are in touch with the source of their life purpose sometimes are able to act freely and courageously without the usual fears and limitations of their personal egos. This is because they are committed to something larger. They are not trying to prove themselves, or protect themselves, or hold onto anything they have gained. At least at times, they transcend these concerns and live from a higher place. This is a wonderful feeling!

Circumstances

This exercise needs to be done in a setting where people have some access to the natural world (see second half of the exercise). It may be used in a social transformation workshop or a regular workshop.

Working with a Partner. When working with a partner, take turns leading each other through the guided fantasy part, and then perform the ritual together.

Time: 25 to 30 minutes depending on the group size.

The Exercise

First we are going to do a guided fantasy to help you get in touch with the source level of your life purpose, with something that you would like to dedicate yourself to. Then we will perform a ritual in which you will make the dedication. Please arrange yourselves for a guided fantasy.

♪ "Crystallite" (from *Crystal Meditations* by Don Campbell, as much as needed; suggesting depth and descent)

[Leader begins with an induction.] Now imagine that you are exploring in a rocky, mountainous area. Notice your surroundings. . . . Is there any vegetation? . . . Is it sunny or windy? . . . As you climb over the rocks, how does your body feel? . . . Climbing, exploring. . . . Looking around, taking note of what you see. . . .

Now you come to a particularly large rock. You climb it, and looking down on the other side, you notice a cave going deep into the mountainside. You approach the cave, and as you enter you pick up a lighted torch to guide your way. . . . You move further into the cave, exploring it. At the back of the cave you find a series of steps rough hewn out of stone, slanting downward. You are drawn to follow them. . . .

Moving downward, noticing the walls of the stairway, the material, the texture, the play of light and shadow. . . . Passing an opening leading off to the side into a corridor, continuing down. . . . Feeling the rock of the stairs under your feet, the feeling of climbing down. . . . Deeper and deeper into the earth. . . . Walking down, feeling a sense of quiet, a sense of stillness. . . .

Coming to another opening leading into a passageway, you stop to look at some carving in the wall over the doorway. You touch the letters with your hand, then hold up the torch. You make out the words "Life Purpose," and you know that you have come to that deep place of inner direction. You enter that passageway and walk along it, exploring. . . . You come to a door and wonder what is behind it, but you know with an inner sense that this is not what you seek. You continue on passing other doors, searching for the right one. . . .

You finally come to a door that draws your attention. You look at it carefully and see carved above it the word "Source." You know that you have reached your destination. In a moment you will open the door and walk into a room in which you will encounter the source level of your life purpose, in which you will commune with your deepest reason for being. You may encounter a being who will interact with you, or you may find something in the room that embodies the source of your dedication, or you may just sense it in your body.

You carefully open the door, and step through. You will have a few minutes now to encounter the source of your life purpose. [Allow about two minutes.] Now your time is almost over; see if there is something to bring back with you from this place. It could be an object, or an image, or even a feeling. [Allow half a minute.]

[Direct the participants to leave the room and return to the surface by reversing the journey down through the cave. Then bring them out of trance.]

Now everyone please go outside and find a bit of nature that represents for you the source of your dedication. It might be a twig, a leaf, a flower, a stone, or something unique that you find. Bring it back in with you to use in the dedication ritual.

[While people are outside the leader constructs a sacred circle six to eight feet in diameter out of some natural objects such as stones. When people come back in, they line up for a procession. This should start far enough away from the circle so that people will take some time walking toward the circle.]

As the music plays please walk very slowly toward the sacred circle holding the object in your hands and contemplating your dedication as you walk. When you reach the circle, place your object in the center in some relationship to the other objects placed there. We will be forming a totem in the center, representing all our dedications. As you place the object, say aloud, "I dedicate myself to _____." Then sit around the edge of the circle to witness the other dedications.

Wait until I give the signal to start the procession, and leave about five or six steps between each person in line.

♪   *Ignacio* (first and third movements, by Vangelis, as much as needed; sweet and grand processional tone, very slow)

Take a deep breath and turn your attention inward. Reconnect with the part of you that is dedicated to a higher purpose. Focus your attention on the object you hold in your hand as you contemplate your dedication.

[There is an introductory section to the music before the processional part. Give the signal when the processional part begins.]

[After all have finished:] Now as you observe the totem we have formed, see that you are not alone in your dedication, your calling. Just as these objects have come together inside this circle, so you will have people to help you and to work with you in your life task. Sense your connection with the people in this room, and through them to the larger humanity, each person with their own purpose, their own part to play in the unfolding human story.

♪   Simplified music: Use *Ignacio* as above.

Experiences

People are sometimes wary of this ritual, because of the serious nature of making such a dedication, and perhaps because of discomfort with rituals in general. However, when the leader adopts an attitude of reverence and conviction, invariably people enter into it and are quite moved.

Our friend Sandra (the plant that grows back) explored her sense of life direction over the months in the Inner Journeys group, and found herself more and more drawn to artistic endeavors. However, she kept feeling that she was not talented enough or worthy enough to pursue art as a life purpose. In the guided fantasy, when she entered her source room, she was deeply moved to find it full of art materials. As she spent time exploring the room and reflecting on its meaning, she felt a profound sense of self-acceptance and permission to follow her artistic inclination. We will pursue this further with her in subsequent exercises.

Another woman chose a stone and a leaf for her objects. She identified with the stone, because "while stones can seem dull, when you put them under water, interesting lines and colors are revealed." She feels that she came from a potentially dull background but has consistently allowed waves of change to wash over her to bring out her essence. The leaf was important for her because its colors represent fall, which is an introspective time when she can see all the changes she has gone through in the year. She dedicated herself to helping other people through their important periods of change.

The Children of the World

Bill is the man from last chapter who was concerned about the nuclear threat. When he entered his source room, he found a group of children who were frightened of nuclear war, who were afraid they would never grow up. Even though he had known what his dedication would be before doing the guided fantasy, it was very important for him to spend some time in the room with the children. He listened to them and comforted them, and he told them that he would dedicate his life to protecting them. At that time he had no children of his own but wanted one very much. He felt that he was speaking to his own unborn child as well.

He decided that the object which best expressed his dedication was not outside in nature. He was drawn to a little porcelain figure of a child, which he placed in the circle to represent his love of children. He dedicated himself to ending the threat of nuclear war to the children of the world, so that they might grow up without fear to lead full lives.

When Bill placed his object in the circle and made the dedication, he spontaneously bowed to the ground. This act expressed and confirmed how much the dedication meant to him; it "sealed" the dedication for him. He was also moved by witnessing other people's dedications. This gave him a sense of "everyone being a product of the earth and drawing power from her, and having a drive toward healing her."

He came away from the exercise with a strong determination to get to work on his goal. By this time Bill had also done significant work (described in chapter 3 and later in this book) on overcoming his difficulties with confidence and follow through. Soon afterwards he threw himself fully into the peace movement. This was during the early Reagan years and he felt caught up in an emergency situation that demanded his full commitment. He became intensely involved in his local nuclear freeze organization and devoted countless hours to that work over the next year and a half. It was a time of high excitement, sustained effort, and great satisfaction.

10

Gaia

SOMETIMES PEOPLE EXPERIENCE their life purpose as a spiritual "calling." They feel called to be a certain way in the world. They sense that a higher power desires to work through them to accomplish certain ends, a divine power has chosen them to act as a channel for its love or wisdom or purpose on the earthly plane.

This can take extreme, obvious forms, such as channeling written or verbal material that the person does not claim to have authored. Occasionally people will even feel that they are receiving direct instructions from a divine presence. However, most of us experience a calling in subtler ways—feeling a strong passion for some ideal, being unexpectedly moved at certain times, receiving creative inspiration that seems to come from somewhere else, vaguely sensing a project that needs to be birthed through us.

I will not attempt to resolve questions about the metaphysical reality of such a higher source. It could be a separate being, or universal intelligence of some sort, or an aspect of one's own superconscious. For this book I am interested in the experience of being called and how it affects our lives, not its origin.

My Experience

During the last eight years I have come to recognize that I feel a strong sense of purpose or calling connected with the planetary crisis. Given my scientific background, the idea of having a calling was quite foreign to me until I was introduced to it by Jean Houston. In her workshops she has frequently suggested that we consider the idea that a higher power could move through us to accomplish a purpose in the world. When I have tried this out experientially during her exercises, I have been deeply moved, feeling a yearning and attunement and a deep sense of direction, even while at first not believing in the concept.

The strength of my sense of calling was brought home to me by the following incident. During the first year of my work with Jean Houston, I was opening up spiritually, feeling a greater sense of grounding, peace, and openness. However, during a period of four or five months I was unable to attend a workshop and unable to renew that sense of spiritual connection on my own. At that time I was scheduled to lead one of my own socially-oriented empowerment workshops. On the morning of the workshop, I took a few minutes to open myself to a deeper sense of my purpose for the day. I closed my eyes, grounded myself, and almost immediately was flooded with that sense of peace and loving connection that had been missing during those months. I realized that because this work is my calling, the higher connection was available to do the work, even during a time of spiritual drought.

To feel called in this way, to feel something nobler moving through you, to open yourself and allow yourself to be taken is an exquisite experience: you feel both humbled and lifted up. You know that you are not of great importance, but you feel yourself as part of something vast and meaningful. "Oh the wonder that bubbles into my soul!" writes D. H. Lawrence about such a time.[1]

Gaia

Gaia is the ancient Greek goddess of the earth. Recently James Lovelock has proposed the "Gaia hypothesis," the idea that our

---

[1] D.H. Lawrence from "The Song of a Man Who Has Come Through."

planet is actually a living organism.[2] He supports this by elucidating the various properties and functions of an organism and then showing how the earth performs these. In addition to understanding this intellectually, we need to learn how to relate to the earth as a living being.

Up until now, our mechanical and industrial mentality has led us to see the earth only as an object to be used. As a result we are destroying much of the fragile beauty of the natural world and even our own natural life support systems. We need a new sensibility that integrates our scientific knowledge with an ability to relate personally to animals, trees, rocks, oceans, and the planet as a whole. The earth has much to teach us if we are only willing to listen. In this exercise, you have an opportunity to relate to Gaia and to hear the calling she may have for you.

Circumstances

This exercise is designed for social transformation workshops but is appropriate for ordinary workshops as well. It is a good exercise to use as a short workshop in itself, since it covers many of the elements of the work of empowerment for social transformation.

This guided fantasy uses a reincarnation theme. If you are uncomfortable with this idea, please understand that I don't intend this as a literal statement about the nature of reality, but rather as a powerful psychological metaphor.

The Naming Ritual is a perfect exercise to use immediately following Gaia because the message from Gaia sets the stage for the ritual. The exercise Manifesting Your Intention contains a section which involves imagining Gaia healed from the hurts and dangers that are visualized in this exercise. These three exercises are excellent to use in sequence.

Time: 25 minutes.

---

[2] James Lovelock, *Gaia: A New Look at Life on Earth* (Oxford, Eng.: Oxford University Press, 1979).

The Exercise ――――――――――――――――

[People arrange themselves for a guided fantasy. The leader starts out with an induction.]

♪   "Great Wall of China" (from *Silk Road* by Kitaro, twice, as much
     as needed; hypnotic, outer space tone)

Now imagine that your body is getting very light, . . . that it begins to float up into the air. Imagine yourself gradually floating up into the room, rising toward the ceiling, and as you rise higher into the air, you go deeper into yourself. . . . You now find yourself near the ceiling and able to look down and see everything in the room. . . . You float right through the ceiling and out into the air, feeling no discomfort as you do this. You can now look out and see the area around this building. [Mention significant landmarks.] . . . You continue to rise in the air, and as you do you go deeper into trance. . . .

[Leader continues suggesting that they rise into the air and see more and more of the earth and go correspondingly deeper into themselves. Continue mentioning the sights one might see in this process based on the time and place of the exercise. For instance, if you are on the West Coast in the afternoon, you might mention the sun glinting off the ocean. Continue until:]

Looking around, you now notice that the horizon looks slightly curved. You are beginning to see the earth as the sphere that it really is. As you continue to rise, what had been "the ground" gradually condenses into a globe that you are observing at a distance, and what had been "the sky" expands to become outer space completely surrounding you. And still you feel no discomfort. . . . There before your eyes is that beautiful little blue-green ball, and you feel that you could almost reach out and touch it. You also have a zoom lens so that you can zoom in and see or feel whatever is happening on the surface of the planet. . . .

♪ "Sequence in Earth Natural" (from *Mother Earth Lullaby* by Synchestra, as much as needed; soft, gentle tone with nature sounds in the background)

Envision the planet, now, not as a dead hunk of rock as we usually think of it, but as Gaia, a living organism, with all the normal life functions of a living creature. Feel the rhythm of night and day which is Gaia's pulse. . . . See the atmosphere and ocean currents swirling around her surface, circulating nutrients and carrying away waste products much as the blood does in your own body, feel the swirling movement and the sense of being cleansed. . . . See threadlike rivers swinging first one way and then another as they accommodate themselves to the changes of the land. The surface of Gaia's body is also marked by high, majestic mountain ranges, rich, teeming forests and jungles, flat expanses of fertile grasslands, and great arid deserts. . . .

Inside of Gaia you can sense an enormous churning current of liquid rock flowing back and forth between the core of the planet and the crust, sometimes oozing through volcanic pores to supply the minerals essential for life. . . . Notice how Gaia maintains the optimal conditions for the existence of life: the right temperature, the right balance of nutrients in the oceans and gases in the atmosphere, and a protective ozone layer over all. . . .[3]

Envision the various living creatures that inhabit Gaia and are analogous to her cells and organs. . . . Imagine the vast network of human beings as being like her nervous system, bringing communication and consciousness, . . . or, on the other hand, image us as a great profusion of malignant cancer cells, growing out of control and bringing disease and destruction. . . . And finally let yourself sense Gaia as a being with

---

[3] Parts of this paragraph were taken from Peter Russell, *The Global Brain* (Los Angeles: J.P. Tarcher, 1983).

awareness and feelings, who lovingly provides a life support system for her creatures and who feels pain when her integrity is threatened. . . .

♪   "Time Travel" (from *Silk Road* by Kitaro, twice, as much as needed; heavy, discordant tone)

Now you begin to notice that there are a number of dangers and threats to Gaia's health. Her air and waters are polluted with chemicals. . . . Toxic wastes are buried in her body, as well as nuclear poisons, which will last for thousands of years. Even her rains, which generally bring life and growth, are sometimes poisoned with acid. . . . Her protective ozone shield is breaking down, threatening her life forms with radiation, floods, or freezing temperatures. . . .

Many of her people are oppressed and exploited, making it difficult for them to have the basic freedoms and necessities of life. . . . A large number of her people are starving, or living without adequate shelter, or suffering from untreated disease. . . . Violence is widespread in the form of crime, terrorism, torture, war. . . . The very makeup of Gaia's air has been so altered that her temperature is going up, as if she had a fever, threatening to destroy her ability to support life as we know it.

Why is this happening? The human race has acquired the powers of gods, but in doing so has lost reverence for life. We do not see that Gaia is alive! We treat her as an object to be used. We see other life forms and other people as objects to be used. We even see ourselves this way. . . . But there may be a change coming. . . . This object consciousness may have run its course. It may be replaced by a new reverence for life and personhood and spirit. Envision these two kinds of consciousness now in dynamic tension over the face of Gaia, between groups, between people, within people, within organizations and governments. . . .

♪   *Heaven and Hell* (fourth cut on side two, by Vangelis; medieval chant with female lead, no words, spiritual tone)

Now we are going to switch to a different realm altogether. From the ordinary realm of space and time we move to a mythic realm where you are no longer a human body but a soul, and Gaia is no longer a planet but a goddess. Imagine what Gaia looks like as a goddess. . . . We are going back in time to a point shortly before your conception. You are having an audience with Gaia. Feel what it is like to be in her presence. . . .

Gaia is speaking to you about your coming incarnation. She tells you about the hurts she is suffering, and the threats to her that are coming, and about your role in helping her to overcome them and be healed. She tells you about the special talents, understandings, and inclinations you will be born with to help you in your task. And she may indicate how you are to use them. Your role may be explicitly political in helping to deal with one of the many threats to Gaia's health. Or it may be directed more at the necessary change in values and consciousness. Gaia may be very specific about what you are to do or quite vague. She may speak to you in words, or show you images, or you may just sense her message in your body. Take a few minutes now to listen to Gaia as she tells you of your calling. . . .

[Allow until just before the music ends, about two minutes.] She tells you that you will only dimly remember these things after you are born, and only when you are deep inside yourself. But they will always be there to guide you if you listen. She blesses you and ends the audience. Thank her for her guidance. . . .

You now find yourself back in outer space watching Gaia from a distance. You begin to float back down toward the planet. [Reverse the initial trip into outer space, bring them back down to earth, but more quickly than on the way up.] You float back through the roof of this building and gradually settle down into your body on the floor. [Bring them out of trance. People then share their experience in pairs.]

♪ Simplified music: Use the cut from *Heaven and Hell* as above. This piece seems to be important for this exercise because of

its ability to evoke such a potent experience of Gaia. It should
be used if at all possible.

Experiences

Feeling Worthy

Don is the man we met earlier who was working on opening
his heart and feeling his passion for social transformation. He
described his experience with this exercise as follows: "The journey up into the stratosphere was exhilarating. It was great to see
the earth whole from a distance like that, and it made perfect
sense to see it as a living organism, the cyclical nature of things.

"When we saw all of the things that are wrong, it had
quite an impact. I mean I knew all those things already, but to
experience it all at once really made the tragedy come home.
When we met Gaia, I saw her at first as a young goddess with
long blonde hair. Then she became half black, half white, divided
between the left and right sides of her body. Then she assumed
a lot of other forms in sequence, representing all the different
peoples on earth."

Don had been thinking about doing some research on an
idea of his having to do with the historical causes of our current
societal situation. In the fantasy, he was deeply moved to be told
by Gaia that this project was his special gift to the world. He was
also filled with feelings of unworthiness, because his project is in
an area where he doesn't have the normally required academic or
professional background. He started to cry, asking "Why is it my
job to offer this to the world? I'm not qualified. I'm not worthy
to do this."

In the Naming Ritual (chapter 12) which directly followed,
Don described this experience to his partner and shared with her

some of his frustrations and doubts about himself. Having heard about his insecurities, she was eager to empower him in the ways he needed, especially by affirming his project as innovative and worthwhile. This had quite an impact on him. He came away from the evening having uncovered an unconscious block to his work and replaced it with renewed confidence and a sense of purpose.

Further inner exploration also confirmed that this particular project *was* important for him to pursue. This awareness was grounding for him because he tends to generate ideas easily and spread himself thin working on too many things at once. In this case, the affirmation he received made it possible for him to stay focused on this project and move ahead with it.

A Big Heart

Another participant, Liza, reported her experience as follows: "When you suggested that we see all the different things happening to Gaia, I didn't see them so much as feel them. It felt like my body was being polluted and my protective shield had holes in it. It was visceral and unpleasant, but I'm still glad to have experienced it. I feel like I know more from the inside what's going wrong in the world."

During her audience with Gaia she was enraptured by the lovely female voice in the music. "Then I started hearing a voice saying 'Beautiful healer.' I could feel myself on the planet being instrumental in helping everyone to transform the heat of their destructive rage into heart energy. It happened as a result of people being able to deal with their rage. The heat was like a silver cord between all beings. On the planet, in addition to the usual activity, there was this great heart thumping; the earth was a big heart rather than a big head. And the joy was incredible, actually unspeakable. No matter what was going on, life was a celebration."

Other Experiences

Another person experienced the Gaia fantasy kinesthetically through her body. She saw Gaia dancing as she rotated on her axis and revolved around the sun, and she felt herself dancing with Gaia. Then she experienced herself *as* Gaia dancing and then finally as everything in the world dancing. Her message from Gaia was, "Walk this earth and touch people gently." This meant to travel the earth (like Johnny Appleseed), moving from place to place and touching people, bringing love and healing where she could. She was to avoid getting involved in small, ego-oriented concerns, and was instead to find ways to reach out and make people conscious.

Sally was told by Gaia that her work in the world was to *be* who she already is in the world, not to *do* something specific. This meant cultivating her gentleness and generosity, and being a "therapist in the world" with everyone. Gaia also told her, "Open your heart. Open your mind. Say what you see and feel and know." This underscored what she was currently working on—trusting what she had to say and using her voice to speak out. She came away from the evening (which also included the Naming Ritual) "feeling grounded and whole, and with a profound sense of having been seen and appreciated." The next day she was able to speak out in new ways at a conference she attended.

Another man identified Gaia with his wife in some way, and as a result became more accepting of her moving out into the world. He also got a message from Gaia that it was time to make his poetry available to people. He became more accepting of his work and also more flexible about how to circulate it, letting go of the idea that it had to be in the form of a book. He began putting this into action immediately.

11

Finding Your Contribution

IN MY SOCIAL transformation workshops and other work with people, I frequently hear: "I'm very concerned and I want to do something, but I'm not really a political person. I don't like writing letters, or canvassing, or going to political meetings. What can I do?" This exercise is an attempt to help answer that question.

I see making a contribution to social transformation as an aspect of life purpose. You can make an important contribution by following your talents, your interests, and your deepest sense of calling. Even though people are needed to do the nitty-gritty, routine electoral work, to organize and demonstrate and speak, you can make the greatest impact by following your heart wherever it leads. (Of course, some people's hearts lead them to do the more traditional political work.)

For example, my friend Diana is very interested in culture and aesthetics, likes to read, and is concerned about the nuclear threat. Diana has a friend Hetty who was working with the Hiroshima-Nagasaki Touring Museum Exhibit. This show was designed to raise people's consciousness about the nuclear threat by demonstrating what happened in 1945 when we bombed those cities. Hetty was in charge of coordinating volunteer work for the museum, and needed someone to do research on what Japanese culture was like just before 1945. She saw this as a perfect opportunity to use Diana's interests, and so recruited her for that task.

In that way Diana found her contribution for that time. Since then she has moved on to contribute in other ways. This story could be multiplied thousands of times over with innumerable variations. It is a matter of finding the right match for your interests, your talents, the issues which concern you, and the people and projects to work with.

The Search

Finding your contribution isn't necessarily easy. It involves both inner and outer searching: inner searching to find what really fits your deeper sense of life purpose, and outer searching to find how you fit with an existing organization or project, or how you can create one.

This searching may take much time and energy, but it is well spent. In the process you are learning about yourself, influencing others, and participating socially. And your contribution will be so much more valuable for you and for the planet. After all, we're working toward the kind of society where each person can develop their full potential. This should be reflected in *how* we work toward it.

The search invariably involves trial and error, as you experiment with many different projects, all of which stem from your deeper life purpose and planetary concerns. You will learn how each project feels to you and how well it seems to contribute to the world. Those efforts which don't work out should not be considered failures or indications of your lack of worth. They are simply part of the inevitable feedback you receive from life as you learn more about how to manifest your purpose.

The search also involves a process of successive approximation, where at first you find something that only partially meets your criteria for a fully satisfying contribution. Perhaps you find a volunteer project in an area of interest which allows you to gain skills and experience. After that you can get a paying job in the same field which also gives you increased responsibility and autonomy. During this time you develop higher level contacts and refine your ideas of exactly how to use this work to make a social contribution. This might enable you then to move into a situation that really uses your creativity in higher service.

As you gain experience, your interests and skills will become refined, and you will create newer and more exciting ways to fulfill your purpose, ways that use more of your creativity, that reach more people, that flow from your deepened understanding of what is needed. Each time you will find or create a situation that fits you better and allows you to have a greater positive impact on the world. Throughout this process, you continually refer back to your higher self. Each decision involves evaluating your feedback from the world and consulting your inner guide so that you remain true to your life purpose and avoid traps and sidetracks.

During my searching I have engaged in many different activities:

1. leaving my career as a computer scientist to become a psychotherapist;

2. offering free individual counseling sessions to help others find their social contributions;

3. doing administrative and organizational work with three different organizations, each of which combined psychological, spiritual, and social concerns;

4. leading workshops and giving talks on personal growth, social transformation, and life purpose;

5. reading, studying, and doing research on the psychology of social change and on life purpose;

6. beginning to write three different books on these subjects and so far finishing this one.

Some aspects of these projects didn't work out, some worked partially and led me on to more appropriate efforts, and some have been very successful. Some were right for a while, some I am still pursuing, and some I may return to at a future time. All have evolved from one form to another over time, and I'm constantly coming up with new ideas for projects to pursue.

Even after finding a satisfactory contribution, your interests and concerns will probably change in the long run. People who are working creatively at their edges tend to move on to new projects after a while, even if the underlying thrust of their purpose remains unchanged. Each time you move on, you will need to search again, in both the inner and outer dimensions. The search for your life purpose and your social contribution is never completely finished; it becomes an exciting and continually evolving endeavor throughout your life.

Circumstances

The exercise as described is for social transformation workshops; a variation for regular workshops is included. Like Gaia, it involves a reincarnation theme, so remember that this is only being used as a psychological metaphor.

Working Alone. When working by yourself you must do the guided fantasy and the interpretation of symbols on your own. The storytelling is best done in writing. Skip the eye contact part.

Working with a Partner. When working with a partner you can take turns leading each other through the guided fantasy. The interpretation and storytelling can be done as described. As with earlier exercises, one person can lead both of you through the eye contact part.

Time: 1 hour and 45 minutes. The full exercise as described here is considerably longer than others in the book. If you don't have enough time to complete the whole exercise, an appropriate shortened version would consist of just the guided fantasy and the interpretation in pairs.

The Exercise

[First the above viewpoint on finding your social contribution should be discussed with the leader providing an example. Then members of the group can give additional examples of people contributing in ways that are different from the usual modes of political activity.]

The following writing exercise[1] will help to stimulate your thinking about your contribution. You should have a pen or pencil, a blank sheet of paper, and a copy of the exercise. You will not have enough time to go into any of these areas in as much detail as you might like. The exercise is just to get you started and stimulate you. You may want to continue this exploration on your own. [The leader reads each of the nine areas to the group and gives people about a minute to think about each and take notes or draw.]

[After the writing exercise.] Pair up with someone you don't know very well and spend five minutes sharing with each other what you learned from the exercise.

Writing Exercise

1. Skills. Things you have learned or been trained to do; e.g., therapy, administration.

---

[1] For more extensive exercises of this sort without the social emphasis, see Richard Bolles, *What Color Is Your Parachute?* (Berkeley, CA: Ten Speed Press, 1970).

2. Interests. What you are drawn to or enjoy doing, what you're concerned about in the world, the kinds of people and physical settings you like.

3. Abilities. Your natural talents. Those qualities of yours which have enabled you to do things well and to be successful; e.g., empathy, perceptiveness, organization.

4. Combining these. Where are there overlaps among these three areas? Where do you have the interests or abilities but need to develop the skill? How could you combine areas in a single project? For example, combining networking, writing, and administrative abilities in doing promotional work.

5. Existing work: changing values. How does your current work serve to promote the values of a healthy society? How could it? For example, mediation promotes cooperative values.

6. Existing work: raising consciousness. How does your current work serve to increase people's awareness of the planetary crisis and its relationship to their lives? How could it? For example, making the connection between societal and personal problems in doing therapy.

7. Existing skills applied to political work. How do you or could you apply your existing skills to work that is more directly political? For example, making a peace quilt.

8. Teachers. Who have been important people you have learned from? What sort of teachers might you now need to find or be open to learning from?

9. Peers and projects. What people and projects have you found to work with? What do you now need to look for—a political or cultural organization, an affinity group, people to collaborate with on a project, a job opportunity?

[Now people arrange themselves in pairs in positions for a guided fantasy (see chapter 4). The leader starts out with an induction.]

♪   *Starmusic* (by Don Robertson, side 1 and side 2, as much as needed; hypnotic, outer space tone)

Now remember a scene from about a year ago in your life. Any scene will do; just let one come to mind. Don't try to figure out what was going on a year ago. Just let it come to mind and experience it as clearly and vividly as possible. See exactly what is happening, hear the sounds, feel your emotions, notice your body sensations. Now share this with your partner. . . . Now let that go and let another scene come to mind from two years ago. And share that with your partner. . . .

[Continue going backward in time. As you get to the younger years and beyond, mention that people may be imagining the scenes rather than actually remembering them. The entire sequence of scenes is as follows:

a year ago,
two years ago,
five years ago,
ten years ago,
your early twenties,
your teenage years,
your childhood,
when you were a baby,
from your birth,
from your conception.]

Now we are going to go back to a time before your conception, and we're going to move into the realm of mythology. Imagine that you are at the top floor, the ninth floor, of an old stone tower, in the receiving room of a god or goddess who is in charge of life plans. You are being briefed by this being on your coming incarnation and the plans for your life. Let yourself visualize this being as he or she receives you in the top floor of the tower. Sense what it is like to be with them. . . .

This being, who is your guide, explains your life plan as follows: "Planet Earth is approaching a crisis. It is the usual spiritual and political crisis that happens when the intelligent species of a planet passes through its industrial era. The human race will pass through the height of this crisis during your lifetime. It will either grow in consciousness enough to control the technical power that it is developing or it will destroy itself and much of the planet as well.

"You will live in a place, a nation which will be pivotal in this crisis, and you are destined to have a significant role in helping to resolve the crisis. This doesn't mean, of course, that the future is determined. You will have choice and opportunity for creativity all along the way. The outcome for the planet is not clear.

"But you will be born with special talents and powers and interests to help you in your task of contributing to healing the planet and transcending the crisis. You will be presented with the right experiences in your life to prepare you for this task and the opportunities to carry it out. Of course, once you are born you won't remember any of this very clearly, but nevertheless let me show you what is in store for you. Follow me."

Your guide leads you out of the room on the ninth floor of the tower, and leads you down a stairway to the eighth floor. Each floor in this tower has special windows which show special kinds of images related to your calling and your coming life. They may be explicit scenes or they may be symbolic images. You may hear words or you may sense the messages in your body. Remember whatever images or messages you get, even if they don't make sense at first, because this is wisdom from your deep psyche.

You are now on the eighth floor of the tower. As you look out the windows you see images related to the talents and powers and special qualities you will be born with to help you in your calling. When you have a sense of your message or image, share that with your partner.

Allow people about 30–40 seconds on each floor. The complete sequence is as follows:[2]

8th floor: The talents and special qualities you will be born with to help you in your calling

7th floor: The interests and inclinations you will be born with

6th floor: The education and learning you will receive to prepare you to make your contribution

5th floor: The hardships and pain you will go through on your path, which will also prepare you to meet the challenge

4th floor: The growth you will make and the changes in values and consciousness you will go through

3rd floor: The persons in your life who will be significant in preparing you for or helping you carry out your task

2nd floor: The signs and portents you will see that will let you know that you are destined to contribute and that point out the way to go

1st floor: See yourself actually making your contribution, carrying out your life purpose]

[Gradually bring people out of trance.] Now spend some time remembering and taking notes on the images you received in the tower. Write a description or make a drawing of each one. Ask your partner for help if you need it. You will have 5 to 10 minutes.

---

[2] The use of a tower for viewing a sequence of images occurs in a number of Jean Houston's exercises. See "Being Reeded and Gathering the Golden Fleece" from Psyche and Eros, *The Search for the Beloved*.

Now spend some time with your partner interpreting the images in terms of what they may mean for your life purpose and contribution. You may not have enough time to process each image thoroughly, so you may want to concentrate on one or two that seem particularly important. Partners, let the person try to interpret the images first, while you guide them and ask questions. Wait to offer your interpretations until they have explored theirs. [Allow 5 minutes for each partner.]

You will now each become a storyteller and tell your partner your life story as if everything significant in your life was leading toward your making your contribution. You may use material from the writing exercise, from the tower fantasy, from your life history, and anything that comes to you spontaneously as you are telling the story. The story may just go up to the present, or it may also continue into the future.

Tell the story in the third person. Let yourself be creative. Pretend that you are a bard from ancient times telling the story of a famous hero whose entire life was integral to their great calling. You might start out, "Let me tell you of the story of the sorceress (name) who saved her kingdom from the invading hordes. She was born in a small village near the sea." And so on. Let yourself play with it. You will each have about 12 minutes.

♪ "Abraham's Theme" (from *Chariots of Fire* by Vangelis; or other heart music)

Now sit comfortably, facing your partner and make eye contact. Let your breathing slowly synchronize with each other. . . . Consider this person. You have been on a long journey together this last hour. This person has shared some of their life with you. Take a moment and really receive them. . . . Honor them and their life journey—their natural abilities, their struggles and their pain, the growth they have made, their moments of triumph. . . . Honor them from the deepest, most evolved part of you, . . . and know that you are honored in return. [Allow music to end, about half a minute.]

♪   *Chariots of Fire* (part of side 2; gentle heart music which then
     builds to an expansive tone)

And now look deeper, past the story you have heard, to the
essence of this person. See them as they truly can be in all their
potential. See this person as they were meant to be—whole, free,
balanced, fully alive. . . . Rejoice in their beauty, their strength,
their creativity. See those hidden potentials which this person
only vaguely dreams of. . . .

   Most of all, see this person's great capacity for helping others,
for helping to heal the planet and transform our society. . . . See
them following their calling, finding their contribution, carrying
out their part in this great project of creating a new society. . . .
As you do this, feel your desire for their success, your joy for
them, your loving. In doing this, you are empowering them and
enriching yourself. [Allow music to end, about half a minute.]

Variation

For use in a regular workshop, this exercise can be modified so
that the emphasis is on finding one's life purpose in general
without the specific social orientation. Delete the writing exercise
or modify it to exclude the social areas. And delete the paragraphs
in the guided fantasy in which the guide tells the person about
the planetary crisis.

Experiences

A Young Adult

Unlike most of the people described in this book, Jenny is only
21 years old. I have included her story here partly to illustrate
how Inner Journeys work is applicable to a wide age range, and

also because this exercise is particularly useful for younger people or those who are new to self-exploration.

Jenny originally came to therapy because of difficulties with low self-esteem and lack of confidence and career direction. Despite being bright, she dropped out of college because she couldn't handle it emotionally. She had a hard time getting along with people because of her tendency to be angry and domineering.

In the guided fantasy, when the planetary crisis was first mentioned, Jenny assumed that things would go badly and the world would be destroyed. When it was suggested that she would help to turn the crisis around, she was jolted in a positive way. "I felt very light and ethereal. I imagined I could fly and be invisible if I needed to be, and I could speak every language. I was thin and had long, red hair and a white gown. I was very calm. I saw open hands that could do anything—creativity.

"As guides I saw my parents, and also some people in back of them whose faces were unknown. I knew that at some point they'd come into my life and then I'd recognize them. There was hardship and cruelty, being made fun of and picked on and being scared. But in the next image I saw myself rising above it and feeling OK about myself, and being able to help others to do that too.

"I would grow a garden and study martial arts and attend a predominately Negro college. Someone very close to me would die, and that would be a struggle for me. I would be very distressed, but somehow I would overcome the pain and continue. R_____ would help me set the world on a constructive course, teaching me patience and how to deal with my anger more productively. I imagined myself as some sort of preacher, though no one would know that I was preaching. I would have a magical way of infiltrating people's minds with goodness toward others. Basically the message seemed to be about helping people and the earth and animals."

Jenny did this Inner Journeys exercise as part of a long-term individual therapy process. After two years of work on herself she is now able to get along better with her co-workers and is feeling stronger and more confident in her relationships in general. She has begun a searching process that will eventually lead her to a sense of life purpose, even though as a 23-year-old she can't be expected to be very far along. She is finding her feet career-wise; she has moved into a responsible, full-time job. She is experimenting with various creative outlets in the arts. Her social consciousness is developing, showing itself as little acts of kind-ness toward people in need. Eventually it will probably become more focused and integrated with her other interests as part of an overall life direction.

A Mature Woman

The following experience comes from Grace, a 40-year-old who is experienced with this kind of work and also with investigating her life purpose. It illustrates how one can fully let go of control in a guided fantasy and allow images to arise that may have no obvious meaning, knowing that they can be interpreted into a coherent whole later.

Grace saw the following images for each floor:

8th: Wings flying upward, symbolizing raising consciousness

7th: An owl superimposed on an eagle holding a pen in its talons, meaning wisdom and writing

6th: The winged heart which is the Sufi emblem. She had re-cently been studying Sufism.

5th: Rough rocky terrain for hardships

4th: A pool with angels coming out of it in all directions, signify-ing spirit emerging out of the emotional

3rd: A spiralling staircase with hierophant figures in red and black ascending the stairs, having to do with male spiritual authority figures and her ambivalence toward them

2nd: Water insects skating in a particular direction on a pond, as a sign of her direction in life

1st: A stylized horse's head arching back, full of life, signifying action, vibrancy, aliveness

This was largely a confirmation of directions in which she was already moving—raising spiritual consciousness through her work as a psychotherapist and also through writing.

Another Experience

Barbara is the woman we met earlier who learned to become a tree in order to ground her compassion. "The images I remembered as you took us back through our lives were fascinating to me. I remembered a dress I made that came out of a medieval court." She realized that she had common attitudes and a common viewpoint at all the different ages. It gave her a pleasurable sense of the continuity of her self over time.

Her tower images had to do with integrating her femininity with a masculine sense of assertiveness in dealing with the material world. "I came up with two guides, my 13th-century monk and one of the forms of the Goddess. The monk has been there for years now to teach me what it is to be religious, and the Goddess is teaching me what it is to be a woman. And they integrate in some very nice ways. It was fun. Having to talk about the images during the fantasy was difficult, but it helped me retain more. If I go off on my own, there's a lot I lose. It was nice at the end talking to [her partner] about it because she made more sense of some of them than I could."

Barbara was apprehensive about the storytelling at first, because she didn't see herself as good with words. However, she gave herself permission to play with being a bard, and she ended up enjoying herself and having her verbal side validated by her partner.

SECTION FIVE

Empowerment

Introduction

THIS SECTION DEALS with personal power—the power to be who you are, to assert yourself, to take risks; the power to accomplish your life purpose in the world, to take action in the service of social transformation. This kind of power is cooperative; your own power is increased when those around you also feel empowered. Personal power is not to be confused with power over others or the power to dominate or control, which is the kind of power frequently exercised in our society. Personal power means the freedom to act assertively and spontaneously, with confidence and courage. It means projecting your intentions into the future and acting to carry them out.

Personal power depends on feeling good about yourself—your innate qualities and talents, your personal worth, your previous accomplishments, and your potential.

As children we grow in our sense of personal power as we learn that we can affect our surroundings in the way we intend and accomplish what we want. In order for this to happen we need support and encouragement from our parents and others around us. As developing beings, we frequently take on tasks that we cannot handle without help, and we sometimes encounter difficulties and rejection from others. At these moments we need understanding and guidance and a consistent reminder of our positive qualities and potential.

Many children do not receive this encouragement, or worse, they are judged and made to feel inadequate. They are made to feel that they have failed because there is something intrinsically wrong with them. This message can come from parents, from other children, or from the school system. We live in a highly competitive, judgmental culture, where people are evaluated rather than appreciated, where only a few can receive top honors. This makes it difficult for us to grow up feeling powerful and good about ourselves.

Once you have internalized a view of yourself as not being able to accomplish what you want, it becomes a self-fulfilling prophecy. You enter into projects or relationships expecting problems, expecting to fail. This expectation may make you timid or uncooperative. You may give up at the least sign of difficulty. If something doesn't work out, you may assume that it was entirely your fault, thus confirming your negative view of yourself.

These tendencies are exacerbated by the size of our institutions, our work situations, and many of the organizations that affect our lives. In so many of them we feel anonymous, like just one person in a large impersonal bureaucracy. By ourselves we have little opportunity to affect the things that matter in our lives and even less power to affect our society. We are taught to think only in terms of what we can accomplish by ourselves. We rarely contemplate what we might accomplish by working with others. This contributes to our feelings of powerlessness.

Women and Men

In addition, women are often taught that it is not OK for them to be powerful. As girls they are taught it is not feminine to be strong and self-confident, that instead they should be "nice" and placating. They learn that boys like girls who are coy and who will build up the male ego. They are taught that it is dangerous to do well or to stand out, that they may be disliked for it.

As a consequence a woman may grow up with a fear of her own power and a tendency to undercut herself whenever she is becoming strong and assertive. She may become afraid of success and may sabotage herself whenever she approaches it. A woman may choose men who are arrogant and willing to exercise the power she denies herself, who may even want to dominate and control her. Then she is forced to turn to covert and manipulative means to get what she wants.

Men have a different problem. We are taught to identify masculinity with power and to feel that our manhood depends on our strength and power. So in order to bolster low self-esteem, we may turn to exaggerated macho stances, to arrogance, or to a driving, workaholic ambition. We have such a need to feel powerful that our power turns destructive.

On the other hand, those men who are sensitive to what is going on in the world see that our society is riddled with destructive extremes and perversions of power. Competition, domination, and hard-heartedness are all contributing to the breakdown of our society. In recognizing this and in working to develop our soft, gentle, feminine sides, we must be careful not to throw the baby out with the bathwater, rejecting our power and our masculinity altogether. Robert Bly has made this point very clearly and has become the leading spokesman for men's empowerment, calling for us to discover the life-affirming power of the deep masculine.[1]

For men and women to extricate ourselves from these webs of disempowerment, we must put ourselves in situations where we will learn to feel good about ourselves. We must choose to be with people who value us and want us to be powerful, and who also value our gentleness and our vulnerability. We must choose relationships in which our self-esteem and confidence are enhanced. We can seek out groups in which mutual support and

---

[1] Robert Bly and Keith Thompson, "What Men Really Want." *New Age Journal* (May 1982).

empowerment are the norm. We can learn to value and appreciate our own strengths and special qualities. And we can join with others in tackling our larger institutional and societal problems, so that we feel our collective power to affect change.

This Section

In the exercises in this section you are sometimes empowered by yourself, sometimes by an archetypal figure from the deep psyche, sometimes by a partner from the group, and sometimes by the group as a whole. The experience of being empowered by others in the group is especially important because it empowers them as well. In these exercises, love and power, those two great poles of human existence, come together in a beautiful way.

In a sense all of the exercises in this book deal with empowerment. However, some emphasize it more than others. The exercises in this section are:

The Naming Ritual
Manifesting Your Intention
The Flight of Empowerment
Expansive Movement
Affirmations

Those exercises outside this section which emphasize empowerment are as follows:

The Child and the Higher Self
Reowning the Shadow
all Social Transformation exercises
all Life Purpose exercises
The Expanded Body

12

The Naming Ritual

LET YOURSELF REMEMBER times when someone has really seen your specialness, has recognized how much you have to offer and let you know. These are memorable experiences! This kind of naming is one of the greatest gifts we can give each other.

The naming exercise in chapter 6 dealt with recognition and acceptance. This one deals with a slightly different, but equally important aspect of naming—honoring a person's strengths. Just as we all need to be fully accepted as we are, we also need to have our positive qualities encouraged and celebrated. We need to have people in our lives who see and rejoice in our talents, our accomplishments, and our special qualities, and who also see our potential. We need people who can imagine us growing, developing our abilities, and realizing our dreams of who we can become and what we can contribute to the world.

This naming function grows and develops through your life. As a child, you clearly need to receive this kind of encouragement and empowerment from your parents and other adults. It forms one of the pillars of healthy self-esteem. If you receive this consistently during your early years, you learn how to give it to yourself more and more as you grow. Ideally as an adult you are able to name yourself fully and lovingly, recognizing your strengths and visualizing your potentials. This gives you the confidence, courage, and sense of personal power that will enable you to take risks, to create new projects, and to believe that you can make a significant contribution to the world.

This exercise fosters this sense of empowerment by arranging to have you name and be named by another person in a ritual format that facilitates the process of taking in very deeply the sense of being honored.

Circumstances

This exercise is best done after an exercise in which you have an opportunity to sense your life purpose and to acknowledge the gifts you have to help you carry it out, exercises such as Gaia and Finding Your Contribution. If it is done by itself, there may need to be an introduction to the concept of life purpose and some time for each person to explore what their purpose might be. The exercise can be used in regular or socially oriented workshops.

Rituals tend to cause discomfort or embarrassment because they are foreign to what is normally acceptable in this culture. Therefore before this exercise can be used, a group must have had enough time to develop trust in each other and confidence in the leader. In order to ease people into the ritual, the leader can provide a context for the experience by explaining the value of ritual. I usually say that it is a way of speaking directly to the deeper levels of the psyche. It is also useful to acknowledge the problems that people may have with a ritual and to encourage them to try it in a spirit of experimentation.

Working with a Partner. This exercise cannot be done alone. When working with a partner, switch leadership along with the roles of the exercise. The one who is naming should be the leader for that part of the exercise.

Time: 40 minutes.

The Exercise[1]

[People pair up with a partner they don't know particularly well. Each person will go through a sequence of exercises with the partner as helper, then they will switch roles, and the other person will go through the sequence.]

People who are going first, begin by talking to your partner about those qualities of yours that are especially important in helping you carry out your life purpose. These can be insights you gained from the previous exercise, or qualities you were already aware of in yourself—talents, strengths, interests, abilities. Partners, listen attentively because you will need to remember these things later. [Allow 3 minutes.]

Next, talk about your intentions to use these abilities to serve the world in the future. You may be very clear at this point about what you intend to do, especially if you have thought about it a lot. Or you may have vague hunches and intuitive sensings that you can explore with your partner during this time. You are not expected to come up with a specific path of action right now. This exercise is one step in an ongoing process that must take its own time. Partners, help this exploration by listening, by encouragement, and by asking questions that help develop your partner's ideas. [Allow 3 minutes.]

[Go over the following instructions before the ritual starts. Then ask people to assume the ritual positions.]

Now we will do an empowerment ritual in which your partner will name you by acknowledging your special qualities and your potential for contributing to the world. You will kneel and your partner will stand behind you with their arms held high and wide, making their body into the shape of a vessel or chalice. [Leader demonstrate.]

---

[1] This exercise is adapted from Jean Houston's Naming Ritual used in her workshop "The Myth of Times to Come," and many other workshops.

When the music starts, partners, you will breathe deeply and let the energy of the universe flow into you. Then begin to acknowledge the personal qualities that your partner has to offer the world and the things you see them doing in carrying out their life purpose. Give them names which affirm their unique essence. You might say things such as:

"I recognize your wisdom and patience,"

"I see you organizing people with energy and enthusiasm," or

"I name you subtle teacher."

Don't be afraid to say exactly those things that your partner has already said, as well as anything else that you want to add. Let yourself be creative in thinking of interesting names for your partner. [Mention examples. One of my favorite names that someone used was "Eagle of Compassion."] Let yourself experiment with using a ritual voice, speaking in dramatic, incantatory tones. This is a way of talking directly to the unconscious.

As the naming is progressing, gradually bring your arms down as if the vessel which you have become is slowing tipping and pouring its goodness onto your partner. As the music reaches its climax, place your hands on their head, and let the energy flow into them as they receive the power of their naming.

Now ask people to assume the ritual positions.

♪   Credits (from *Starman* soundtrack, last five minutes; or other music which combines heart and celebration, such as "Pachelbel's Canon")

Partners, now raise your arms, breathe deeply and let the energy of the universe flow into you. Become a vessel of loving confirmation for your partner. People who will be named, put yourself in an open, receptive place to take in what you are about to receive. Now as you become ready, begin to name, recognize and acknowledge your partner.

[This last paragraph should be spoken by the leader in a ritual voice. You may have to remind the partners to lower their arms and to place them on the participant's head at the appropriate time. Allow until the music ends.]

And now, feeling yourself fully recognized in your powers and abilities, knowing yourself named and confirmed as one who has a significant contribution to make to the world, spend a few minutes in silence, taking this into the deepest part of yourself, and knowing yourself. [Allow half a minute.]

[Then have the partners go through the same sequence of exercises with roles reversed. After that, allow time to share experiences with each other.]

Variations

When this exercise is used after the Gaia fantasy or in a social transformation workshop, the following invocation can be used after the music ends:

And now, sitting there, letting the energy of your naming flow into you, the energy from your partner's hands, from their heart, imagine this energy to be the energy of a greater force wanting to work through you to heal our world. Open yourself to that greater power. Let it shine down on you, and into you. Let it move through you to act in the world. Know yourself called to a sacred task. Know yourself affirmed as one who has an important contribution to make to building a loving society. Know yourself named: peacemaker. Take a moment in silence to be with this.

Experiences

As a result of being named, some people come to accept or appreciate themselves more fully, and others come away with a heightened sense of who they can become. For some, the naming triggers interesting and empowering images. The exercise also tends to encourage a deep bonding between the partners. It is a wonderful way to end a day or workshop. Some people feel awkward with the exercise at first, but once they try it, they usually get a great deal from it.

The Eagle and the Hands

Sandra is our friend who has been developing her strength and her interest in art. Afterwards she reported, "I have done so much fretting about what I'm supposed to be doing and how I'm supposed to be doing it. Now I see that I don't need to do that. I am already there now, evolving in the direction I need to be going."

She had done the Gaia fantasy before the naming ritual, and had experienced herself as an eagle flying high above the planet. Her message from Gaia was to "rise up and be strong and help others to do the same." During this exercise she was named "Eagle of Compassion," and she experienced her entire body as that of an eagle, feeling great power and clarity of vision. As her partner mentioned "perspective," Sandra imagined being able to fly out of herself during a difficult interpersonal interaction so as to gain a larger perspective on it.

She had shared with her partner her sense that sculpting was part of her life direction, and in the ritual her partner also said, "I see your hands of creativity. I name you Shaper of the Life Force." As she heard this, Sandra felt a tremendous rush of energy from her heart down her arms and into her hands, charging them with vibrancy and potency. Sandra again felt affirmed and empowered in her choice of this life direction.

Other Experiences

Another woman reported, "At first I was skeptical, wondering where I was going, but it was amazingly impactful. I was surprised

that I felt so touched, so there, so present, and so vulnerable."
She was given names which meant a great deal to her: "Deep
One," "Dedicated One," "Noble One," "Generous One." She
found that the most empowering part was taking the risk to speak
when she was the namer. "When I stood up to work with [her
partner] a part of me went, 'Oh, my God! What was it she said?
What can I say now?' But I know enough to know you can't do
it that way. I opened myself up to let it come from a higher place
and trusted what came through, but it was still a risk, especially
when I said things she didn't say. But it was wonderful! I felt so
open and giving—and powerful."

Susan and Judy had been affirming their playfulness in an
earlier exercise. In the ritual, Judy named Susan "Rascal," which
prompted Susan to image herself as a mischievous raccoon. During Judy's turn, she shared that she sees her calling in terms of
bringing light into darkness. Susan named her "Sunshine" and
imaged her as a yellow chrysanthemum.

Group Naming Ritual

With a small group of people (not more than seven or eight) who
know each other well, a group naming ritual can be done which
is even more powerful than the exercise just described. In the
pair exercise, individuals are empowered by partners whom they
don't otherwise know well, and in the process a deep connection
is sometimes created. Part of the power of that exercise comes
from being seen deeply and honored by a stranger. In the group
exercise, the empowerment happens, but it comes from people
who know the person well, and without prompting from the
person being named, so it has a special meaning.

People start by taking a few minutes in silence contemplating the other members of the group, bringing to mind their
particular strengths, talents, and abilities, and envisioning them

manifesting these in the world in fulfilling their life purpose. Then the ritual is enacted as described above with each member of the group in turn taking the receptive position. The other group members stand in a circle around the member who is kneeling, all holding themselves as vessels and simultaneously naming the member who is kneeling while the music plays. Finally, they all place their hands on the participant's head and shoulders.

Since the ritual must be enacted for each member of the group, it cannot be done with a larger number (without some modification) for two reasons. First, there is not enough room for more than six or seven people to stand around a member to perform the ceremony. Second, the repetition of the exercise would induce boredom after a while, and the last people would likely be shortchanged. In fact, because of this repetition I recommend using two or three different pieces of music with the group ritual to add variety.

For groups that are strongly connected, the usual five minutes allowed for the ritual for each person may not be nearly enough. The group whose experience is described below used about ten minutes a person.

Variations

The following induction was used by my friend Ginny Gardner in conjunction with the group ritual:

Centering ourselves in our heart chakra and raising our arms up into the universe, reaching out into the cosmos and gathering in pure loving energy and holding it, so that we can pour it down all over _____ [recipient] as we name him/ her. And _____ [recipient], all you need to do is open yourself up wide to receive the gifts that we bring and keep them in your heart forever.

Experiences

Even though this form is even more public than the pair ritual, people don't seem to be bothered by this because no one person is responsible for doing all the naming. People have more time to think of just the right names. As might be expected, this exercise greatly strengthens the bonding in a group.

The following are excerpts from the naming done by the close-knit group we met before in Opening the Heart. Sally was named as follows:

I name you feisty fighter for the truth

I name you creator of beauty, preserver of ancient things

I name you lady of the dark

I see you as a witch standing and stirring her cauldron, and finding a bag of gold and bringing it forth to share with the entire world

I name you laughter-bringer

I name you as the one who brings through the arts a way to help people find their place in the healing of the planet

I name you networker and organizer, the one who cuts through bullshit

I name you fun friend and marvelous cook

I name you one with discerning eye and rich voice

I name you one who thoroughly enjoys all the sensual delights

I name you the goddess of the crinkly eyes and the wonderful laughter

I name you nymph of the forest

I name you carrier of soul

I see you brave enough and honest enough to follow your own journey wherever it leads you

Janet was named the following:

I name you planter of gardens, creator of beautiful space, filler of the environment with wonderful energy

I name you carrier of joy

I name you compassion flower

I name you keeper of the cave

I name you wonderful friend, dear heart

I see you gently holding the snowflake in your hand and gifting the world

I see you enhancing the landscape with your long dress and your beautiful hats with flowers in them

I see you moving people deeply with your love and your wisdom

I name you she who stands in the wind

I name you essence of graciousness and gentleness

I name you bringer of the spirit into the world

I name you friend of integrity and great honesty who is dedicated to the truth

I name you lover and creator of music

Janet felt so appreciative after her turn that she spontaneously hugged the whole group. Encouraged by her, the people whose turns came after did the same. The spirit of the group was highly energetic, funny, and loving all at the same time. It was a profound experience of connecting and bonding for everyone.

I was participating as a member of this group. During the first half of my naming experience, I listened carefully to what was said about me, loving it and feeling enriched. Then when people placed their hands on my head and continued, I let go of processing the content of what was being said and just opened myself to a deeper level of experience. I felt as if my entire being was being filled with goodness. Afterwards I, too, wanted to hug the entire group. I felt open and connected and able to reach out in love to a degree that was astounding to me.

13

Manifesting Your Intention

ONCE YOU HAVE a sense of your life purpose, you are faced with carrying it out in the real world. This is exciting and challenging to the utmost and requires you to bring all your powers to bear on the task. One potent aid in this process is visualizing yourself carrying it out.

It is well known that visualizing or imagining an outcome that you desire makes it more likely to occur. This may work directly on reality in some way, or it may simply work through your psyche, changing you so that you act in the world so as to bring about the outcome. For the imaging to work, the goal must be truly aligned with your deeper purpose, with the wisdom of your higher self, and with the larger flow of events. This means that your goal will be appropriate and realistic and in line with your needs and the constraints of reality. It also means that you aren't likely to sabotage your intention unconsciously.

Imagining success in this way helps to counter the programming for failure that many of us learned in childhood by being undermined or judged. You may have picked up a failure mentality because you weren't supported through difficulties, or because your efforts weren't appreciated, or because your parents had unreasonably high expectations of you. We have an extremely competitive and judgmental society, which makes it hard for many of us to believe in ourselves. Because of this, many people actually imagine the worst consequences whenever they take on something new. It's very difficult to move ahead with confidence when your mind is focused on unpleasant results!

Of course, it is wise to foresee a possible negative outcome so you can work to ensure that it doesn't happen or so you can handle it in the best way, but this should be done with hope and confidence. What is destructive is imagining that an unpleasant outcome is likely to happen and being deflated by it.

Positive imagining has been very important in my own development and success in the world. Through the years of working with Jean Houston, I have planned, imagined, energized, and refined much of my work during exercises in her workshops. In addition, I do this frequently during the course of my everyday life. I am naturally a planner and dreamer. Often at night after I turn out the light, without even intending to, I plan the course of future projects, imagining the best possible outcomes and each step of how they will develop. Out of this come specific ideas of what to do, and also the drive and excitement to carry them out.

How to Visualize Your Intention

Visualizing an outcome works best if the imaging is done energetically and the images are concrete and vivid. This way the intention is made real, and images are planted in the psyche that help to energize and organize motivation, planning, and action. Confidence and self-esteem are also enhanced by the energy and the positive imaging.

The imaging is more powerful if you not only imagine carrying out your intention successfully, but also visualize its results, the effect it has on the world. This helps to further charge the project with hope and enthusiasm, and also to remind you that you are serving a larger purpose.

In the case of social transformation, accomplishing your larger goal requires the help and cooperation of many other people, so it is important to visualize these others and their contributions. This helps you to experience yourself as part of a larger movement and prevents you from feeling solely responsible for the world. Imaging the success of this movement, then, instills hope and confidence at this larger social level, hope that we can heal the world and transcend the planetary crisis. Imaging this greater social outcome helps to bring it into reality.

Circumstances.

This exercise needs to be done after one in which you get in touch with your life purpose, such as the Gaia or Finding Your Contribution. In addition, you should have already explored what your next step might be in realizing your life purpose. If this has not yet been done, you can do it in pairs at the beginning of this exercise.

The exercise is designed for a social transformation workshop. It can be used in other workshops by deleting or modifying the sections which refer to social issues—those which use music from *Chariots of Fire*.

Working Alone. When working alone, the guided fantasy and movement parts can be done as directed. I recommend doing the declarations aloud to music and then writing them in your journal.

Working with a Partner. When working with a partner, take turns leading each other through the guided fantasy and movement parts, then do the declarations together.

Time: 30–35 minutes.

The Exercise[1] ————————————————————

[This will not be a quiet trance, but an energetic exercise. People start in a sitting position with spine straight and eyes closed.]

♪   "Spiral" (from *Spiral* by Vangelis, twice, as much as needed; rousing, energetic tone)

Breathe deeply, and with each inhalation imagine that you are taking in the intention of the universe to work through you, you are taking in your calling, taking in your inheritance of power and wisdom, taking in the energy of the whole. With each exhalation, feel the energy accumulating in your belly. Each time you inhale, be open to receive the pattern which is yours. Each time you exhale, expand it, increase it, till your belly begins to glow like a sun. Inhale and take in your gifts and the intention of the universe. Exhale and deepen that power, concentrate it. . . . Inhale, exhale. . . . Take in the power, deepen it. . . .

Now make a low pitched humming sound in order to ground the energy deep in your body. [Leader demonstrate.] Feel the resonance of the hum as far down in your body as you can. . . . Ground that creative intention in your belly, in your buttocks, in the bottom of your spine. . . . Feel your intention being grounded in your root chakra, in your animal nature, in your sexuality. . . .

Continuing to breathe deeply and to hum, now put your individual stamp on that energy, infuse it with your unique personality. Give it your personal sense of how to serve humanity and the earth (even if you don't know exactly what that is). . . . Now let the energy expand outward from the blazing sun in your

---

[1] This exercise is adapted from The Creative Intention exercise from *The Possible Human*, p. 206, and from exercises presented in Jean Houston's workshops "The Myth of Times to Come," Santa Barbara, October 1983, and "Shapeshifting the Social Order: Sacred Psychology and Social Transformation," Ojai, CA, April 1984.

belly, from its grounding in the earth. . . . Expanding outward
more and more, until it fills your whole body. . . . Expanding
outward even further until it fills the energy field around you. . . .

Now let it radiate further out, seeding itself in reality. Send
your intention out into the universe. Send it out in space and
send it forward in time. . . . Send it out to the people you will
network with, to those teachers you will learn from, to those who
you will work with, to those you will influence. . . . Humming,
breathing, building, expanding outward. . . .

Now letting go of the humming and continuing to breathe
deeply, visualize yourself carrying out your intention. Imagine a
particular situation in which you are taking action that flows from
your intention, or in which you are manifesting some of those
qualities of being that you are developing as part of your intention.
Imagine a particular situation in which this is happening. . . .
See yourself in that situation, being and doing what you are
doing successfully, easily, powerfully, lovingly. See it as vividly as
possible. Let your being be filled with the energy of your intention
as you visualize it happening. [Allow half a minute.]

Now in your fantasy, change perspective from seeing yourself
to *being* that self who is carrying out the intention. You will now
see the world from your eyes in the fantasy. You will feel your
body sensations and emotions as you carry out your intention.
Let yourself be there as fully as you can. Plunge yourself into that
experience. [Allow half a minute.]

Now let yourself imagine the results of what you have been
doing. See the works you create, or the people you help, the
structures you bring into being, the healing or the love you help
to manifest. Spend a moment enjoying and appreciating the fruits
of your work, the results of your intention made real. [Allow half
a minute, then fade the music and have people gradually stand
up with eyes closed.]

♪   "Abraham's Theme" (from *Chariots of Fire* by Vangelis, twice, as
     much as needed; or other heart music)

We are now going to do a guided fantasy including body sensation and movement. As the music plays, let your intention move through you, feel the strength of it in your body. If you feel like it, let your body sway gently to the music. . . . Now become aware of all the people in the room and the fact that each of them also has an intention, become aware that each of them has been given strengths and abilities to carry it out, that they are potential companions to you in your life of purpose. . . .

Now imagine all the people in [local organization or local town] who also care about other people and the planet, each with his or her own calling, each contributing in their own way. Let an image come to your mind which represents this to you. . . . Now expand the image to include all the people in [local city or area] who are involved in this life-affirming work, each with their own intention, each helping in their particular way. . . .

Now imagine all the people in this country and around the world, each with a unique contribution to make. People exploring spirituality and consciousness, holistic health, gender, ecology, politics, the new science, art, natural living, race relations, planetary citizenship, and many other things. Let an image come to you of this at the same time that you let your body feel it. So you will be both sensing and seeing this great web of people in action, which you are an integral part of, this great movement of people developing a new set of values, a new view of reality, and a new society. . . .

♪   "Eric's Theme" (from *Chariots of Fire* by Vangelis, twice; or other celebratory music)

Gradually let your body move a little more strongly to the music. Imagine that this great web of movement and change really spreads and gains momentum across the country and around the world. Let yourself imagine that it becomes a great movement, that it really starts to have the impact that we all want it to have. As the years go by and the movement expands, the tide begins to turn on the planet.

Let yourself imagine that reverence for life is getting stronger and stronger, and the old mechanical way of doing things is dropping away. The new consciousness begins to affect larger numbers of people. It begins to affect even institutions, governments, the economy. These changed institutions in turn affect more people. A new society begins to emerge which treats the earth and her people in a caring, loving way. . . .

If you feel like it, let your body movements become larger and more expressive. Begin to dance your feelings and your fantasy. Imagine the human population stabilizing and beginning to work with the rest of nature in an attitude of cooperation and respect. . . . Imagine understanding and appreciation between races, religions, classes. . . .

Cooperation develops between nations to reverse the arms race and dismantle the nuclear arsenals. . . . More and more people around the world are able to live with the basic necessities of life, free from disease and want. . . . More people are free from crippling institutions and ideas which limit who they can be. . . . People are empowered to be fully alive and creative, in tune with the universe. . . .

You now see our society and our planet moving toward being what it was meant to be—healthy, alive, vigorous, supporting a teeming complexity of life in harmony and love. Let your body and spirit move with this new vision. Recognize your part in helping to create it. Celebrate this new world. And dance your celebration! [Allow until the music ends, about another two minutes.]

♪ "Pachelbel's Canon" (one or more times, as much as needed; or other celebratory music)

Let's stand in a circle. Whenever someone is ready, move into the center of the circle and declare to the group your intention. This can be a long-term intention or a more immediate step. It can be very specific or quite general. It can be something you intend to do or a way you are intending to be. This is to empower you and also to empower the rest of us. Let yourself do it in such a way as to embody and express your personal power. Start by saying your name and then your declaration. When you have finished we will respond in unison: "We support you, (name)!"

[If necessary it should be made clear that not everyone needs to do this. Some people may not be ready at this time. If there is reluctance to start, the leader may have to go first to break the ice. People should be encouraged to declare more than once if they like.]

♪   Simplified music: Use some energizing or celebratory music
      throughout—"Spiral," "Eric's Theme," or Pachelbel.

Variations

When this exercise is used after the Gaia fantasy, it brings a nice sense of completion to include references to the healing of Gaia. These come in the section using "Eric's Theme." The last four paragraphs would be as follows:

Let yourself imagine that reverence for life is getting stronger and stronger, and the old mechanical way of doing things is dropping away. The new consciousness begins to affect larger numbers of people. It begins to affect even institutions, governments, the economy. These changed institutions in turn affect more people. A new society begins to emerge which treats the earth and her people in a caring, loving way. The threats to Gaia begin to recede. The damage begins to be repaired. . . .

If you feel like it, let your body movements become larger and more expressive. Begin to dance your feelings and your fantasy. Imagine Gaia's streams and waters beginning to run clear again, the ozone layer repairing itself. . . . The increasing use of renewable energy sources. Gaia's precious forests growing strong again, the greenhouse effect receding, the climate remaining stable. . . . Imagine the human population stabilizing and beginning to work with the rest of nature in an attitude of cooperation and respect. . . . Imagine understanding and appreciation between races, religions, classes. . . .

Cooperation develops between nations to reverse the arms race and dismantle the nuclear arsenals. . . . More people around the world are able to live with the basic necessities of life, free from disease and want. . . . More people are free from crippling institutions and ideas which limit who they can be. . . . People are empowered to be fully alive and creative, in tune with the universe. . . .

You now see Gaia moving toward being as she was meant to be—healthy, alive, vigorous, supporting a teeming complexity of life in harmony and love. Let your body and spirit move with this new, lovely Gaia. Recognize your part in helping to heal her. Celebrate Gaia's beauty. Dance with her! [Allow until the music ends, about two minutes.]

Experiences

Sandra envisioned herself as a student or apprentice to a sculptor. She saw herself in his studio working on a particular piece which she intended to create. She imagined having plenty of time in her life to learn and practice sculpting and to take art courses in other areas that interested her as well. Within a year she made this vision a reality in her life, taking a leave of absence from her job and devoting herself full-time to studying art.

Sandra also imagined a place where people who are in pain could come and be healed. She saw it as a tunnel leading into light, where they would emerge able to be in charge of their lives. She also envisioned herself touching many people briefly during the course of her daily life and giving them something that would help them along their path, though it wasn't clear exactly what form this would take. This aspect of her life purpose will need to be explored further.

A Budding Writer

We have met Judy a number of times, as she has been healing the lack of nurturing in her childhood. Now we see another side of her as she explores her life purpose. She reported on this exercise: "It was especially important to visualize my intention, to have that assignment and to face it squarely. It allowed the fantasy to flow.

"It was a unifying experience for me to feel part of something greater. It was very helpful to know that there are other serious people, and lots of them. I felt lighter, like a load was lifted, a feeling that I'm not alone." It was especially valuable for her because in her everyday life she is not in touch with people who are socially concerned.

"I felt a real connection when we were imagining the world healed. It was a nice way to turn around the heaviness from earlier in the day. [We had done Planetary Compassion.] I liked going through all the different aspects of how the planet was healed. It is so important to visualize peace." As she danced during this part of the exercise, Judy found herself making circles with her arms signifying that things were becoming whole and complete.

"Declaring in front of the group was neat. It was scary, and I almost didn't make the really important declaration—to write plays for peace. It's something I've wanted to do for a long time, but haven't. But when I declared myself, I felt like I had made my commitment. It also made me feel like I could do it. The group support was helpful, too."

Sample Declarations

"I'm going to live from that place that I felt this morning, that place of connection, so that the work that I'm doing is really motivated from a desire to serve."

"I am releasing that part of me that feels passion and creativity. I'll be leading groups and inspiring people."

"I want to learn how to put my words on paper with as much force as they come from my being, so that they can travel where they need to."

"I'm going to demonstrate at the Nevada nuclear test site."

"I intend to accept myself unconditionally, and to use the energy that is freed in healing myself and the planet."

"I want to let go of my fears in order to see people clearly and be with them, to give them the love I hold inside, so that they also can be released from their prisons."

"I would like to reclaim my hostile and angry side, so that I can reclaim my power."

"I want to find a way to feel even a small amount of the openness and the love that I feel right now, all the time in my life."

Even though this part of this exercise can be threatening to people, the group is usually so alive and energized at this point that people are eager to declare their intentions publicly. During the declaring, people feel excited and connected, and some are also deeply moved. Afterwards, it is often appropriate to come together in a circle holding hands or with arms around each other. This is a wonderful way to end a day or a workshop.

14

The Flight of Empowerment

THIS EXERCISE IS best introduced by the story of how a young man was empowered by his mentor, drawn again from the Riddlemaster Trilogy. In this scene, Morgon and his mentor Yrth are flying across the Realm in the shape of falcons.

> [Yrth] shot suddenly ahead, in and out of sun and shadow, in a straight, exuberant flight towards their destination. [His] excitement shook Morgon out of his monotonous rhythm. He picked up speed, soaring to catch up with the dark bolt hurtling through the sky.
>
> He gained on the falcon slowly, wanting with all the energy in him, to overtake the falcon in the pride of its power and pass it. He sprinted toward it with all his strength. . . . And then he was beside it, matching its speed, his wings moving to its rhythm. . . . It would not let him pass, but it lured him even faster, until all his thoughts and a shadow over his heart were ripped away.
>
> [Then, his energy spent, he landed and changed to human shape.] The falcon was hovering above him. He watched it motionlessly, until the wild glimpse into his own power broke over him again. His hand rose in longing toward the falcon.[1]

[1] From *Harpist in the Wind*, © 1979 Patricia A. McKillip. Reprinted with permission of Atheneum Publishers, an imprint of Macmillan Publishing Company, p. 194.

To me, this is a deeply moving rendition of being lured into your personal power through love—your love of the strong person who is helping to guide your life, and their love for you and their desire that you come fully into your own. In an ideal childhood situation this kind of empowerment would be provided by the parents, especially the father. However, because of the social conditioning which removes most fathers from the home and involvement in child rearing, this kind of empowerment is usually not provided. Mothers are often involved and caring enough, but lack a sense of their own personal power to pass on. So most of us have grown up without completely developing and internaliz- ing this support for our personal power. Many men especially are troubled by the lack of a loving, empowering relationship with their fathers.

In this exercise, you have an opportunity to remedy this by finding or creating that support within your own psyche. You will have an opportunity to discover in the depths of your psyche, in the archetypal realm, a figure who can function for you the way Yrth functioned for Morgon, a figure who can lead you on into an experience of your personal power. This figure frequently appears as a male, especially for men doing the exercise. For some women it is important that this figure be female, so that they can fully own their own power and not project it onto men. For other women, their unconscious chooses a male figure because power is archetypally associated with the male. If this happens to you, understand that this male figure is part of you—an aspect of your animus, your masculine side. This power is as much your birthright as it is for a man.

My own internal empowering figure is an amalgamation of three large powerful male figures from some of my favorite fantasy novels: the wizard Yrth introduced above, Treebeard the Ent from the *Lord of the Rings*,[2] and the giant Saltheart Foamfollower from

---

[2] J.R.R. Tolkien, *The Lord of the Rings* (Boston, MA: Houghton Mifflin, 1965).

the Covenant Trilogy.[3] They seem to combine wisdom, love, great power, and a wonderful sense of humor.

Circumstances

Time: 20 minutes.

The Exercise

This exercise is a combination of guided fantasy and movement. In the first part you go into a walking trance while taking an inner journey to meet your empowering figure. Then you imagine taking a flight of empowerment, while expressing this experience through movement. If it is difficult for you to remain standing throughout the exercise, feel free to sit, doing the movement from that position.

♪   "Slopes" (from *Mother Earth Lullaby* by Synchestra, as much as needed; steady, walking rhythm)

Stand with your eyes closed, and begin to walk in place very slowly, taking your attention inward, becoming aware of your internal life, going slowly into a deep place as you move. Focusing inward more and more as we begin our journey. Walking and going deeper, slowly moving and going deeper. Gradually getting into the rhythm, relaxing into the rhythm, quieting inside, focusing, steady, going deeper. Moving into a place where the images of the deep psyche can emerge more easily.

---

[3] Stephen R. Donaldson, *The Chronicles of Thomas Covenant the Unbeliever* (New York: Ballantine, 1977).

Imagine that you are walking through wild mountainous country. Great rocks are tumbled here and there, and there are patches of trees. The land is desolate, tough, and beautiful. You round a corner and emerge over a little rise and before you is a mountain. You find yourself drawn to it. You are intrigued with the challenge of climbing it and seeing the view from the top of the mountain. You see a rough trail that seems to circle around the mountain leading upwards, and you follow eagerly. As you do this, notice your surroundings in detail. What is the trail made of? How does it feel on your feet? How difficult is it to walk on? What vegetation do you see? What do the rocks look like? . . .

The trail leads around the mountain in a circle moving ever higher. You can see more of the surrounding countryside as you move higher along the trail. Notice what you see in the distance as you gradually ascend the mountain. . . . You know with an inner sense that your internal empowering figure waits for you at the top of the mountain. You have been drawn to take this trail to the top in order to reach them. You feel a yearning to be in the presence of this being. And you know with that same inner sense that this powerful being is also yearning to connect with you, and so you continue walking up the mountain. . . .

Moving higher and higher circling the mountain. You are getting closer to the top. The trail is getting rougher, steeper, more difficult to climb. Sometimes large rocks bar the way, sometimes the trail is very steep over crumbling ground. But you feel stronger as you go; your strength seems to grow to meet the challenges before you. Ever circling, moving higher and higher, feeling your strength. . . .

♪ "Horizons Beyond Infinity" (second half, starting at the point where the music becomes dramatic, from *Starmusic* by Don Robertson, as much as needed; powerful, dramatic tone)

You are now close to the top. You can see that you have one very steep part yet to climb, and you will be over the lip of the hill and at the top. You struggle up this last part with a sense of power as you exert yourself to your limit to surmount the obstacle. You finally pull yourself over the top and stand on the flat rocky summit of the mountain. You look out and see the vast sweep of wilderness spread out before you. . . .

You turn and see your empowering figure approaching. You can now begin to make out what this being looks like, or you may just sense the presence. The being approaches and greets you. Feel what it is like to be with them. You have a moment to interact with this being. . . .

Your empowering figure invites you to discover the strength and potential that is ready to emerge in you. He or she beckons you to follow and be lured on into your power. . . . You are both transformed into the shape of swift and powerful birds or flying beasts—falcons, eagles, or condors, perhaps dragons. Let yourself be transformed now along with the empowering figure. . . .

♪   *Heaven and Hell* (next to last cut, side one, by Vangelis; gradually rising to powerful, celebratory tone)

The empowering figure now flies off into the air. And you take off, following them, trying to catch up. As you do this, let your body begin to move into the feel of the flight. . . . The empowering figure flies higher and faster and lures you on. Let your body move more and more with your sense of the freedom and speed of your flight. Let yourself begin to dance the experience as you imagine it on the inside. You may whirl, glide, swoop, soar, just letting your body take over as you focus on your breath-taking flight after the empowering figure. . . .

Feel your yearning for the love of the empowering figure, and let it move you faster and faster, higher and higher, into the experience of your personal power. Feel the wind whipping past you, feel the strength in your arms, your chest, as your mighty pinions take you higher, swifter. . . . See the great distances you cover, the vast landscape below. . . .

♪   "The Oh of Pleasure" (from *Deep Breakfast* by Ray Lynch, begin a little way into the piece, when the momentum is already

building, leaving no space between this and the previous piece;
grand, soaring tone)

The lead bird goes even faster, even higher, and you follow
eagerly. Let yourself be taken; come into your power. Break free
and let your spirit soar with the wind and the sun. [Allow a
minute.]

Now you go into a long powerful glide. You have the sharp
eyes of a great bird, and you look down over the landscape you
are traversing and discover that it is the landscape of your life.
What you see spread out before you, in real or symbolic form, is
your life. But now you have an opportunity to view it from a
place of power and perspective. You may see many things in a
new light. As you look down what do you see? Rocky terrain, a
desert, lush greenery, a smooth road, a bog? . . . What parts of
this landscape are you drawn to? You may get new perspectives
on your past. You may see your current situation more clearly.
You may find a sense of meaning and purpose for your life as a
whole. You may sense where you are headed in the future. Take
a minute now to peruse this expanded view of your life as you
glide through the air. [Allow a minute.]

And now, taking what you have learned from this vantage
point, look into the near future of the landscape of your life, to
see what your next step might be in the overall plan. What does
the terrain look like? A dangerous chasm, a fork in the road, a
hazy mist, a fast moving river? [Allow half a minute.]

[As music ends:] You now glide down to the ground, tired
but exhilarated. You lie down to rest on the earth, and the
empowering figure lands beside you, feeling very proud. You may
rest on the earth here now if you want.

♪   "Falling in the Garden" (from Deep Breakfast by Ray Lynch;
relaxing, shimmering tone)

Take some time to be with yourself, resting and assimilating all
that happened in this journey. Let go now and let it sift through

you, let it deepen in you. Let this glimpse into your power take hold, and know that it is you. [Allow until end of music, a couple of minutes.]

And now gradually come back, bringing with you a sense of your strength and your power and your possibilities, knowing that this is a place you can return to when you need to know what your power is and who you can be. [Re-orient them to the room.]

♪ Simplified music: Use "The Oh of Pleasure" for the entire flight.

Experiences

The Soaring Fire

Judy is the woman who has been working on letting go of her "nice lady" persona and becoming playful. She described her empowering figure as "very beautiful. It came through the sun, so it was very light and bright and pulsating—a human type figure, but moving back and forth between an embryo and an adult shape. Then it became like a space capsule, ready to soar. At the back of the capsule where the fire comes out was a chrysanthemum image with brilliant red and gold colors."

"I was following that fire, moving into and with the fire, being the fire, and then just soaring. We were streaks of fireballs, playing and swirling, zipping and zooming in the skies! It was huge fun! We got beyond the worlds, and there was a wizard-like being who was saying 'Yay, go on with it.' We joined many others and there was so much space to play and run. I sense that when I unleash that fire, that power in me, I'll find powerful fire people to play with. At the very end there was a cylindrical place with a beautiful burning fire; it was like it was *the* fire. And we who had been traversing took this fire and brought it very gently down to earth. That was our gift." Notice how this is a beautiful integration of the playfulness of the child with the spiritual depth of the higher self.

Sarcasm vs. Support

Occasionally, someone resists becoming empowered and needs individual help. Bill is the man we met earlier who has been developing his self-confidence and personal power with regard to the nuclear threat. In this exercise, he started out feeling angry and competitive toward the empowering figure, wanting to "bust out" of something. He became sarcastic, disparaging the exercise.

In his work afterwards, he realized that his father had frequently been sarcastic like that toward him, "poking pins" at his ideals and life goals. He had internalized this and was now doing it to himself. This was one of the main reasons why he had trouble feeling confident about his plans and following through on them. He also realized that he was reacting to the empowering figure as if it were his sarcastic father. I pointed out that this was the opposite of empowerment and asked him to allow himself to imagine what he would want from an empowering figure who could be trusted to care.

His answer: "I have the sense of something being right *with me* or coming into me. Like I'm standing here in my body, and something enters me. It's a very supportive sense, that each step I take, the figure is right with me helping me take the step, instead of digging the ground out from under my feet. I sense myself going step-by-step, with something right behind me helping me, putting energy into my legs."

I encouraged him to feel this physically. He breathed deeply and felt strong energy flowing through his body. He felt his steps being firm and sure, his presence being large and solid. I had him continue this while walking around the room. As he walked he felt himself gathering strength, and sensed many people walking with him lending him strength to accomplish their mutual goals.

This contributed to Bill's being able to support himself through difficulties rather than undercutting himself. It was an important piece of the work which enabled him to become a dedicated and confident peace worker. We will see another piece in the next chapter.

Other Experiences

Another man reported that he met a bear as his empowering figure. He had been working on becoming stronger and more assertive, and the bear represented his emerging power—finding his own space, standing up to challenges, and commanding respect. Then he felt the enjoyable sensation of a cold wind, and the empowerment figure become "an immense bird whose wings were moving very slowly and powerfully; its eyes were shiny black with no irises. I really loved the sense of solidity from the bird; it let out a huge screech with deep vibrations." The overview of his life showed him how his lack of assertiveness had caused difficulties in his marriage. He saw his next step as reclaiming his power.

A woman described her experience as follows: "The figure I met at the top of the mountain was clearly my masculine side. I expected that the empowering figure would be feminine, and instead it was a man who was gloriously beautiful. He was exquisite, and I felt such a sense of love for him. It was a moving and beautiful experience. I'm happy to know that he is part of me." She found the flying freeing and strengthening. As she viewed her life below, she saw three tasks for herself: loving her family, creating a particular work of art, and setting up a support group for herself and others doing peace work. These tasks seemed easily accomplished and integrated with each other.

Sandra reveled in the physical aspects of climbing the mountain and flying. "My empowerment figure was a combination of human and animal, full of red and orange light. It was female and really powerful. At first it frightened me because I didn't see any compassion along with the power. But when I went down on my knees to this figure, she touched me on the shoulder and I felt totally cared for. She kissed me and I was filled with energy. We flew away together like sisters. It was fascinating; I got really lost in the experience of being a strong, powerful bird." This provided another step in the development of Sandra's strength.

Another woman, Mira, reported that she saw "the spiritual mother symbol from *Clan of the Cave Bear*[4] (a neolithic Great Mother image). She was a massive, 30-foot-tall granite figure, but she could communicate with me." During the ensuing months, Mira formed a very significant relationship with this figure. She met her again during the Gaia fantasy, and "she's been with me ever since. I meditate and talk with her daily."

She continued, "During the flight, I could see everything below so clearly; it was beautiful. I flew between two ranges of mountains. While visualizing my past, some of that pain from this morning started coming up again, but I just flew by it and let it go. When I got to the end of the journey, I was stronger. I could look back on the pain as a place I was, but no longer am. It was a good feeling."

---

[4] Jean M. Auel, *The Clan of the Cave Bear* (New York: Crown Publishers, Inc., 1980).

15

Expansive Movement

AN IMPORTANT ASPECT of empowerment is feeling free and loose enough to act in the world with confidence, spontaneity, and expressiveness. Many of us are held back by fears, constrictions, and lack of self-esteem. These constraints manifest themselves in the body as well as the psyche in the form of chronic patterns of muscle tension. They may or may not restrict normal movement, but they do restrict movement that is spontaneous or expressive, such as reaching out to hug someone or demonstrating passion while delivering a speech. This holding back may also show itself in the body in a lowered energy level which might prevent, for example, the forceful expression of your point of view or sustained commitment to a difficult project.

Since these restrictions are partly physical, the body is a useful avenue for working on them. I have found that movement mobilizes my energy in a way that overcomes my normal fears and inhibitions and makes a profound difference in the freedom I have to express myself. I am normally quite shy in large unfamiliar social situations. People who have known me only in these settings are often very surprised to see me on the dance floor or playing sports. They say that I seem like an entirely different person. I am outgoing and spontaneous; my energy level is raised past the threshold of my defenses, and my body is freed.

This exercise takes you out of your normal patterns of constriction by asking you to become certain animals through move-

ment and to experience the expansive qualities that are archetypally associated with these animals. This freedom is then
transferred back into the human realm and applied to your life
through movement and dance. You have an opportunity to experience yourself as expanded and empowered through experimenting with movement that is far more dramatic and expressive than
would be appropriate in most situations. This learning is later
unconsciously translated into the kind of expression that will
work in your everyday life.

Circumstances

This exercise is good to use as an introduction to expressive
movement for people who are unfamiliar with it. (See the discussion of movement on page xxxv in "How to Use the Exercises.")
It starts out with movement that is not too difficult or uncomfortable and builds gradually to more expressive and potentially
threatening kinds of movement at the end of the exercise.

Time: 20 minutes.

The Exercise[1]

You will be becoming different animals through movement. You
are free to choose whichever animal of a given kind you are drawn
to and would like to incarnate. For instance, when asked to
become a lion or other great cat, feel free to choose a panther,
cougar, or anything else that fits for you. In addition, we are
working with the archetypal lion here, not necessarily how lions
actually behave. If you think, for instance, that lions are actually

---

[1] The first four parts of this exercise were designed by Deborah Bedford-Strohm
when she was assisting me in leading Inner Journeys groups.

lazy, don't let that detract from the exercise. Let yourself become the archetypal lion, strong and fierce and proud.

♪   *La Fête Sauvage* (second cut, side two by Vangelis, as much as needed; dreamy, sinuous tone)

Curl up on the floor and become a cat dozing in front of the fireplace, or maybe lying in the sun. Take a minute to go inside and find your sense of catness. Get in touch with the cat qualities in yourself—the languor, the pride, the sensuality, or whatever qualities you associate with being a cat. Let yourself become all cat. . . . Now begin to wake up and stretch in the warmth of the fire or sunlight. Take your time as you do this, feeling the warmth prickling on your skin, slowly unrolling a paw and feeling each muscle as you do. Continue unfolding slowly, relishing each movement. . . . Then stretch your whole cat body, breathing deeply, yawning, purring, letting out whatever sounds your cat body wants to make. [Allow another minute, then fade the music.]

Now you are going to become a different animal. Let go of the cat sense and just sit quietly for a moment.

♪   "Celestial Soda Pop" (from *Deep Breakfast* by Ray Lynch, as much as needed; playful, bouncy tone)

Now let yourself become a playful puppy. Maybe you just woke up and are looking for someone to play with. Get in touch with the excitement, the anticipation, the lightness, the carefree feeling. Let this sense of playfulness begin to take over your body and move with it. You might feel your tail wagging, your muscles alive and quivering, ready to romp. . . . Begin to move around the room, looking for something or someone to play with. You're a happy-go-lucky puppy looking for fun! If it feels appropriate, feel free to interact with others. . . . And feel free to bark or growl or let out any other puppy sounds that feel right. [Leader may need to initiate the sounds.] . . . You'll have a few minutes to play to your heart's content. [Allow 2 minutes, then fade the music.] Now let go of the sense of puppy, and feel yourself calm and empty.

♪   *Oxygene* (first rhythmic section, by Jean Michel Jarre, as much as needed; powerful, driving tone)

Come to a standing position. . . . Now go inside and find the essence of a great cat, a lion, a tiger, a panther. Find the power, the presence, the aggressiveness, the pride of a lion or lioness or other large cat. As you sense these qualities, let your body grow into them. Feel how the pride raises your head and drops your shoulders. Feel the presence of your whole body, how all your muscles are alive and alert, the power in your haunches. . . . Imagine yourself in a forest or savannah. You might begin stalking another animal. Feel the power, the grace, and the sureness of your movement. [Allow a minute.]

Let a growl come from your great throat. Let the sound rise from deep in your belly. Let it grow into a roar. Let the sound come out full. Let the whole forest know that you are here, that you are powerful! [Leader roar to stimulate people. When people are finished roaring, fade the music.] Now let that go and come to stillness again.

♪   "The Oh of Pleasure" (from *Deep Breakfast* by Ray Lynch, as much as needed; lilting, soaring tone)

Stand up, close your eyes, and go inside. Let yourself become a great soaring bird or animal, an eagle, a hawk, a falcon, a condor, a dragon. Get in touch with the qualities of eagle or falcon or other great flying being in yourself—the strength, the calmness, the expansion, the perspective. . . . Then let these qualities take over your body. Begin to soar over the earth. Spread your wings and feel them beating slowly, steadily, powerfully. Feel your breath deep, calm, and energizing. Move as a powerful, expansive, great flyer. Feel the air moving by you as you soar, playing on the air currents, letting the wind take you, moving effortlessly and gracefully. . . .

Sense the great height at which you fly, the wide landscape within your view. Feel the power of your wings, the speed with which you can fly. You might suddenly swoop down towards the earth, and then glide on an updraft. Let the wind and the music take you! [Allow 2 minutes, then fade the music.] Now let that go and come to stillness again.

♪   *Equinoxe* (first cut side two, as much as needed; rhythmic, danceable, uplifting tone)

Now let yourself become a combination of the great cat, the soaring bird, and the puppy all at once. Feel the expansive perspective, the driving power, and the playfulness simultaneously, and let your body move with that sense. Don't try to figure it out; it can't be done. Just let the movement come from inside as you feel yourself to be that integrated being. . . .

Let yourself also be an integrated human being as well as an integrated animal. Let yourself be an integration of your adult, child, and higher self; your puppy child, your lion adult, and your eagle higher self. Let the movement be a dance of celebration of your fullness of being, your complexity. You are spontaneous like a puppy, powerful like a lion, and expansive like an eagle. You move in the world with vigor and purpose. You are strong and open; you are not afraid to be yourself out in the world, to initiate, to risk. Dance this expressive, powerful you! . . .

Now let a sense come to you of your life purpose, your potential, what you are here to do and to be. It doesn't have to be specific. You may only sense it as unexpected images, or body sensings, just a hint of the direction in which you are moving. . . . Now imagine yourself carrying out that purpose, passionately, expressively, creatively, lovingly. Imagine yourself moving in the world expansively, accomplishing your goals, sharing your gifts with humanity. And feel the strength and the inspiration moving through you. . . .

Feel in your muscles and sinews your passion, your calling, your strength. Dance your action and purpose. Move into the world with no fear to hold back your natural power. Soar with your eagle self and roar with your lion nature! [Allow until the music ends, about 2 minutes.]

♪   Simplified music: *Equinoxe* cut as above.

Experiences

Like the Child and the Higher Self, this exercise is about integrating the best of our various selves, except that here it is done symbolically through animals and through movement so that it is less threatening to people. Notice that only after people have become each animal and are moving as the integrated animal, do I suggest that they become the integrated human being and consider their life purpose. This way the momentum of the earlier stages of the exercise carries over into the most difficult part.

License

Bill is our friend who has been working on self-confidence and follow through. He reported, "The theme of it for me was 'license.' As a cat, I felt I had license to feel sensual in my body. As a puppy, I felt I had license to be stupid. It was OK; I didn't have to watch it. As the eagle, with the incredible eyesight I could see the overall picture of things. With the lion, it was OK to feel dangerous." As himself he had permission to feel proud of some of his accomplishments. He sensed that he had power that was veiled, and it felt very good to be without his usual guilt about not yet using it. He imagined manifesting his power in front of large groups of people, projecting his presence, and setting an example for others just by being himself.

"It was very powerful for me. While I was moving, I got a strong sense of confidence, expansiveness, of not having to hold myself back. I want to translate that into the way I live my life. I realized, 'Wow, I can be that person!' " Indeed, in the ensuing months he was able to use some of this energy and this permission to be himself in his peace work.

In the Forefront

Sherry is our friend who has been working on self-esteem, who had the tornado as shadow. "I saw the eagle scouting out new things and new ideas, seeing the lay of the land, getting a sense of direction. The tiger was on the ground, leading into the new part of the forest, stalking whatever comes next. The puppy was nudging everybody else into the act. Then I became the eagle again scouting new territory. So there was this sequence of seeing and leading and nudging. My purpose was to serve as an example to others of taking risks, of being in the forefront of things.

"When we were through, I was so buzzed up I felt, 'OK, let's go out and do something right now.' It was so powerful! If you had a group of people doing that, it would be tremendous to move right into a shared purpose." This exercise was done about a year after her first Inner Journeys experience, when she had trouble owning her higher self. You can see how far she had come.

A Playful Dance

In this exercise, Judy was again working on her playfulness. She had progressed to the point of being quite playful in guided fantasies, as we saw in the last chapter, and this exercise provided the next, more difficult step, living it out in public. She reported, "At first I had difficulty letting myself be playful as a puppy, especially making sounds. It was much easier to roar as a lion. You were great as a puppy, S_____. You really inspired me. I especially liked the part when we were snuggling up and falling asleep together." A dragon image had been coming up for Judy during the previous few months, so she chose that for the flying animal, enjoying its power and force.

During the last part, she found herself walking a lot, as in walking her path, feeling her power in her solar plexus. She worked through her discomfort with playfulness by overcoming symbolic barriers—she jumped over a big log and moved around a body of water. "Once I got past those obstacles, my body movements became more fluid and I was able to bounce around and be playful. I did a little dance around my third eye area, feeling that there was power coming in there from the cosmos so that I could pursue my new goal in school and handle it intellectually." Notice how the playfulness empowered her in what would seem to be a totally different area—intellectual development.

Other Experiences

Marcy reported, "I loved being the various animals." As she danced her own empowerment, she found herself making a heart-shaped movement with her arms, "surrounding me, and then surrounding everyone I came in contact with. I imagined living my life with that motion in me, and it felt revolutionary. To allow in the spirit, the source of energy coming from the earth, and to trust what happens."

Lena had been single for a long time and had almost given up on finding a mate. But while she was an eagle flying, she "was delighted that another eagle joined me, and it was a wonderful dance. No matter what kind of tricks I did, he could follow me. And sometimes he led and I followed. Two powerful and mature animals flying over the world."

She got a clear sense that her work in the world is in speaking and performing in front of large groups, letting people know that we need to change the way we live in order to save humanity and the planet. Intermixed with the music of the exercise, she heard a song with words. "Everything was golden and sun lit. There was a collective sense of a new dawn of awakening and of people being able to take things in their own hands and make a difference." She realized that she needs to accept the gifts she has been given that make her a charismatic speaker and to use them in service to the world.

16

Affirmations

LIKE VISUALIZATION, affirmations are a well-known method of attempting to bring about a desired future state. The idea is that you are more likely to become who you affirm yourself to be. Using positive affirmations is an excellent way of countering negative programming you may have received as a child, especially with regard to self-esteem. Self-esteem is one of our most fragile and most important needs throughout our lives, and one of the most crucial determinants of our well-being and growth.

If you had experiences as a child that planted negative messages about yourself in your deep psyche, they will interfere with your sense of well-being and your ability to act in the world with power and confidence. Affirmations are a way of reversing this by planting positive messages. In addition to the content of the affirmations, an attitude is conveyed that it is OK to feel good about yourself and that you can grow and change.

For an affirmation to be effective, it must be aligned with the true direction of your growth and it must reach the deep psyche. In the absence of an opening into the depths, mechanically repeating affirmations accomplishes little.

You may have noticed that many of the exercises in this book involve affirming who you are and who you can be. In each case, the exercise must be structured so that the affirmation is done when you are in a receptive state, so that it speaks to the deep unconscious. The receptive state is sometimes achieved by opening yourself to buried pain from the past or by inducing a particular emotional or spiritual state. The exercises are set up to speak to the deep psyche by using trance, music, movement, and the leader's tone of voice. This particular exercise also relies on the power of publicly declaring the affirmation and receiving group support.

Most people recommend that affirmations be done in the present tense.[1] For example, saying "I am strong" even if you don't currently feel that you are very strong. This speaks directly to the unconscious in a way that other forms such as "I am not weak" or "I will be strong" do not. However, I think that even though using the present tense may speak to the unconscious, it may not make sense to the conscious mind. As I am saying "I am strong," a part of my conscious mind may be saying "But I'm not really." Therefore, I favor a form that affirms what one is becoming or learning to be, such as "I am becoming stronger" or "I am learning to be strong." This avoids activating self-judgment while retaining the positive present-oriented statements.

Circumstances

A variation of this exercise for socially-oriented workshops is provided.

Working Alone. When working alone, read the beginning instructions silently to yourself and then speak the affirmations aloud.

Working with a Partner. When working with a partner, you can do the exercise together, with one person reading the directions and both of you taking turns saying the affirmations.

Time: 20 minutes.

---

[1] Margo Adair, *Working Inside Out* (Berkeley, CA: Wingbow Press, 1984), chapter 3.

The Exercise[2] ———————————————

[People begin by standing up, with eyes closed.]

♪   "Pachelbel's Canon" (or other celebratory music, as many times
    as needed)

Visualize yourself or get a sense of yourself as being on a lifelong
journey of growth and development. You began as a child many
years ago with wonderful potential, and gradually over the years
you've been realizing more and more of those possibilities. . . .

    Along the way you have been hurt, wounded, and as a result
of this some of your possibilities have been suppressed for a time.
But also as a result of that pain, you have been encouraged to
look more deeply into yourself, to heal yourself. You have released
the protective covering of innocence. You have let go of the
safety of not knowing. Your experience of shadows has brought
you new depth of vision. It has also made you deeper and more
mature, more compassionate, seasoned. . . .

    See yourself now in the middle of a lifetime of expansion
of potential. See the many ways that you have grown over the
years. . . . Now see yourself continuing to grow in the future.
See or sense all the ways that you will develop, all the ways
you will become enriched and deepened, all the hidden potential that you will realize in the future. . . .

    To help you do this I will speak sentences of affirmation.
You may want to say them to yourself after me; they apply to you.
Feel free to move to the music if it feels appropriate so that each
affirmation becomes grounded in your body. [Allow a little time
after each sentence for people to take it in.]

    I am getting stronger and healthier, in body and mind.

———————
[2] This exercise is adapted from Jean Houston, "The Art of the Mensch," *The
Possible Human*, p. 127.

I am becoming more supportive and healing and loving, and also more able to take in support, and take in healing, and take in love.

I am becoming bolder and more expressive, able to show myself more fully and inspire people.

I am learning to connect with people more easily, so I can participate constructively and joyfully in the life of my family and community.

I am becoming more compassionate toward the suffering in the world.

I am learning to integrate my intellect and my intuition, my passion and my endurance, my assertiveness and my receptivity, so that I approach life from a place of balance.

I am becoming more perceptive of what goes on inside myself and others, and also more perceptive about what is happening in my community and the world.

I am growing more confident and more centered in myself. This allows me to risk more and to turn difficulties into challenges. It allows me to bounce back from failures or defeats.

I am becoming more aware of the great social issues of our time — the fate of the human race and of the planet.

I am becoming freer from convention, able to think creatively, able to make new, unusual connections, to see and experience and do things that haven't been done before.

Now you are going to get in on the act. Whenever you feel ready, declare to the group one of the ways that you are developing, or a way that you will develop in the future. After each person makes their affirmation to the group, the rest of us will support them. So after a person says, for example, "I am becoming strong," we will reply as a group, "You are becoming strong." You will have a chance to make more than one affirmation. So whenever someone feels ready, begin to make your affirmations. [Allow as much time as people need.]

♪   "Eric's Theme" (from *Chariots of Fire* by Vangelis; or other celebratory music)

And now a few more affirmations for all of us:

Life flows through me. I feel my connection with the peoples of the world, with all life, with the universe. The creative intention of the universe flows through me, quickening me with purpose.

As I reach more and more of my potential and my life becomes richer and more satisfying, I also can contribute more to helping others and healing our beautiful and troubled planet.

I am the developing human being, the planetary person, the being of love, the next step of evolution.

Now let yourself move more fully to the music. Ground the sense of possibility in your body. Dance your potential, your purpose, and your being! [Allow until the music ends, a couple of minutes.]

And now, knowing yourself to be all these things, if not already, then in potential, spend a moment in silence taking this into the deepest part of yourself, knowing yourself, resting in this.

♪ Simplified music: Use either Pachelbel or "Eric's Theme" throughout.

Variations

In a social transformation workshop, substitute the following for the initial part dealing with lifetime growth:

Invoke an image of someone who represents for you a person who has contributed greatly to social transformation and planetary healing. It might be Gandhi or Martin Luther King or Mother Teresa of Calcutta, or it could be someone closer to home such as Helen Caldicott or Ron Dellums, or even someone you know personally. Call them forth and in your imagination let their best qualities flow into you. Imagine yourself taking on those qualities with your own particular stamp on them. . . .

Now also imagine developing your own high qualities of service even more than you have already. Imagine yourself becoming a planetary healer, a contributor to social transformation in ways that use your particular gifts. . . .

Use the following affirmations:

I am becoming more aware of the great social issues of our time.

I am becoming more concerned about the fate of the human race and of the planet.

I am developing my creativity and wisdom.

I am searching for ways to use my talents in the service of social transformation.

I'm becoming more open to the possibilities for contributing that may arise.

I am getting stronger and healthier.

I am becoming more compassionate toward the suffering in the world.

I am becoming bolder and more expressive, able to show myself more fully and inspire people.

I am learning to connect with people more easily, so I can network well and participate constructively and joyfully in political and cultural groups.

I am learning to integrate my intellect and my intuition, my passion and my endurance, my assertiveness and my receptivity, so that I bring a more whole person to this great work.

I am becoming more perceptive of what goes on inside myself and others, and also more perceptive about what is happening in the world.

I am becoming more supportive and healing and loving, and also more able to take in support, and take in healing, and take in love.

I am growing more confident and more centered in myself. This allows me to risk more and to turn difficulties into challenges. It allows me to bounce back from failures or defeats, to maintain my commitment.

I am becoming freer from convention, able to think creatively, able to make new, unusual connections, to see and experience and do things that haven't been done before.

Life flows through me. I feel my connection with the peoples of the world, with all life, with the universe. The creative intention of the universe flows through me, quickening me with purpose in this time of great need.

As I reach more and more of my potential and my life becomes richer and more satisfying, I also can contribute more to the great projects of our time.

I am the planetary healer, the true revolutionary, the one who engenders social transformation, the peacemaker.

Experiences

This exercise generates high energy, laughter, and strong group bonding. There is much love and empowerment expressed and much teasing and joyous humor. The affirmations used tend to be shorter than those said by the leader because of the need for the group to repeat them. The following are the affirmations used by one group:

I am becoming wiser.

I am moving into living my full potential.

I am at ease in using my power.

I am powerful.

I am becoming more loving in a wider variety of situations.

I am expressing freely.

I have access to energy.

I am getting lighter and more grounded every day.

We are one, and we're all coming into the awareness of that.

I am getting more centered in myself.

It's easier and easier for me to know and set my boundaries.

My confidence in myself grows every day.

I'm getting more comfortable in putting myself out in the world.

I am filled with energy.

I'm getting freer and freer in expressing who I really am.

I'm feeling safe to feel sexual.

I feel joyfully happy being alone.

Sherry is our friend who was working on self-esteem and who had a judgmental monk as her shadow. This exercise was very important to her. "I had a real feeling of strength and power; the energy was running all through me. There was a feeling of freedom and openness. The most important thing was feeling that I was a good person and that I deserved to feel good about myself."

She continued, "It was scary to make my own affirmations, but that made it even more powerful when I was able to take the risk to say such positive things about myself. And nothing bad happened! I got a wonderful supportive response from the group instead. That had quite an impact. The kidding around was really fun, too. I feel so alive!" This exercise added another piece to her growing strength and self-confidence.

Another woman, Martha, reported on how it helped her with self-acceptance: "It was energizing and empowering for me. I really saw that my tears [referring to some deep crying she did earlier] are that very evolution that's taking place—my tears of joy, tears of recognition, tears of coming home. [Affirmingly] I just have a lot of crying to do."

SECTION SIX

The Spiritual Realm

Introduction

WE TAP INTO the spiritual realm at those rare moments when we are deeply inside ourselves, profoundly at peace, when we glimpse a higher meaning to our existence, when love just pours out of us. We experience at once the letting go of self and the fulfillment of self, the most exquisite pleasure and the transcendence of pleasure.

The spiritual realm is the part of the psyche that is the wellspring of the higher human capacities and our touchstone with the divine. It may be thought of as the higher part of the unconscious. Psychosynthesis calls it the superconscious: "From this region we receive our higher intuitions and inspirations . . . and urges to humanitarian and heroic action. It is the source of the higher feelings, such as altruistic love; of genius and of the states of contemplation, illumination, and ecstasy."[1] The higher self, discussed in the introduction to section one, is the part of the self that extends into the spiritual realm.

In the spiritual realm you may encounter the divine in the form of God or the Goddess or an archetypal divine being (see chapter 19). Or you may experience unity with all of creation or an insight into the meaning of existence. The spiritual realm is sometimes experienced as light, as wholeness, or as liberation.

---

[1] Roberto Assagioli, *Psychosynthesis* (New York: Viking, 1965).

Entering into this realm has been described as a return to the source, as an awakening, or as death and rebirth. The process of spiritual transformation may be experienced as journeying to a place of vision and power, as uncovering the veils of illusion, or as purification by inner fire.[2]

Many people who have come close to death have had powerful experiences of what must be the spiritual realm. These experiences have had a commonality to them that is independent of people's previous religious beliefs. Some of them reported receiving unconditional love and acceptance from a divine presence and feeling a strong desire to unite with this presence. Some felt deep peace, joy, and love; others saw sights or sounds of unearthly beauty. Some felt they received an understanding of their unique purpose in life or even of the workings of the universe.[3]

Spiritual Traditions

It is important to distinguish between religion and spirituality. Many religions have become formal and bureaucratic and have partially lost touch with the spiritual essence that inspired them. Though some people within these formal structures retain a living connection with the divine, many are simply caught up in outward forms and dogmatic teachings. I hope that those of you who have turned away from religion for these reasons will not discount the spiritual aspects of Inner Journeys work. I have had profound and moving spiritual experiences which have affected my own life and growth deeply. Whatever its ultimate nature, I know from personal experience that our spirituality is an important part of our makeup which cannot be ignored.

---

[2] Ralph Metzner, *Opening to Inner Light* (Los Angeles, CA: J.P. Tarcher, 1986).
[3] Kenneth Ring, *Heading Toward Omega* (New York: Morrow, 1985).

You may have noticed that I am using the term spiritual realm in an ambiguous way, to refer to a part of the human psyche and also perhaps to a separate realm of reality. Of course, many spiritual and esoteric traditions do believe that there is a spiritual realm that has its own reality, perhaps even the primary reality from which the physical world is derived. I prefer not to take a stand on this, leaving it to be explored by each person. Whether the gods and guides and spirits of this realm are actually separate beings or simply higher forces and constellations within our psyches is an open question for me.

Most spiritual traditions not only assume that the spiritual realm has a separate existence, but usually make very specific pronouncements about the ultimate nature of that reality. They tell us the identities and natures of specific divine beings, the nature of consciousness and the self, the meaning of existence, etc. There is a danger in this because the greatest value to be obtained from this realm is in what we learn from our direct experience of it, not from the teachings of others. Too often people unquestioningly accept a belief system that is handed down to them rather than doing their own searching through inner experience. My own feeling is that ultimate reality is probably far beyond our understanding at our current level of development. It seems presumptuous to think that we are even capable of comprehending it at this point. We have learned so much in the last century about both the human psyche and material reality, and this knowledge is just beginning to be applied to larger philosophical questions.

On the other hand, some spiritual traditions are thousands of years old and have very sophisticated psychologies and cosmologies. Within the mystical core of these traditions, there is a common underlying viewpoint on ultimate reality. This has been called the perennial philosophy.[4] It talks of the underlying unity of all things and how this has been experienced by mystics

---

[4] Aldous Huxley, *The Perennial Philosophy* (New York: Harper & Row, 1970).

throughout the ages. Indeed, this is one of the reasons why it makes sense to me to speak of a spiritual realm at all.

Despite this commonality, however, enormous differences exist among the various traditions in their views on spiritual reality. They present widely disparate and even contradictory teachings, and they all seem to be strongly bound by the cultures and religions that spawned them. This doesn't prompt me to believe that any of them has pinned down the final answers to these profound questions.

The personal search for these answers can be very fruitful because it can lead us to experience some of the deep mystery of existence. For this reason I strongly resist any premature closure. The quest seems far more important than any answers we might find.

Spiritual Development Today

As I see it, the goal of spiritual development is twofold: first to experience ultimate spiritual reality directly, to love God, to be in union with all that is; second, to bring this experience into the way we live our lives, to actualize our divine purpose in the world. This dual goal seems to be present in most spiritual teachings, but sometimes divine union is emphasized almost to the exclusion of service. I have been grateful to Jean Houston for emphasizing the importance of using the fruits of the spiritual journey to green the world. We are here not simply to experience the divine, but to bring the divine into form. Our task is to bring love, creativity, and wisdom into the world. At this time in history, with the future of the human race possibly at stake, it seems critical that we keep this goal firmly in mind.

Each spiritual tradition has grown out of a particular culture at a certain time in human history and has been partially a response to the needs of that time. Each tradition has been a way of bringing some divine wisdom to bear on the struggles and aspirations which were current then. We now have access to the riches of all these different traditions, and we need to drink deeply from this well of experience. However, the needs of our time are unique, and we cannot be content with simply following one of the ancient traditions.

Our age has its own particular problems and its own understandings of the human condition, which must be incorporated into any spiritual system that can truly speak to us today. Today's issues include the equality of women, the honoring of the body and sexuality, the celebration of cultural diversity, the need for action on behalf of social transformation, and the need for autonomy and responsibility on the part of each spiritual aspirant. We need to evolve a spiritual tradition (or traditions) that includes these factors, that reaps the harvest of our past and goes on to address our deepest spiritual yearnings and social responsibilities of the present.

The exercises in this section, which provide an introduction to the spiritual realm, are as follows:

Journey to the Spiritual Realm
The Expanded Body
Surrendering the Heart

In addition, you may visit the spiritual realm during the following exercises:

The Child and Higher Self
Opening the Heart
All Life Purpose exercises
The Flight of Empowerment

17

Journey to the Spiritual Realm

IN THIS EXERCISE you take a journey to the spiritual realm in order to deepen your access to this part of your psyche and to bring something back to enrich your life and the world.

At one point during this journey, it is suggested that archetypal or mythic elements will appear in the images you are constructing. Archetypal images are those universal images that have inspired entire cultures through the ages as opposed to those with purely personal significance. These are the kinds of images that Jung designated as belonging to the collective unconscious.[1] They typically include images of gods, devils, spirits, giants, strange beasts, medieval and other mythological or fantastic scenes. They deal with birth, death, initiation, transformation, and other spiritual themes.

Circumstances

Working Alone. When working alone you will need to think of images for yourself to imagine in each of the sense modalities, and you will have to go on the journey by yourself. Even with

---

[1] June Singer, *Boundaries of the Soul* (New York: Anchor, 1972), p. 89–96.

taped instructions, going on the journey by yourself may be difficult unless you are proficient at guided fantasy.

Working with a Partner. When working with a partner, you can
tape the instructions, or one person can lead both of you through
the exercise together.

Time: 40 minutes.

The Exercise[2] ──────────────────

[The group should have an understanding of the spiritual realm
and of archetypal images. People then arrange themselves for a
guided fantasy in pairs (see chapter 4).]

First, you are going to suggest things for each other to imagine,
taking turns. We will start with smells. So if I were paired with
[co-leader], I might say: "Imagine the smell of freshly baked
bread." She would do that, and then [co-leader] would say, "Imagine the smell of the ocean." And we would continue back and
forth. Do that now. [Allow a minute.]

Now we move to imagining tastes. For example, "Imagine
the taste of a hot fudge sundae." [Co-leader], "Imagine the taste
of a rich curry sauce." Now you continue with tastes. [Allow a
minute.]

Now ask your partner to imagine body sensations—touch or
movement. "Imagine the sensation of petting a cat." [Co-leader],
"Imagine swimming in a cold mountain lake." Now continue.
[Allow a minute.]

Now we will do sounds. "Imagine the sound of thunder."
[Co-leader], "Imagine an orchard full of bird song in spring." Now
continue. [Allow a minute.]

──────────
[2] This exercise is one used by Jean Houston in the 1985 Mystery School.

An now things you would see. "Imagine a beautiful sunset." [Co-leader], "Imagine what your bedroom looked like when you were a child." [Allow a minute.]

Now we do multi-sensory images. "Imagine riding a bike in heavy city traffic, seeing the cars, feeling the bike under you, hearing the traffic sounds, smelling the exhaust." [Co-leader], "Imagine walking in a meadow in summer in your bare feet, seeing the beautiful wild flowers, feeling the sun on your body and the earth beneath your feet, hearing the soft wind in the grass." Now continue. [Allow 2 minutes.]

You are going to create a story together. You are going to go on a journey together. One of you will begin the story, describing what is happening and you will each imagine yourselves there. Then that person will stop and the other person will take up the story from there, and you will continue back and forth. For example, I might start as follows: "We are walking through a forest which is shrouded in fog. It is cool and damp and somewhat ominous." [Co-leader], "The trees are ancient, gnarled giants. We come to a clearing in which there is a mound of earth with a dwarf tree growing on it." Then I would continue on from there. Now begin your journey together. [Allow 3 minutes.]

Now each of you will dream on the story separately, silently for a while. [Allow a minute.]

Now come back together and tell each other what happened in your story. [Allow 3 minutes.]

Carry on the story as a joint journey again, going back and forth, beginning at the point where you separated and incorporating elements of each other's stories into the joint story you are weaving. [Allow 3 minutes.]

♪ *Ecstasy* (fifth cut, by Deuter, as much as needed; enchanted, medieval tone)

Now continue your story, allowing archetypal or mythic elements to enter the story if that hasn't already happened. [Allow 3 minutes.]

♪   *Ignacio* (first movement, by Vangelis; spiritual tone)

Soon in your journey, you will cross a bridge or pass through a mist or a doorway or in some other way cross a boundary which clearly means that you are entering the spiritual realm, the realm of light, wisdom, and love. This is the realm of creativity, inspiration, and deeper meaning, of union, joy, and peace. In this realm your story will contiue, and at some point you receive something from this realm to guide your life and evoke your deep potential. You may encounter a being or receive a gift. You may see a vision or sense something in your body or hear words or sounds. Continue your journey now and see what emerges. [Allow until music ends, about 3 minutes.]

♪   *Ignacio* (third movement; grand, spiritual tone)

Now each of you will continue on in the spiritual realm separately to receive the insight or experience that is most important for you at this time. [Allow until music ends, about 3 minutes.]

[Slowly bring people back out of trance. Partners then share with each other the rest of their stories.]

♪   Simplified music: Use *Ignacio* as above.

Experiences

Trading sensory images back and forth serves to take people deeply into a mutual trance which seems to be somewhat different from the usual kind of trance. People are generally not very still, and they are capable of chatting and joking with each other in relatively normal voices. Yet you will see from the results that the trance is quite effective.

People invariably have an easy time combining their separate stories even when there is little commonality. However, they often report that there is an underlying thread of unity or a surprising amount of similarity to their different journeys. Some people even report that at times they know what will happen next before their partner speaks it aloud.

The combination of individual and shared fantasy is very important. A deep sense of human connection is engendered by sharing the depths of each other's psyches for a time. The sharing also keeps people focused during the long guided fantasy without requiring much direction from the leader, making it possible for the fantasy to be created entirely by the participants. The individual parts of the fantasy are necessary to allow for the fullest play of the person's unconscious, to allow the deepest layers of the psyche to be tapped, unencumbered by the need to verbalize to one's partner. This is especially important at the end of the exercise, when people have entered the spiritual realm.

The Seal Convention

Our friend Sherry was paired with a woman named Marcy for this exercise. They both took part in describing their experience to the group: "We started on the beach, and as we were walking into the ocean to get around this cliff we noticed a big seal. All of a sudden a giant wave came and took us out into the ocean underwater, and the seal went with us. He was a wise, old seal. We held onto him, and he pulled us and guided us down into a long tunnel. We knew he was taking us somewhere for a special reason, and we weren't afraid because we knew he was good.

"Then we came to an underground cave filled with light, which was a meeting room full of seals. There was a king and queen seal, and the queen seal was just incredible. She was golden and glowing and magnificent. There was a light which radiated from the queen seal like a comet or fireball and went inside of us. It went down into your pelvis and it went down into my belly, and it felt warm and wonderful. We knew we had been brought there to receive the light.

"We knew that they were the basic power of the earth, and their purpose was to transform all the evil that we had done to the planet and make it good again. That was what they did in this little meeting room. She was giving us the light so that we could do the same thing. Then all the seals started playing with us and shoving us, bouncing us from one seal to the next. They were saying, 'It's OK to play, it's OK. Now you have the light.' "

Marcy: "The other piece of it was making eye contact with the seals—their big huge seal eyes, their big, brown loving eyes. I knew I would never lose that image in my whole life. And they said to us, 'You can come back here any time you want.' "

Sherry: "I separated and started swimming out. I took this trip all around under the water. The colors were wonderful, blue and green, brightly lit. I touched fish. A giant squid was waving at me; I wasn't afraid. Then a porpoise came along and pulled me back to shore, and after a while you came swimming along back to the beach, and we sat there peaceful and happy and content. We knew we had these lights within us. My light had worked up to here [indicates chest]. The sun was setting. It was very beautiful and calm. We were sitting there on a log for a long time with our arms around each other."

This confirmed Sherry in her growing sense of self-worth and personal power. It was the second exercise of the day in which Sherry and Marcy had been paired, and they clearly made a deep bond even though they had never met before. After the exercise, I heard one say, "I feel like we're sisters forever."

The Bear Woman

Melissa and Linda reported their journey as follows: "We started walking up a mountain pass. We took a path off to one side and discovered a beautiful spring of water in a meadow. We each took a drink, and then we fed each other water from the spring. It was like a ritual. The water was the clearest clear and the purest pure, and at the same time was so nourishing that it filled all the taste bud sensings. It had the quality of being like sweet food. Then a wolf came out of nowhere, bowed to us, took a drink of water, and made it clear that we couldn't stay in the meadow, we had to go on.

"So with some reluctance, we started going further up the pass, and it started to get dark and cold and snowy. We started looking for someplace to shelter for the night." They spotted a cave and went in. There were frightening shadows, and they smelled something cooking. They followed the cave far back, finally coming into a wide circular area. There was an old woman with long white hair, wearing a bear skin cloak, sitting at a table. At that point their story lines diverged.

Melissa: "In my case, we smelled the most wonderful smell of stew in the entire universe, and we were both so hungry that we would've killed for a pot of that stuff. The old woman said, 'I'll feed you dinner, but there's a price. Both of you can eat, but one of you has to stay with me forever.' Our mouths watered and our legs shook and we both broke out into a sweat. We looked at each other for a long, long time, and at the same instant, we both said, 'I'll stay.' And the old woman said, 'You've learned what I needed you to learn. You've learned the lessons of humanity and good manners and taking care of each other, so you can both go, after dinner.' " [cheers from the group]

Linda: "In my story, the old woman becomes a bear, and then we become bears. And then she becomes a raccoon, and we become raccoons. She's our teacher, like a shaman, and we're learning from her without words how to become the different animals. It's communicated just by being in her presence. Then she says, 'I want to communicate to you how to become spacious.' And she has us become the night sky. I had a very powerful bodily experience of being the night sky and losing all the limits of body and where I begin and end, becoming limitless."

Bodies of Light and Sensuality

John: "We started in a forest, and after walking along a path, came to an unusual moss-like ground cover. We stopped, looked at it, tasted it, put our palms down on it, and were immediately filled with gold-pink energy. It went right up the arms and by the time it had made the circuit back down to the ground, it had completely transformed us into what you might call our light bodies. At the same time the whole landscape changed into another dimension, much like seeing everything as pure energy and not the physical forms."

Lena: "As these light bodies, my experience was as a golden molecule, bopping around and flying and diving. As the pure energy, we could transform anything. I cleaned up the air and then the water, and then I asked everybody in the world to be happy and stop fighting. Through this energy we were able to transform the whole universe. John's experience was having this consciousness and my experience was being able to bring all the other elements into this blissful, euphoric, and perfect state with me. It was like a fountain of energy that we kept re-immersing ourselves in, diving and playing in.

"Then at a certain point, the lady of the fountain appeared. I saw her as shimmering, clothed in sparkling silver and gold. She told us that while we could experience this, we would have to make some kind of choice as to whether we wanted to go back to being human. At this point we began to see people from our families and to realize that not everybody would choose to experience this aspect of their consciousness. We could go back to being human and take it with us, but we wouldn't be able to bring all our friends and relatives to the fountain, so to speak. She offered to give us a special glimpse into the great mystery, an opportunity to look behind the window, to understand or experience the great plan. And then we went off on our own."

John: "It was like going through a curtain. My experience was that my light body broke apart into millions of pieces of light. And while there was a sense of the limits of my body, at the same time there were so many different facets, all aware at once. The pieces of light gradually rose into outer space, and my feeling was one of being home. I had given up my self and was more than willing and happy to do so. It just felt completely right—this sense of being all things at once."

Lena: "When I looked behind the opening that this magical woman opened for us, I saw God, and she was just as large as the universe, and I fell into her. I was falling into the softest and most cushioned feeling in the world. It was white feathers and cotton puffs and cloud. I was falling into this endless cushion of love, and I was able to look into her eyes and to see that everything was love. Then I was like a child being held in her arms and her bosom. God became all these sensuous feelings; she was breasts and vagina and penis and mouth. She was every imaginable kind of soft, sensual skin. I had this sensation of being completely surrounded by love and softness, and protected. It was delicious, very blissful."

These experiences speak for themselves. People have clearly reached the spiritual realm and received a variety of boons to bring back with them: insight, purpose, love, power, surrender of self, experience of higher powers. The depth and richness of these journeys is not unusual for this exercise.

18

The Expanded Body

YOUR HIGHER SELF is that part of your self that resides in the spiritual realm and embodies the higher capacities of love, wisdom, and purpose. This concept was introduced in chapter 1. This exercise provides a means of reaching the higher self through empowerment.

One of the reasons we stay locked into our ordinary selves is because of our needs and fears about dealing with the world. In this exercise you have the opportunity to experience yourself as large and powerful, thus encouraging you to feel safe and to let go of the worries and petty concerns that keep all of us small. As these drop away, you can more easily experience the side of you that resides in the spiritual realm, the side that is larger than your local self, that is perhaps as large as the universe.

I created this exercise out of an experience of my own higher self. After a workshop with Jean Houston, I came away from one trance exercise[1] feeling a profound sense of depth and maturity. I experienced a sense of purpose and motivation in the world that was quite different from what usually moves me. I felt that the

---

[1] Jean Houston, "Being Reeded and Gathering the Golden Fleece" from Psyche and Eros, *The Search for the Beloved*, p. 173.

most important thing in life was to be fully present to all the levels of my experience in the moment. I felt larger and deeper than my usual concerns about pleasure, belonging, or status. It was a wonderful feeling of freedom and solidity.

Later, I did some trance explorations on my own to continue that work. As I retrieved the experience, I felt as if my body was spontaneously growing larger and larger. I became a giant version of myself. The expansion and depth of my psyche at that moment was concretized in an expanded body image. This has continued to be an important way of experiencing my higher self. For example, I usually imagine my internal empowering figure as a giant (see Flight of Empowerment).

The Imaginal Body

This exercise uses the concept of the imaginal body from the work of Jean Houston.[2] The imaginal body is a reflection of our ability to imagine movement, emotion, size, and position in our bodies. I like to explain the imaginal body in terms of the channels we use in guided fantasy. Visualization is not the only channel operating during a guided fantasy. Just as we can imagine seeing anything in a fantasy that we could see in reality, we can also imagine feeling anything that we could actually feel. We also can imagine hearing things and occasionally even tasting or smelling. The visual channel is the major one, but the channels of hearing and body sensing are also important. In the most vivid fantasies all channels are operating, and each contributes something different to the experience. The imaginal body is simply a name for the kinesthetic or body-sensing channel in guided fantasy.

---

[2] Jean Houston, *The Search for the Beloved*, chapter 7.

Circumstances

Time: 40 minutes.

The Exercise

Assume a comfortable position for a long guided fantasy, and close your eyes. . . . Now tighten the muscles of your feet. . . . Now relax them. Now tighten the muscles of your imaginal feet. This means imagining that you are tightening your feet and feeling these sensations without actually doing it. . . . Now tighten your calves. . . . Relax them. Now tighten your imaginal calves. . . . And relax them.

[Then move on the the thighs, and on up the body, doing each segment in turn with both real and imaginal parts of the body. Make sure not to skip any parts of the body. The person is actually constructing an imaginal body during this part of the exercise, and any parts of the body that are skipped may later turn out to be missing.]

Now let your imaginal body feel sleepy. Feel waves of lassitude and tiredness fill you. . . . Now let that go.

Now imagine that you are being nurtured in a very loving way. Feel the warmth and comfort, the safety, the good feeling in your imaginal body. . . . Now let that go.

In your imaginal body be a happy, playful puppy. Feel your enthusiasm, your love for your owner, your energy. . . . Now let that go.

Now feel yourself in your imaginal body as a tiger prowling through the jungle. Feel your strength, your sure-footedness, your agility. Feel your body as if you were stalking prey, sensing the great power just waiting to be unleashed in you. . . . Now let that go.

Imagine yourself as a hawk or other great bird soaring through the sky. Feel your imaginal arms become wings, gliding effortlessly throught the sky. Looking down with your sharp eyes at the great vista laid out before you. . . . Now let that go.

Feel yourself as a large, powerful bear striding through the forest. Feel your tremendous size, the great strength of your arms and claws, the great power of your body, how confident you feel, how little fear. . . . Now let that go.

Feel yourself as a redwood tree, rooted in the earth, stretching high up into the air. You are a quiet, serene giant of the forest. Feel your sap flowing slowly through your body, your leaves rustling in the wind. You are ancient, standing in your wisdom and watching the centuries roll by, seeing countless creatures live and die, and growing and learning from it all, in your rootedness. . . . Now let that go.

Now let yourself become a whale. Feel the great size of you gliding effortlessly through the ocean. Feel very large and at the same time very light, buoyed up by the water. Breaching the surface of the water and then diving deep. Moving with power through the oceans. . . . Now let that go.

Let yourself become a meadow and feel your warm moist body teeming with life. You spread out for a distance and form a rich ground of abundance, full of flowers, grass, earthworms, little animals. Feel yourself spreading out in the warm sunshine full of richness. . . . Now let that go.

Feel yourself now as a mountain, a great rocky mountain, your firm rockiness rising out of the earth to a great height. Feel your strength, your solidity, your agelessness, the great size of you, the great vantage point you have from your peak. . . . Now let that go.

[This part of the exercise can be summarized as follows:[3] sleepy, nurtured, puppy, tiger, hawk, bear, redwood tree, whale, meadow, and mountain.]

---

[3] This kind of shape shifting in the imaginal body occurs in "Evoking Your Imaginal Form," *The Search for the Beloved,* p. 72–75.

Now in a minute when I tell you, your imaginal body will begin to expand and develop in your own particular way, both physically and spiritually. You may sense your body expanding to be that of a giant, or a large animal, or some formation from the natural world. Or it may simply become an extended version of your normal body. Or you may find yourself stretching to fill the sky, or becoming the planet earth perhaps, or even the entire galaxy. Or something entirely different.

♪ "Horizons Beyond Infinity" (second half, starting at the point where the music becomes grand and powerful, from *Starmusic* by Don Robertson, as much as needed)

Whatever it is, begin to let your imaginal body expand. Find yourself extending, blossoming forth, building, amplifying, increasing on many levels. . . . As this happens, feel the quality of that expanded body, experience what it is like to be so large— the power, the perspective, the reach. What is it like to live from there? . . .

Find yourself expanding in the emotional and spiritual sense as well. Find yourself becoming more developed, more advanced, more mature; becoming more solid, stronger, deeper. Becoming naturally invulnerable, not because you are defended in any way, but rather because you are simply too large, too strong, too evolved to be hurt. Feel the security in this body, the great strength, the personal power that is yours. If you chose to act, who knows what you might accomplish. . . .

Also feel the depth you have in this expanded body and expanded psyche, feel the richness, the complexity. Notice the deepened insight you have into people and situations. You aren't distracted by the needs and fears of your ordinary body and psyche. In this place you are developed enough to transcend these fears of the local self. In this place, if any problems confront you, they are problems that are much larger than your personal issues. . . .

You may also notice that you are motivated differently than usual. You may find that ordinary pleasure, security, and achievement have less importance for you in this state. This advanced version of you may feel a different kind of responsibility, a different kind of maturity. It may seem more important to be fully present or to love or to serve others than to go after pleasure or avoid pain. You may find that your ordinary ego and security needs have greatly diminished or vanished in this expanded version of yourself. Feel that now in whatever form it takes. . . .

♪ "Pachelbel's Canon" (extended version, from *Timeless Motion* by Daniel Kobialka, as much as needed; or other heart music)

Now whatever form your expanded body has taken, it has a heart. Find the heart of your expanded body, and feel it. Feel its warmth, its openness, feel the enormous love that emanates from it. Feel your heart expanding even farther so that it becomes larger, capable of containing great sorrows and transmuting them to light, capable of powerful healing energy, capable of warming and supporting great numbers with its love. . . .

Now visualize the ordinary you, the part of you that resides in the ordinary world with all its demands and fears, its pleasures and pains. Open that huge heart of your expanded body and let the loving energy pour out to your ordinary self. Surround yourself with love and light, with acceptance and compassion.

Now from this higher and deeper place in you, begin to look at things in yourself that you might have considered faults or weaknesses from your normal consciousness—things you feel guilty or ashamed about, things you perhaps didn't like about yourself. Look at these traits from this larger perspective, and see the pain you have suffered that may have caused you to act in ways that you consider weak. Let yourself see the hurts and difficulties behind your problems. And feel compassion and love for yourself. . . .

Now let yourself also see the hidden strengths behind these so-called faults. Perhaps, for instance, you see yourself as touchy, and hidden within that is a positive vulnerability. Perhaps you see yourself as selfish, and hidden within that is assertiveness. Look at each of these things that you may have thought were not OK, and see the positive side, the hidden strength in each one of them, see your hidden strength. . . . Continue looking at yourself from this place of the expanded body and psyche, and from this deeper, evolved place, feeling your full acceptance of yourself, all of you. . . .

Now also celebrate your positive side. Take a look at your talents, your strengths, your special qualities that are unique and important, your potential. . . . Look inside yourself and see your inner beauty and the deep wisdom that resides in you. . . . Notice how lovable you are. Appreciate what a special person you are. . . .

Now also let this love and acceptance flow out to others. Let it go first to those you are closest to—family, lover, good friends. Extend your compassion and acceptance to those qualities in them that you might have thought of as faults. Let your heart flow out to them just as it has to you. Also honor and celebrate their strengths, their richness, and their special qualities. . . . Now let your loving flow out even further to others in your life— acquaintances, co-workers, people you run into occasionally. Open your heart to them, too, accepting their faults and appreciating their strong points, widening the circle of your love. Feel the love flowing out of that deep expanded place of strength in you. You are strong enough and large enough and deep enough to let your love spread out to all these people.

Now let it flow out even further, to all people of all nations and races and classes and religions, all over the world. Feel yourself great enough, and expanded enough, and open enough to have your love flowing out to all people. . . . And also flowing out to animals of all kinds, to the earth, to all of the natural world, . . . encompassing the whole planet and everything in it with your love, your accepting, honoring, healing love. . . .

Now also from this expanded place, sense, however vaguely, your purpose in being here on this planet—sense your calling, see the great potential you were born with. What is that deeper sense of mission that vaguely tugs at you? In this deeper place you can feel it more easily. It may only be a sensation in your expanded body, or it may be much more specific. Sense what your life direction is. . . .

Now very gradually begin to stretch and move your real body. Very slowly, let the sense you have of your expanded imaginal body begin to flow into your real body. . . . Feel that sense of depth and power begin to transfer into the real body that you are now gradually beginning to move, creeping into your muscles, into your bones. Bringing each part of your real body to life and infusing it with the power of love of your expanded body. . . . As you do that, slowly begin to move, then sit up, and eventually come to standing, keeping that sense of depth and power. [Wait until people are standing.]

♪   "Eric's Theme" (from *Chariots of Fire* by Vangelis; or other cele-bratory music)

Gradually come to a standing position, keep with you that sense of your expanded body and psyche. As you stand, continue moving and swaying a little, feeling that sense of power and openness in your body. Take some deep breaths, letting the energy in your body begin to come alive along with the sense of expansion. Filling your flesh with the strength and love of that expanded body. Grounding those qualities in yourself and ground-ing yourself to the earth. Begin to move with the music as you express this sense of your expanded body. . . .

Now let your body move more fully to the music. Feel the power of your body and let this come through you in movement. Celebrate this higher, deeper you in your body as it moves. . . . Let your movements become even larger. Let your celebration become a dance, moving freely and expansively. Flow out to the stars and deep into the earth! Let the expanded body come fully into you. [Allow until the music ends, a couple of minutes.]

♪ Simplified music: Use "Horizons Beyond Infinity" as above.

Experiences

From the expanded place, people get a larger perspective on their lives, one that encourages them to see what is really important. A perspective that allows them to forgive themselves and others, one that encourages a sense of being rather than doing.

Touched by God

Claire reported on her experience: "I liked being a meadow, the warm earth and feeling the flowers growing. The most exciting was being the animals. It was a different experience of perceiving the world. I loved stalking as a tiger. I had such power in my muscles, and I was so graceful and sure-footed as I went through the jungle. I knew what I had to do. It was marvelous. And I loved being a whale! Bounding through the water with my sides all wet. And I *am*! I very much am."

She continued, "The imaginal body was wonderful because it overcame my mind-set about not being able to do things because of having flaws. I grew and grew, and my arms and my legs became two triangles with my head in the middle extended up on the top of the world." She saw herself as the figure in the painting in the Sistine Chapel with her finger being touched by God.

She felt she was given the power and the right to just *be* instead of having to *do* all the time. "I remember when my daughter died I felt I had to compensate by being the best God-damned teacher in my work with young women. Now I know I don't have to be the best anything. The greatest impact was the powerful feeling of being, and the trust that I could deal with whatever was going to come at me. I think that's what it is to be powerful, rather than wanting control as I have for so long. A great revolution for me. I had an inkling before, but now it's a knowing, in a very internal place."

The All and the Family

Our friend Judy reported, "I had a wonderful experience. As soon as you said to expand, I was the stars, the cosmos. I was without body, without any kind of form. It was like I was all form within this expansion. There were gorgeous colors and excitement and movement within my boundaryless boundaries: It just felt really incredible. Meteors were passing through me. I had a sense that I could incorporate it all. I could allow it all to be there just as it is."

Judy found it very easy to feel love for herself and for people in general, but she found it much harder to love her family, because she felt resentful about not getting support from them during recent hard times. "But once I felt really expanded and open and loving in other ways, then I could allow it to seep back into the family. I could see that I close myself off when I haven't received love that I think is my due. Then I was able to open my heart and feel an incredible amount of love even for the people I have been hurt by." This was an advanced step for Judy in her emancipation from dependence on others.

Other Experiences

One man reported, "I could feel myself growing and becoming larger and joining with others here, in being one much larger entity. It was a wonderful reminder about putting my local self in perspective. The everyday, petty stuff that I stumble over and get all revved up about, it was very helpful to see that from this grand perspective. It put those things in their place, and I felt much more connected to the larger essence.

"And then it struck me: I'm *being*, but I don't know how to *be*. I know how to *do*. My whole life I spent in training, learning, and practicing doing, but not being. So when I reached this wonderful being-connection, very powerful, all-interconnected, my immediate reaction was, 'What now? What am I supposed to do with it?' That was a wonderful insight."

A woman described her experience, "I found myself going back in time and acting as chief priestess to the Goddess. It was a very powerful experience. I had this incredible blue cloak with little gold threads and stars, a blue and white mantle that looked like a waterfall, and a wonderful wreath of ivy. Everybody was being loving with each other."

Our friend Sherry's expanded body took the image of an apple tree bursting in bloom. Then she became a willow, which was solid and rooted, and also flexible in the wind. She received an inkling of her life purpose through the symbol of the tree. Her purpose was to offer shelter and nurturing and a sense of being for people. She also became a reference point for travelers, with directional signs on her trunk.

Another woman said, "I was a bit of everything, mostly the earth and the ground and the flowers, and then I became the tree, the mountain, the sky, and the soaring eagle. But I was a part of the whole unity. I was really aware that I was the whole thing, looking down, but being down as well. I had this tingling all over me, like the grasses were spurting up and the flowers were opening! It was wonderful. I wondered, 'How do I know what I am, if I'm everything?' It made me think that the purpose of the universe is to know itself. That's why the universe makes separate things."

19

Surrendering the Heart

THIS EXERCISE DEALS with letting go, opening the heart, and surrendering in love to the divine. To encounter the spiritual realm in such a personal way can be very powerful, experiencing the divine as a being or presence, the "beloved of the soul."[1] Since this may seem strange or unfamiliar, let me discuss in more detail what is involved.

You may experience the divine in any of the traditional ways such as God, Allah, the Goddess, Jesus, Buddha, Gaia, or Kali. If you follow or are familiar with a religious tradition that recognizes a personal god, then these experiences will make sense to you. If not, experiment with an open mind and see what happens. You may find that an archetypal figure that is your unique representation of the divine will emerge from the depths of your psyche. For example in Journey to the Spiritual Realm, people encountered the seal queen, the bear woman, and the sensual god.

On the other hand, your experience of the divine may be less well defined. That is what has happened to me and to most people doing this exercise. You may sense your heart opening and love radiating upward without any specific object for your love.

---

[1] Jean Houston, *The Search for the Beloved.*

You may feel a desire to surrender and be taken lovingly by some higher power without knowing who or what that is. You may sense a letting go and opening of your being. Please do not devalue your experience if you do not see a divine figure. People have had very profound experiences without this.

To love fully and completely means to let go of boundaries, to surrender the self, to become one with the beloved. This means letting go of personal desires, fears, and even the sense of who you are and how you are separate from others. This can be a wonderful, freeing, ecstatic experience. The goal of this exercise is for you to allow as much surrender as you are ready for at this time, and then to return to a clear sense of yourself. In other words, it is a temporary experience, and you will return to your separate self afterwards, hopefully changed as a result.

Rumi

During the exercise, we will be reading selections from the great 13th century Sufi poet Rumi. Rumi had the experience of loving God through loving another person; that is, he fell in love with a person whom he saw as the embodiment of God, and this triggered an intense ecstatic love relationship with the divine, seen first in his beloved and then everywhere. He wrote mystical love poetry about this experience in which the references to his beloved are frequently ambiguous as to whether he is referring to his human beloved or to God. As you hear the poetry, don't try to make rational sense of it or even to follow it clearly in detail. Just let it take you deeper into the experience.

I have had memorable experiences of surrendering to the divine. This has happened in doing a variation of this exercise in Jean Houston's Mystery School and at other times during her workshops. It has also happened several times while doing the Sufi practice of "turning" or whirling for which the whirling dervishes are known. (This practice also derives from the genius of Rumi.) During these times I felt a strong desire to let go and be taken by a higher force, to give over control and direction to something other than myself, although I had no idea what it was. I remember crying out silently "Take me!" Then I was swept up in a joyful sense of love and freedom. It felt like being out of control and centered at the same time.

Circumstances

Working Alone. When working alone, I suggest that you put the directions and poetry on tape so that you can fully concentrate on the humming and surrender. You will have to skip the second part.

Working with a Partner. When working with a partner, take turns leading each other through the first part, then do the second part as directed, each partner in turn massaging or rocking the other.

Time: 50–90 minutes.

The Exercise[2]

[This exercise uses a special breathing pattern which the leader should practice beforehand. You breathe very slowly, taking about five seconds on the inhale and five more on the exhale. During each exhale, you hum three times.]

---

[2] The first part of this exercise is the Zikr of the Ultimate Communion of Love, from *The Search for the Beloved*, p. 212.

Sit upright, one hand on your heart, and make a humming sound so that it resonates in your heart. Try it. . . . We will breathe slowly and deeply, humming three times on each exhale. [Leader demonstrate.] Now try it with me. . . . It is important that we all stay together so that the pace of the breathing is right. The breathing is an important part of this because we are using it to transform our state of consciousness. As we proceed and you get used to the mechanics of the humming, let go into it. Let it be a hum of pleasure, as in "Mmm mmm good," a hum of joy, of love, of ecstasy.

At times we will stop the humming for a few moments and then continue again. While you are humming, I will be reading Rumi poetry and making some suggestions. Just continue humming while I am talking. Let us begin now.

[The leader should get them started and coordinated by leading them in the breathing. Allow a minute or so for them to get used to the humming. If there is a co-leader, he or she can continue leading the humming while the leader speaks.]

As you hum, know that you can let go into the humming, and that your heart will open as much as is right for you at this time. . . . You can surrender to the joy of communion with a greater power. . . . You can let go and be taken by a loving force, be taken over and carried into a sweet sense of union. . . . You can feel the melting, the wonderful sensations of oneness, of being bathed in love. Feel your boundaries loosening, flowing together, blending, so that you are larger, more open, diffusing outward, coalescing in love with all around you. . . . Knowing that you are loved deeply and desired, as well as loving deeply and desiring, desiring union with the great mystery. . . . Continue humming, allowing any images or body sensings to arise. . . . Now come to silence and allow yourself to be with the sense of communion. [Allow 30 seconds.]

[Begin the humming again.] As we continue, if it is appropriate, you may get an image or sense of who or what is the object of your love and surrender.

[Allow 3 or 4 minutes, during which time you read selections of Rumi poetry[3] especially the short quatrains. Rest for 30 seconds and then hum again for 3 or 4 minutes, reading more Rumi poetry. Then repeat this a third time. Then rest for 30 seconds once again.]

Now one by one each person will lie in the center of the group to be taken even deeper. We will surround the person in the center and gently touch them in ways that encourage them to let go even further. You may do any of the following:

• Simply place your hands on the person.

• Gently massage the person.

• Lift the person's head or a limb and hold it or gently move it to encourage them to completely relax it.

• Rock the person gently to encourage their whole body to let go. This can be done by gently pushing the person from side to side at the hips, or by sitting at the person's feet, picking up the ankles, and rocking the whole body up and down. [These should be demonstrated.]

♪   "Pachelbel's Canon" (extended version by Daniel Kobialka, as
      much as needed; or other heart music)

[Each person in turn lies down on their back and the rest of the group gathers around them. Begin the experience for the first couple of people with an induction such as the following:]

As you feel ready, move in and touch ——————— in whatever ways you like. As you do this, let yourself feel your love for him/her and your desire for him/her to have the best experience of opening and loving that is right for him/her at this time. Let

---

[3] John Moyne and Coleman Barks, *Open Secrets* (Putney, VT: Threshold, 1984); John Moyne and Coleman Barks, *Unseen Rain* (Putney, VT: Threshold, 1986); Daniel Liebert, *Rumi: Fragments, Ecstasies* (Santa Fe, NM: Source, 1981); Edmund Helminski, *Ruins of the Heart* (Putney, VT: Threshold, 1981).

that love move through your hands as you touch him/her and move him/her deeper into the letting go and the opening. Feel free to express this in humming or singing as well if that feels right.

[Read more Rumi poetry during part of the experience for each person. The group members can do this as well as the leader, allowing the leader the option of participating in this part of the exercise. If there is enough time, allow 10 minutes or more per person. If not, 3 or 4 minutes for each will do.]

[After the last person finishes and returns to the circle.] Now let's all move in and hug or touch each other in whatever way feels right, closing your eyes, feeling your connection with each other, with the group as a whole. . . . Feel yourself united with the whole group in a loving connection, part of a larger unit, the one in the many, the many in one. . . . And let that connection, that openness connect you also to the greater whole, the great mystery, the divine reality. Feeling a communion with that presence, and knowing that you are loved as well as loving, that you are love, that you are one with the all. Letting yourself be taken and feeling the joy of that and the wonder, and being deeply at peace. . . .

Now let an image come to you, or a body sensing or a sound or a phrase, that represents for you the state you are now in. Let something arise from your unconscious as a way of knowing this place of love and surrender and union. . . . In the days to come, keep this with you as a way of returning to this time, this state of consciousness, bringing it into your life when you choose.

Experiences

A Shield of Light

Our friend Sandra reported that during the first part of the exercise she felt energy coming through her body and a strong sense of openness. "Being touched was really wonderful! Everything that people did felt good to me. There was a unity, a wholeness about it. The words are inadequate, but I felt like I was in a wonderful fluffy down cushion, very light and floaty, with all this yummy stuff around me. I wanted it twice as long. At the very end, there was light, spiralling and funnelling down inside my body, so that my energy could come out. The light was also like a shield so that anything that came in was purified first. I could be open and be protected by this light, but not in a rigid way." In this manner she was integrating her open, loving nature with her newly developing strength.

She continued, "Suddenly I thought, 'This is exactly what I've been wanting. This energy is available to me all the time, and I get lost in the illusion that it's not, but it actually is.' I really loved touching people, too. I started out feeling totally awkward, but once I started on your feet and found myself dancing with the music, then I was into it."

Other Experiences

Another woman reported, "I was having such incredible visuals that when you asked us to move into the group, it was very hard for me. I didn't want to stop. I was really out there, feeling very much like I was on a drug trip. So I decided to go first so I would stop grumbling about doing it for anybody else. Once I'd had my turn and it felt so nice, it was OK to give to others. To feel the love in my heart was much easier than to share it physically. But the sharing was wonderful once it happened, and so that was a very valuable lesson for me.

A man described his experience, "At first I didn't think I'd like it, but it was so marvelous! It really felt like incredible opening happened. It felt like everything matched and was timed perfectly, like one giant organism was working on me. I especially liked being rocked or having my head held; being moved like that encouraged me to let go. The image I got at the end was a body image—the feeling of my arms encircling people and my head and eyes tilting and opening upward."

SECTION SEVEN

Organizing and Designing Exercises

Introduction

I N THIS SECTION we look at how to put the exercises together—in your life journey and in structuring a group or
workshop. Chapter 20 discusses how the exercises are related to
your personal growth process. It includes a detailed outline of the
process of finding your life purpose. These concepts are useful for
knowing how to sequence the exercises in a workshop. Chapter
21 provides further information on organizing an Inner Journeys
group or workshop. Chapter 22 discusses how to design your own
exercises in the Inner Journeys style.

20

Your Life Journey

L ET'S DISCUSS HOW Inner Journeys work fits into your larger life story. We will see how the exercises flow together to facilitate the various stages of your personal growth and the process of finding your life purpose. This will give the general reader a perspective on your development and a program of steps to follow in searching for your life purpose. For group leaders and peer groups it will provide guidelines on how to sequence Inner Journeys exercises in a group or workshop.

For this discussion I will divide inner Journeys work into two general areas—personal growth and life purpose. I have combined psychological and spiritual development under personal growth because I see them as essentially part of one continuum, with the higher levels of the psychological shading into the spiritual.[1] I have included social transformation work as one aspect of life purpose. I will lay out a developmental sequence for each of these two general areas. Exact order is not important; human development is far more varied and complex than any scheme can show. Where appropriate I indicate the relevant Inner Journeys exercises for each stage.

---

[1] Ken Wilbur, "The Developmental Spectrum and Psychopathology: Part I, Stages and Types of Pathology," Journal of *Transpersonal Psychology*, Vol. 16, No. 1, 1984.

Personal Growth Work

Much has been written about the different aspects of psychological and spiritual growth, so I will just sketch a general progression of three broad stages of development.

Healing Pain from the Past

The beginning and most fundamental area of personal growth involves bringing to awareness buried pain from your past that affects the way you live now. This pain can then be healed by experiences which provide what you needed in the past, thus encouraging self-acceptance and new ways of being. This is the domain of much of psychotherapy. It is dealt with in the exercises Child and Higher Self, Nurturing Touch, and Reowning the Shadow.

Developing Personal Qualities

You can also work directly on developing positive personal qualities such as self-support (Befriending Yourself, Child and Higher Self, Acceptance), compassion (Acceptance, Planetary Compassion), and personal power (all the empowerment exercises). Here you are moving from the domain of psychotherapy to growth work.

Spiritual Development

Finally you can work on developing capacities which reflect the highest of human aspirations, such as love, life purpose, wisdom, unity, and inner peace. This is traditionally the domain of spiritual desciplines. It is dealt with in the Spiritual Realm exercises, the Life Purpose exercises, the Child and Higher Self, and Opening the Heart.

• • •

You can't be rigid in deciding which exercise deals with which area. For instance, for one person Opening the Heart may deal with higher love, for another it may deal with compassion and self-support, and for a third it may even bring up old pain to be worked on. Use your own intuition about when an exercise is right for you to do, and don't be surprised if something completely unexpected happens.

In designing a workshop it can be valuable to use the sequence of areas to order the exercises. For example, a workshop or class on Opening the Heart might have the following sequence:

Child and Higher Self
Opening the Heart
Surrendering the Heart

There is no straightforward correspondence between the exercises presented in a workshop and any particular person's growth stages. It may take a given person years to travel the ground represented by the above workshop, and in any given group, there will be people at all different levels of development. Nevertheless, a workshop will flow better for the participants if the order of exercises fits the natural direction of their growth.

Life Purpose Steps

The following is an outline of a program of steps that will guide you in discovering and manifesting your life purpose. They are listed roughly in the order they are to be done, though not every step needs to be completed, and they don't have to be followed in exact order. At any time, you may also need to go back to an earlier step in order to work more on a certain issue.

1. Preparation
    A. Personal concerns
    B. Need for a life purpose
    C. Planetary perspective

     D. Emotional response to social issues
     E. Interconnectedness
     F. Social vision
     G. Personal power
     H. Personal development

2. Discovery
     A. Interests
     B. Innate gifts and skills
     C. Way of being
     D. Source of life purpose
     E. General direction of purpose
     F. Validating existing contributions
     G. Specific goal

3. Action
     A. Personal vision
     B. Investigating possibilities
     C. Staying mobilized
     D. Support group
     E. Successive approximations
     F. Changing projects

4. Working through blocks
     A. Guilt
     B. Success and failure
     C. Personal vs. altruistic motivation
     D. Others

Preparation

The preparation steps can be done in any order, and they need not all be completed before the discovery steps begin. In fact it may be wise to mix in some discovery steps with the preparation.

Personal Concerns

Before you are ready to focus your energy on life purpose issues, you must get some of your basic life needs met, needs for security, belonging, and self-esteem. If you suffer from physical or psychological difficulties which prevent your meeting these needs, then this healing must be attended to first. We each move through this process at the pace that is right for us, given our history and circumstances.

Let yourself view this process of attending to personal concerns as the first step toward finding your life purpose. This is especially important for those of you, mainly women, who have been trained to ignore your own needs in serving others. Don't confuse this self-denying attitude with the higher service of life purpose, which includes taking care of yourself. It is perfectly appropriate for you to learn how to take care of your own needs for a fulfilling life, and this may need to come first, before focusing on a higher purpose. Those of you who have spent significant time and energy on personal healing may also recognize that you gain compassion, insight, and depth through the healing process which will enable you to make a fuller contribution to the world.

At some point you will be healed enough so that your attention can turn to wider questions. Nonetheless, personal healing usually continues even after you move on to the next steps. Occasionally you may also need to return to healing as your exclusive focus for a while before moving on again. Healing exercises in this book are Child and Higher Self, Nurturing Touch, and Reowning the Shadow.

Need for Life Purpose

Everyone has a need to be involved with a deeper purpose that gives meaning to their lives. This need may not be very prominent as long as more basic needs are unmet or serious healing work is yet to be done. Once this has been accomplished, feeling the need for a life purpose is the next important step. You may sense this need in a very clear and specific way, such as a passion for a certain cause, or you may feel it as a general yearning for more out of life or a vague dissatisfaction with your life as it is. Sometimes guilt, inadequacy, or other fears must be worked through in order for this need to emerge. This issue is dealt with indirectly in the Life Purpose exercises and the Social Transformation exercises.

Planetary Perspective

Gaining a perspective on how our current planetary crisis grows out of the larger flow of human history will give you a better grasp of what is happening in the world and how you might want to respond. In addition, if your sense of purpose begins to focus on certain social and political issues, your response will be greatly aided by understanding how the issues you care about are related to each other and to your personal life. This is touched on in the introduction to section four. This perspective can be gained through experiential exercises or through reading and discussion.

Emotional Responses to Social Issues

Many of us emotionally deny the possibility of nuclear war and other threats to our future. We also may repress our feeling responses to the oppression and violence in the world. Breaking through this numbness and feeling our natural emotional responses to these situations allows for the possibility of creative and powerful action. Feeling our compassion for the pain and suffering in the world also allows us to sense those situations which most move us to a life of service, thus pointing the way to our life purpose. This is dealt with in Planetary Compassion and Gaia. Joanna Macy also has some very powerful exercises on this theme.[2]

---

[2] Joanna Macy, *Despair and Personal Power in the Nuclear Age* (Philadelphia, PA: New Society Publishers, 1983), chapter 5.

Interconnectedness

Even though it is healthy to exercise our individuality, we are nourished and empowered by experiencing ourselves not as separate isolated persons, but as a part of the vast web of life. This connects us with people in need and with the natural world, promoting our compassion and igniting our passion to help. It also links us with our ancestors and with future generations, and with the universe as a whole, reminding us that we are part of a much larger story. This experience happens in Planetary Compassion, Gaia, and some of the Spiritual Realm exercises. See also Joanna Macy.[3]

We also learn from feeling our connection with the negative forces in the world and those we consider enemies, sensing our own dark sides and empathizing with people who seem to be supporting destructive ends. This awareness will ultimately help us to be more effective in influencing them.

Social Vision

We are empowered by envisioning a positive future—by imagining a changed society and the social process that might lead to its development. This provides specific goals to work for, mobilizes energy and excitement, and encourages a hopeful attitude concerning the impact you can have on the world. This topic is dealt with in Envisioning a Healthy Society and in Manifesting Your Intention.

Personal Power

Self-esteem. Many people are held back from pursuing their life purpose by low self-esteem, a feeling of inadequacy, or a sense of not deserving to be successful. It is very important to cultivate

---

[3] Macy, Exercise 13, Exercise 47, and all of chapter 6.

an attitude of acceptance, respect, and loving and enthusiastic support toward yourself. This is dealt with in the Naming Ritual, Affirmations, Acceptance, the Flight of Empowerment, and other exercises.

Courage. We must develop the confidence and courage to take the risks that are necessary to put ourselves out in the world and effect change. This is dealt with in Expansive Movement and Manifesting Your Intention.

Social Power. Some people feel powerful in their personal lives but don't feel that they can have any larger influence on the world. This can be overcome by experiencing yourself as part of the larger movement of people who are working to better the world. This helps you to realize that you don't have to solve all the problems by yourself. If you want to contribute to social transformation but are not drawn to traditional political work, you can find many other ways to have a significant impact on the social problems that concern you. It is valuable to sketch out the connections, no matter how subtle and indirect they may be, between your personal contributions and the world issues you care about. This is touched on in Planetary Compassion and Manifesting Your Intention.

Personal Development

Engaging in personal growth, artistic, and spiritual disciplines can result in far more than just personal enrichment. This work can enhance such qualities as creativity, intuition, spontaneity, and the ability to connect deeply with others. It can help you develop groundedness, love, wisdom, and reverence for all being. These qualities will make you more effective in carrying out your life purpose. Most of the Inner Journeys exercises aid in personal development.

Discovery

Interests

You need to discover your most important interests and inclinations—the kinds of activities you enjoy, the settings you prefer, and the sorts of people you like to be with. This will lead you to activities that will spark your excitement and enthusiasm, work that will tap your creative edge, and a lifestyle that will be deeply satisfying. See Finding Your Contribution.

Innate Gifts and Skills

An important step in finding your life purpose is recognizing the gifts you were born with—your unique talents, strengths, and special personal qualities. You also need to honor the skills and knowledge which you have acquired during your life. This is dealt with in Finding Your Contribution and Gaia.

Way of Being

It is important for you to sense the way of being in the world that represents your ideal for personal development. This could mean, for example, being loving to all people, being deeply attuned to the earth, trusting your inner knowing, or being courageous. This way of being may come from actualizing the essence of your most important innate personal qualities or it may come from meeting challenges in your personal growth. People often sense this during the Gaia fantasy.

Source of Life Purpose

This means getting in touch with the motivation for your life purpose, the things that concern you most deeply about the world and other people, the issues that stir your passion and

commitment. The source level is the topic of the Dedication
Ritual and also comes up in Gaia and Finding Your Contribution.

General Direction of Purpose

The previous four steps may prepare you for viewing the larger
flow of your life in terms of its meaning, imagining that the events
of your life can form a coherent pattern pointing toward an
overall purpose, allowing your own personal myth to unfold. This
includes exploring the possibility that you have a spiritual calling
to a certain life purpose. This will allow you to see the general
direction of your life purpose—perhaps focusing on the area in
which you would like to make a contribution or the deeper values
that underlie whatever you do. Tentative projects also emerge at
this time. Most of the life purpose exercises provide an opportunity to sense your general direction.

Validating Existing Contributions

Recognizing the ways in which you may already be contributing
to the world helps you to be more aware and appreciative of the
impact of your life as it is. For example, you may be living
out values that promote a healthy society or influencing people
positively in your everyday contacts or in your work. Understanding your current contribution may help you to be more effective
by doing what you do with the conscious intention of serving a
higher purpose. You can then explore how to expand your influence further, for example, by collaborating with others, gaining
more power, or reaching more people.

Specific Goal

At this point you are ready to hone your thinking to a specific
goal—a new career or job, a volunteer project, a program of
learning and growth, or a changed way of being. This goal may

be refined or changed as you begin to take action, but it needs to be specific now so that you can make concrete plans.

Many people have more than one deep concern about the world and a number of innate gifts or ideal ways of being. In choosing a goal, explore how these areas may be integrated so that as much of your excitement and talent as possible is included. This integration may also occur later during Successive Approximations.

Remember that it is valid to remain in your current work situation and transform it so that you are making a higher contribution. For example, if you do corporate personnel work which you really enjoy, instead of quitting to join the staff of a peace group, you could remain and work to raise consciousness about peace issues or to bring spiritual values (which in the long run would promote peace) into the corporate culture.

Action

For those whose goal is primarily a way of being, some of these steps will be irrelevant because your work will be primarily through personal healing and development.

Personal Vision

Be sure to envision actually carrying out your life purpose, as well as a sequence of events that will lead to that goal. You might write out a life plan or a flow chart of specific actions. This process creates excitement and passion, makes your ideas more concrete, and provides a guide for taking action. It happens in Manifesting Your Intention.

Investigating Possibilities

At this point you have a sense of what you are looking for, e.g. a specific job, a certain type of organization, a particular kind of apprenticeship, or a teacher from whom to learn a skill. You conduct a thorough investigation of the possibilites, through reading and talking to appropriate people. You then try out the ones that seem most promising through interviews, attending meetings, and perhaps beginning a project. Approach this process in a spirit of experimentation, knowing that you will need to test a number of possibilities before you find one that really fits your needs. Give yourself permission to move on when something is not working out, so that you are not afraid of getting stuck in the first thing you try.

Staying Mobilized

In order to get started, decide on a first step of action that isn't too threatening, even just making a single phone call. Once you are started, you can maintain your momentum in various ways. Planning your actions week by week, making commitments to yourself, checking in with a friend, using a support group, rewarding yourself for taking risks, keeping track of your progress.

Support Group

Throughout this process you will need to get emotional support and encouragement from group members, friends, family, and others in your life. This happens in the Naming Ritual and Manifesting Your Intention and generally from working together with others in a supportive group. When you get to the action stage, be sure to involve others in order to receive their feedback, support, suggestions, and networking help.

The next step is to become part of an ongoing group that provides this support. This might be a group of people who are working together on a life purpose project, or a group that provides support to its members in their various projects. Time should be set aside for this process in any ongoing Inner Journeys group.

Finding or creating such a group is an invaluable aid in attempting something difficult or unusual.

Successive Approximations

You probably won't find your ideal life project right away. You will likely have to go through a process of successive approximations. You may work on a series of projects, each of which only partially meets your criteria for a fully satisfying contribution, but it is wise to stay with each one for months or years, gaining experience, skills, and contacts. Each time you can find or create a situation that fits you better and allows you to have a greater positive impact on the world.

Changing Projects

Even if your deeper mission is constant, the specifics of how you carry it out are apt to change over time. This might happen because you finish a certain project, because your interests unfold in new directions, because you discover new talents in yourself, because the world situation changes and you become aware of an emerging need which draws you. When this happens, you will need to cycle back to earlier steps in this model with your new direction. The life purpose process is a lifelong one.

Working through Blocks

The following need not be done in any particular order. They are issues to be aware of because they can block your progress at any point.

Guilt

Some people tend to avoid the whole issue of life purpose because they feel guilty about their lack of a purpose. This usually comes from "shoulds" which they have internalized from others about how to serve the world. For example, "If I really care about poor people, I should help them by going to live in their circumstances." If this doesn't fit for you, it can produce unconscious guilt and resistance. You can free yourself from this by expanding your understanding of the possible ways to contribute to the world and by giving yourself permission to search for the ways that really fit who you are. This comes up in Finding Your Contribution.

Success and Failure

Success and failure are important feedback from the real world about the wisdom of your choices as you search for a way to manifest your life purpose. However, too often failure is taken as proof of your inadequacy or unworthiness. The need for success and fear of failure can block flexibility and distort priorities. When a project doesn't work out, the best response is to see it as a learning opportunity, not a blow to your self-esteem. You might learn how to approach the project differently or discover other directions which fit you better.

The fear of success may also block you at various points in this process. You may fear that you will be ostracized if you are too successful, or that some calamity will befall you because you don't deserve success, or that it is disloyal to your parents to be more successful than they. Making these fears conscious goes a long way toward dispelling them.

Personal vs. Altruistic Motivation

You will need to find a balance between taking care of yourself and serving larger ends. Even while doing a project from an altruistic motivation, you will probably also have strong personal motivations for doing the work—prestige, money, being liked. If these become too large a factor in your motivation, the project can be stymied or diverted from its real purpose.

On the other hand, if you devote yourself totally to a project that does not meet even your minimum personal needs, you will become stressed, burned out, or at least sterile and uncreative. Your work on the larger issue can become compromised or unproductive.

Others

The possible obstacles to manifesting life purpose are as varied as our psychological issues. Many of the Inner Journeys exercises deal with specific blocks. At times you may need to return to Personal Concerns to work through one of them.

• • •

Take some time now to ask yourself the following questions about your current progress through these steps:

1. Which steps have you already taken?

2. Which step (or steps) are you currently dealing with?

3. What blocks are holding you back from progressing?

For group leaders, remember that this outline is to be taken only as a rough idea of the placement of exercises. Some exercises touch on a number of different areas, not necessarily in the exact order mentioned above, and not all of these areas need to be included in any given workshop. The following is an example of a two-day, six-exercise social transformation workshop:

Planetary Compassion
Envisioning a Healthy Society
The Dedication Ritual
Gaia
The Naming Ritual
Manifesting Your Intention

21

Group and Workshop Structure

I N THE LAST chapter we looked at the sequencing of exercises for a group or workshop based on people's overall growth trajectories. This chapter discusses other concerns that bear on the choice of exercises for a workshop, and presents detailed procedures for the all important beginnings and endings. This chapter will be of value primarily to group leaders and peer groups.

Inner Journey Forms

Inner Journeys work can be done in a therapy group, a spiritual group, a political support group, or a group which combines these areas. Depending on the nature and goals of the group, Inner Journeys work may only be one of the processes used. The group could be led by a professional or a lay person, or leadership could be shared among the group members. An Inner Journeys group can be ongoing, or limited in time, or a one-time workshop. The length can be as short as one hour or as long as many years. The principles discussed in this chapter apply (with some modification) to all of these forms, and I will use the term "group" or "workshop" to refer to them generically.

Inner Journeys work can also be done alone or with a partner, as indicated in the exercises in this book. I use Inner Journeys work individually with people in my professional capacity as a psychotherapist. In that case it is done rather differently than in working with groups. The individual setting allows Inner Journeys work to be done with all the sensitivity and individual attention of psychotherapy. I am able to guide a person on a journey that follows their unique personal process. They keep me informed verbally about their experience as the exercise progresses, and I modify my directions according to their pace and direction.

When resistance arises, that is, when something emerges in the person's process that blocks the intended direction of the exercise, I change my focus to helping the person explore the resistance. This can involve going off in an entirely different direction than planned. In fact, you can think of individual Inner Journeys work as an integration of group exercises and the follow-up individual work.

There are important advantages of the group setting which are missing in individual work, however. You do not have the support, sharing, and possibilities for interaction inherent in a group. In addition, a person working individually does not have the power of the group energy to help them go deeply into the exercise experience. There is something very potent about doing an exercise in a group, even when you are in trance and on a very private journey of your own.

Using a Story

In addition to designing a workshop around a theme and ordering the exercises as described in the last chapter, you can also design the workshop around a story. In this case, the inner journey that the participants go through in the workshop is analogous to the outer journey of the protagonist of the story. Jean Houston frequently designs her workshops around famous myths, such as the Odyssey or Psyche and Eros. The participants are thus taken on a journey of transformation that follows the underlying symbolic meaning of the story. This process is described in detail in her book *The Search for the Beloved*.

Each exercise is designed around a different incident or theme from the story and they are ordered according to the chronology of the story. I have designed a workshop around The Riddlemaster Trilogy. Two of the exercises from that workshop, Acceptance and the Flight of Empowerment, are included in this book.

Choosing Exercises

Avoid beginning a workshop with an exercise that may be too threatening, such as a ritual or Nurturing Touch. Pay close attention to the level of trust and cohesion in a group. When it is high, you can afford to use exercises that are more threatening interpersonally (such as the above) or more risky internally (such as Reowning the Shadow). When it is low, such as in a new group or one that has had a large turnover of members, it is wise to use exercises that involve work in pairs and group contact because these promote trust and connection.

Gauge your exercises to the level of sophistication and personal development of the group members. By sophistication I mean how skilled each person is in using the various modalities (guided fantasy, movement, ritual). Highly suggestive guided fantasies are appropriate for people with little experience and skill with the modality. Fantasies that give only general suggestions and allow long periods of time for the participants to image on their own are best for more experienced people. The same general considerations apply to movement work.

It is also helpful if you understand each person's level of psycho-spiritual development. Some exercises are more appropriate for people at earlier stages of personal development (Nurturing Touch, Befriending Yourself), and others for those at more advanced stages (Surrendering the Heart).

Exercises can often be modified slightly to take into account the level of development and experience of your group. Of course, many groups will have a mix of beginners and advanced participants, so the exercises have been designed as much as possible to work for a wide range of people. Nevertheless, by paying attention to these issues you can choose exercises to conform to the needs of your group.

Include a variety of modalities in each day or each workshop. For example, it would be boring to use three solitary guided fantasies in one day. I try to include in each day at least one exercise that includes pairing and one that includes movement. I also find it wise to design workshops that provide for a variety of internal experiences for participants. For instance, I try to include in each workshop exercises providing heart, expansiveness, and spiritual depth.

Other Suggestions

When you are designing a workshop where a number of exercises will be done in one day, remember that earlier exercises will provide context and material for later ones. Frequently a theme or image which emerges for someone in one exercise will be further elaborated in a later exercise, even when the topics of the exercises are unrelated.

In a long-term group, the question of repeating exercises arises. The more projective an exercise is, the more it can be repeated, because the participants are likely to have a different experience each time, depending on where they are at the moment and what material emerges. The exercises that are more directed can sometimes be repeated usefully, but you run the risk of simply taking participants to a place they have already been.

It can be very valuable, however, for participants to repeat an exercise of either sort when they are just learning to use the modality effectively, for example when someone is first learning to allow images to flow or to move spontaneously. The repetition helps them to develop their skills, and they will often derive more and more out of the exercise each time.

I allow 30 to 45 minutes for group sharing and individual work after each exercise. Since most exercises average 30 to 75 minutes in length, I leave about an hour and a half for each exercise. This means that in a one-day (six-hour) workshop, there is usually time for three exercises plus the check-in at the beginning of the group.

Beginning a Workshop or Group

At the beginning of a workshop or at the first meeting of an ongoing group, I find it useful to include the following four processes:

Leader's Introduction

Explain the focus of the workshop or group, what is to be covered, the structure, and any other general information that is needed. Convey your excitement about the work and the topic to be dealt with.

At the beginning of a peer group, you will need to discuss the sharing of the leadership role. One of the conveners of the group should assume the leadership for the opening meeting.

Members' Introductions

Go around the circle giving all participants some time to introduce themselves. In groups of more than ten or twelve this may need to be modified in some way because of time constraints. The function of these introductions is to begin to build trust and a sense of group connection.

Ask each person to give their name and to talk about why they are interested in the group. They should be encouraged to say something personal about how the topic of the group is important to them in their lives right now. You may even give them a specific question to answer which encourages them to be personal. For example, in a workshop on life purpose, you might ask, "Where are you right now in your search for a life purpose?" In a workshop on the nuclear threat, you might suggest, "Tell us one thing that you love about the world that you would hate to see lost in a nuclear war."

The leader usually begins this go-round. This gives you a chance to get things off on the right foot by modeling the personal quality of sharing you want from the members. You may choose to answer the same question you ask of the members. If that seems inappropriate, you can talk about your personal reasons for leading this group or doing this work in general.

Attitudes

After the introductions, people should be prepared for the best way to approach Inner Journeys work by discussing the points made under Participants' Outlook in "How to Use the Exercises."

Resonance Circle

As an opening exercise, we will use the resonance circle (adapted from an exercise by Gay Luce). This exercise moves the group members out of their ordinary consciousness, attunes them to each other, and encourages them to open their hearts, thereby setting a tone for the rest of the time together. This helps to delineate the group time as something special, something outside ordinary life, and encourages people to let go of some of their everyday worries and defenses and judgments, so they can enter more fully into the group.

This exercise uses energy that naturally flows through the human body and our ability to focus and direct it through attention. You can change your consciousness by shifting attention to particular energy centers in the body, and you can produce a more cohesive group consciousness by focusing on the flow of energy between people and around the group (group resonance). Some people may not believe in this energy, but everyone can be made comfortable with energy work by presenting it as a psychological metaphor. I often direct people to feel or imagine the energy.

The Exercise

♪ "Seapeace" (from *Seapeace* by Georgia Kelly, as much as needed; or other heart music)

Let's sit in a circle, holding hands, each person with your left palm up and right palm down. . . . Close your eyes, center yourself, and go inside. . . . Feel or imagine energy coming in your left hand from your partner on that side, passing up your arm, across your chest and through your heart, and then down your right arm and out your right hand to the person on that side. . . . Imagine the energy going all the way around the circle.

Now feel your place of grounding where you are sitting on the floor. Feel yourself rooted deeply into the earth, energy flowing up into you from below, grounding you, centering you. . . . Allow your heart to open as the energy passes through it, allow it to open just as much as feels right for you at this time. . . .

Feel yourself a part of this circle of caring and compassion that we are creating today to guide our work together. . . .

Variation

The following variation can be used in a social issues workshop. Start with the first two paragraphs above, using the same music:

Feel yourself a part of this circle of heart energy, this circle of compassionate people, who care about what's going on in the world, who are interested in exploring their inner realities and also desiring to act in the world to help heal the planet. . . .

Open your eyes now and take each person in. Let your eyes meet briefly with each one. You will be spending the day (evening, weekend, etc.) with each of these people, perhaps sharing some important parts of yourself with them. Like you, they are here today out of a heartfelt concern for our world. . . .

We will become a little community, a mini-society for the day. And we can be creating a new healthy society in microcosm right here in this workshop, in our openness to each other, in our trust, allowing each person to be themselves, to find their truth without judgment. . . .

Now close your eyes again, take a deep breath, and feel the circle we're creating for the day, a circle of caring and love. . . .

Beginning Each Group Meeting

In an ongoing group or class, begin each meeting with a resonance circle and then a period of time for each person to check in with the group. During this check-in people talk about any of the following:

1. What they are experiencing at the moment.

2. What they are going through in their life right now.

3. How the last group meeting has affected them.

4. If they are working on manifesting their life purpose, what steps they have taken toward this since last meeting.

The group members should be encouraged to give feedback and support to the person checking in. The check-in is a very important process, because it helps to build a bridge between the inner work and the person's outer life. On the other hand, it can easily take too much time if you are not careful. Setting a time limit on each person's check-in may be necessary. The group may have to struggle with the trade-off between check-in time and time for the exercises.

Ending

The following two-part process is a useful way to end workshops and to end each meeting of an ongoing group.

Bridging Discussion

People talk about how to take back into their lives what they have gotten from the group. This can be done in two ways:

First, a person may have experienced an important moment during the group, when a higher state or capacity was evoked. Discuss with them how to elicit that state in their everyday life and, if they are ready, how to begin to live from that place. Other group members may be able to give helpful advice on this.

Second, a person may have gained some insight or inspiration on manifesting their life purpose or their work for social transformation. They can talk about what concrete steps they plan to take in the near future, again with advice and encouragement from the leader and group.

If there isn't time for both the bridging discussion and the ending resonance circle described below (as would often be the case in an evening ongoing group), an abbreviated bridging discussion can take place during the resonance circle.

Ending Resonance Circle

At the end of a workshop or group it is important to reaffirm the group bond and individual connections by having people express appreciation to each other. This gives people a real experience of giving and receiving love and affirmation. The process is powerful in itself and also provides rich emotional fertilizer for the growth of seeds (insights, inspiration, depth experiences) that have been planted during the workshop. The opening and connecting that occurs at the end can facilitate the germination of these experiences into lasting changes in a person's life.

In an ongoing group, it also helps to hold the group bonding until the group meets again. And it is a natural place to welcome new people into the group and to say good-bye to and express appreciation for people who are leaving.

The circle is a valuable place for people to make explicit and public important things they have experienced during the group but not yet shared. This makes the experiences more real for the person sharing, and also empowers others by setting an example.

The Exercise ─────────────────────────

[Start out with the resonance circle instructions as above (the first two paragraphs), using the same music, shortening it as appropriate.]

Feel that circle of heart energy, of loving energy. . . . Feel how much has happened here today, the connections that have been made. . . . Open yourself to the group, feel yourself as a loving part of the greater whole. . . .

Let's take some time for anyone who would like to share with us something valuable that you will take away with you from the group today, an image, a feeling, an insight, something that touched you. And also please share any appreciations you have for the group as a whole or for any individuals in the group.

[Allow time for silence before and during this, as people may take a while before they are ready to talk.]

Variation

The following variation has been used in social transformation workshops. Start out with resonance circle directions as above.

♪ "The Rose" (any version; loving tone, the words are revelant to the suggestions)

Now think back over the day to those things that were most meaningful to you. Those things you learned that were new, or that you felt most deeply; those things that inspired you or affirmed you or moved you. . . . Take each one and place it in your heart. It is a seed, a promise. Hold it in your heart and nourish it, cherish it. At some point it will blossom forth with love and passion, moving you to make your contribution to the healing of our times. [Allow until the music ends.]

Then people share some of the things they just remembered, along with appreciations.

Variation

If a group or workshop ends with an energetic exercise involving the whole group, such as Affirmations or Manifesting Your Intention, then it can be very effective to go directly into the closing from there without sharing about the last exercise. (Some of this sharing will happen during the closing).

While people are still standing, move directly into holding hands (or a group hug if people are feeling particularly close), continue using the music from the previous exercise, and share appreciations and important experiences from the workshop as above. This maintains the open, expansive energy of the previous exercise and uses it as a springboard for the closing.

Experiences

The ending is an extremely important part of a workshop or group. When things have obviously been going very well, it serves as a celebration of what has happened and of people's connections with each other.

Sometimes, however, people are feeling very good and connected but it has not yet been made explicit, and sometimes things are just coming together by the end of a workshop. In these cases, the ending can really be a catalyst for evoking the caring and connection that are emerging. It often creates a snowball effect, as one person after another expresses love and appreciation. People are left feeling loving, affirmed, and empowered.

22

Exercise Design

THIS CHAPTER DISCUSSES how to design Inner Journeys exercises. This will be useful primarily for group leaders and experienced members of peer groups who would like to design the exercises they lead.

Inner Journeys exercises are based on the exercises designed by Jean Houston, which have their own unique and extremely effective style. This chapter is really an analysis of the form of her exercises and what makes them so powerful. I want to delineate a key element in the way these exercises are designed that makes them different from other workshop exercises or methods of using guided fantasy.

Suggestive and Projective Elements

There are two contrasting elements of an exercise that contribute in different ways to its impact on a person. The suggestive elements are designed to take the person into a particular emotion or state of consciousness or to elicit certain capacities. For example, the leader might say, "Feel the strength in your arms, your chest, as your mighty pinions take you higher, swifter." The projective elements encourage the person to allow certain thoughts, feelings, or images to emerge from the unconscious (or superconscious). For example, "You look down over the landscape you are traversing and discover that it is the landscape of your life."

Most exercises contain both suggestive and projective elements. The power of Inner Journeys exercises comes from the greater emphasis placed on the suggestive. Most other forms of guided fantasy emphasize projection, using just enough suggestion to induce trance and set up the situation. In Inner Journeys exercises a great deal of attention is paid to inducing exactly the desired state of consciousness for the projection and in helping participants to achieve this state intensely and vividly. In addition, in some Inner Journeys exercises, suggestive elements dominate completely because the main goal of the exercise may be to take the person into a particular state of being which fosters growth or healing, or elicits new capacities from the superconscious.

Inner Journeys exercises contain a wealth of suggestive approaches and techniques—deep trance inductions, various preparatory experiences, long and detailed verbal suggestion, dramatic voice tone, carefully selected music, expressive movement, ritual, and personal contact—derived from the genius of Jean Houston.

An Example

In the Flight of Empowerment exercise, chapter 14, the person takes a journey to the top of a mountain to meet an empowering figure, who then takes them on a flight into their personal power during which they look down on the landscape of their life. (You may want to read over this exercise now or refer back to it.)

The exercise is preceded by reading a selection from the Riddlemaster Trilogy illustrating the empowerment dealt with in the exercise. This is a suggestive element.

The first part of the exercise, the journey to the top of the mountain, is simultaneously a trance induction and the beginning of the guided fantasy. It contains projective elements—the instruction to notice the terrain, the feel of the climb, etc. However, these are mainly for the purpose of inducing trance. The suggestive elements include (1) the fact that it is a journey to the top of a mountain, representing a higher, powerful, spiritual place; (2) the yearning for the empowering figure and its being reciprocated; and (3) the exertion and strength in climbing the mountain.

The first major projective element is, of course, meeting and interacting with the empowering figure. This encourages the emergence of a significant degree of unconscious material. Other projective elements include the transformation into birds or flying beasts and viewing the landscape of one's life.

The suggestive elements during the flight include the following:

• Verbal suggestions of power, expansiveness, joy, etc.

• Free movement, which encourages these same feelings

• The music, which enhances both these and the sensation of flight

• The leader's powerful and exciting, even triumphant, tone of voice

General Schema for Exercises

The following is a general schema for the design of Inner Journeys exercises, which applies to most of the exercises in this book. It consists of eight parts which occur roughly in the following order, although not all are present in each exercise:

Introduction
Altered state
Higher state
Accessing the unconscious
Viewing one's life

Relating to others
Anchoring
Affirming

Introduction

The leader needs to introduce each exercise, as a way of orienting the participants to the goal of the exercise and engaging their interest and excitement in the process. For the Flight of Empowerment, this would involve explaining that the exercise has to do with enhancing feelings of personal power and gaining a larger perspective on one's life. For some exercises, this is all that is needed. For others, it is useful to present some material that more strongly suggests the direction of the exercise.

In the Flight of Empowerment, this is done by reading the section of the Riddlemaster story in which the hero is empowered by his mentor. This gives much more information about what the exercise is intended to do—the power and wisdom of the empowering figure, the fact that he or she wants the best for the participant, the exhilarating quality of the flight. More important, this reading carries an emotional impact that will influence what happens during the subsequent exercise.

In addition to reading or telling a story, an exercise can be introduced by presenting conceptual material related to the goals of the exercise, or by relating incidents from your own life or asking participants to do so.

Altered State

Most exercises start by moving the participants into an altered state of consciousness. This makes it easier for them to allow higher capacities to be accessed and to allow material from the unconscious to emerge. This is typically done by relaxation instructions and trance induction and the soothing music often used with them. The leader's voice should be calm, slow, measured, devoid of inflection.

The beginning part of the guided fantasy can double as an extended trance induction. The sheer act of fantasizing concrete images—specific sights, sounds, body sensations—will gradually take a person deeper into trance. The images must be concrete and specific, however; vague general sensings and conceptual thinking do not work as well. Thus, just remembering your third grade teacher may not be effective, but if you picture her facial expression and see what she is wearing, feel yourself sitting in your seat in the classroom hearing her voice, you will go deeper into trance.

Extended inductions can be done by having the participants imagine a series of discrete images as in Opening the Heart or the Expanded Body, or by taking them through a fantasy story as in Flight of Empowerment and many other exercises. The induction can also be integrated with movement if the movement is repetitive (as in Flight) or if it is intrinsic to the fantasy (as in Expansive Movement).

Higher State

Either during the trance induction or afterwards, we usually want to take the participant into a higher state of consciousness or into a particular emotional state that is part of the goal of the exercise; or we may want them to develop a particular higher capacity. We use a wide variety of techniques for inducing these states:

Verbal Suggestion. The most obvious of these is direct verbal suggestion, such as "You can let go and open yourself to feeling accepted and loved." It's surprising how powerful this simple technique can be when the person is in trance and when you use it in conjunction with other suggestive elements, especially with story elements that are designed to elicit the same state. For instance, in Flight, the climb up the mountain is a story element that elicits strength and the sense of moving to a higher realm of the psyche. Verbally suggesting power and strength works very well in this context because it fits in a natural way with what is already happening and is therefore less likely to generate resistance in the participant.

Verbal suggestion should only be used in the moment, not retroactively. That is, use it to suggest what the person feels as a result of what is happening in the moment in the fantasy. This works well because it induces the feeling in a natural way onto a blank slate, so to speak. Do not suggest what a person is feeling as a result of what happened in an *earlier* part of the exercise, except in a very tentative or general way, because it may conflict with what the person already knows they are feeling. For example, in The Expanded Body, it is OK to suggest various emotional and spiritual qualities that the person is feeling as the body expands— powerful, loving, deep. However, not everyone will feel all of these, so during the rest of the exercise it is dangerous to refer to these feelings specifically because the suggestion may conflict with the person's actual experience and jolt them out of the trance rapport. It would be permissible to refer generally to "the expanded place you are now in" or tentatively to "the power you may be feeling."

Music. The use of music is an effective way to induce a desired state. Inner Journeys exercises are divided into a number of parts, most of which are to be experienced in a particular state. For each of these, it is well worth the effort to choose a piece of music which induces that state. This is done by intuition and by trying out the music on yourself.

For a few parts, however, the choice of music is not straightforward. This is when the participant accesses enough significant material from the unconscious that different people will enter different states depending on what comes up. For example, near the end of Reowning the Shadow, we have people move around the room as their transformed shadow sides. Each person's shadow will be different, so no single mood will be appropriate for everyone. For exercise parts of this kind, I tend to use music that is general enough not to disrupt anyone's experience, or occasionally, no music at all.

Tone of Voice. The leader's tone of voice is an important suggestive element. It might be more accurate to say that the leader's state of being is the suggestive element, though in most exercises people's eyes are closed, so the voice tone is the obvious channel for communicating that state of being. For best results as a leader, you should induce in yourself the state you intend for the group members. Then that state is naturally and powerfully communicated by everything you do. This requires you to have the courage and largeness of spirit to lead with your being as well as with words.

Preparatory Images. During an extended trance induction it helps to include images that tend toward the state that will be induced later. Thus in Flight, which aims at feelings of personal power, during the journey to the top of the mountain the participants are told that they have to exert themselves in the climb, and that their strength grows to meet the challenges. In Opening the Heart, as we count up to 23, the images gradually have more to do with loving. In the Expanded Body, the animals and natural formations imagined near the end of the induction are large and powerful.

Existing Capacity. In order to develop a higher capacity, it is useful to refer participants to a positive memory or to an existing capacity which they can easily access. For example, in Acceptance, this is used twice: (1) people remember a time when they were accepted, and (2) they get in touch with the part of them which is loving and accepting of others. Both of these help them to become accepting toward themselves. Similarly in Befriending Yourself, we access the warm feelings one might have toward a friend, and then transfer them to oneself. In Envisioning a Healthy Society, positive memories are used to stimulate future visioning.

Sharing Images. You can have people share their images with each other while in trance, either in pairs (Opening the Heart, Journey to the Spiritual Realm) or in the whole group (Planetary Compassion, Affirmations). The additional input from others tends to act as an induction into the desired state because the participant is stimulated by the emotional state of the other group members (e.g., their compassion or excitement).

This sharing also provides participants with a broader perspective than they might have had on their own. For instance, during Envisioning a Healthy Society, people hear everyone else's visions as well as their own and are thus introduced to a wealth of inspiring ideas.

Sharing in pairs also tends to increase closeness and affection between the people involved. It is particularly useful for those exercises related to intimacy (e.g., Opening the Heart, Acceptance).

Movement. Free form movement can be used to induce feelings of expansiveness and personal power (Expansive Movement, Flight). Body movement which is flowing and forceful helps to mobilize energy and move through muscular blocks. The self-expression and spontaneity of dance combined with expansive music and verbal suggestion can be very powerful.

The Body. Various other ways of using the body may encourage a desired state. Sitting upright and standing are used to encourage a sense of personal power (Manifesting Your Intention, Affirmations), as is deep breathing (Manifesting, Child and Higher Self). The relaxed posture for guided fantasies encourages letting go into a trance. Physical touch and eye contact are used to enhance personal contact and nurturing (Nurturing Touch, Surrendering the Heart, Opening the Heart).

Other Modalities. In addition to the methods used in this book, chanting, meditation, and body awareness are quite powerful, as are various kinds of expressive art—drama, singing, and drawing.

Accessing the Unconscious

After the group members have moved into the desired state, or sometimes while that is happening, they are ready to access material from the unconscious (or superconscious). Sometimes this is the main goal of the exercise. For example in Reowning the Shadow, uncovering the form and meaning of the shadow figure is central to the whole point of the exercise, and in Gaia, the appearance of Gaia and her message are also central.

Whenever the main point is accessing unconscious matter, participants must be able to interpret its meaning. In many exercises this can happen naturally as a result of the structure of the exercise (Reowning the Shadow, Gaia). However, in some exercises a lot of material is accessed that needs to be understood for further use in the exercise, so it is wise to provide explicitly for interpretation. For example, in Finding Your Contribution, nine different images emerge from the floors of the tower. They are used later in telling one's life story, so have participants spend time in pairs interpreting these images with each other's help. No matter what the exercise, some people may need help with interpretation during the group sharing.

In other cases, the main goal is the state of consciousnes to be achieved, and accessing unconscious material helps to deepen that state and to make it more uniquely personal. For example, in Flight, the main point of the exercise is the state of power and expansiveness that the participant experiences. The exercise could have been designed to eliminate all projective material; i.e., the appearance and message of the empowering figure and the kind of birds. However, by allowing these to come from the participants' unconscious, they become much more involved in the process, the state achieved is more intense and more meaningful to them, and they have personal referents to help them take the experience into their lives.

Though guided fantasy is the primary method, movement may also be used as a means of accessing the unconscious. In Expansive Movement, the participants use movement to explore their embodiment of the various animals. The movement is not just being used to induce an expansive state, but also to access kinesthetically the person's unique experience of the archetypal lion or eagle, for instance.

Internal Channels. In making suggestions to access unconscious material, you need to be aware of what internal channels the participants may be using—visual, kinesthetic, auditory. Even though most people are visual, a significant number of people access best kinesthetically (through body sensing), and a smaller number use hearing, smell, or taste. Some people use one primary channel effectively and find the others dim and vague. Other people can use all the channels well.

Most guided fantasies are visual, in that the material that is accessed is something that would be seen if the internal story were happening in the external world. For example, the participant sees the empowering figure approaching at the top of the mountain. In these situations it is helpful to include suggestions for people who are primarily kinesthetic. Thus, after they see the figure approaching, we suggest, "Sense what it is like to be in his or her presence." This allows kinesthetic people to use their primary channel. For auditory people, one could suggest that they hear the voice of the empowering figure.

Some guided fantasies are naturally kinesthetic, in that material is accessed by having the participant *become* whatever is being accessed rather than seeing it, as when the participant is transformed into a bird in Flight of Empowerment. This also happens in the Expanded Body, the later part of Reowning the Shadow, Expansive Movement, and other exercises. People who are visual rather than kinesthetic are usually able to translate these kinesthetic images into visual ones automatically.

A guided fantasy will be most vivid for people when they can use many channels simultaneously as in real life, for example during the Flight, feeling themselves as a great bird, seeing the landscape below, hearing the sound of the wind, etc. Whenever you can, include suggestions for as many channels as possible. This encourages vividness and makes the exercise accessible to a wide range of people.

Bridging to Everyday Life

Once the higher state and access have been achieved, the influence of this state and material can be enhanced by looking at one's life from this new perspective, by relating to people in the group from this place, by anchoring this new state so that it can be returned to, and by affirming the positive qualities and capacities that have been accessed. These can occur in any order.

Viewing One's Life

The higher state often provides a wider, clearer, or wiser perspective on life. It can be very useful to have the participants look at their lives while still under the full influence of the higher state; for example, viewing the landscape of one's life during Flight of Empowerment. This helps to deepen the understandings obtained while in the higher state; it also helps to make a bridge to ordinary consciousness.

Learning is state-specific,[1] so that what one learns in one state of consciousness does not easily carry over to another. Reviewing aspects of one's ordinary life while in an altered state

---

[1] Charles T. Tart, *States of Consciousness* (New York: Dutton, 1975).

helps to make this bridge. This happens extensively in the Expanded Body. After achieving the expanded state, participants practice self-acceptance and love, then they open their hearts to the people in their lives and in the world, and finally they sense their life purpose. In Expansive Movement, they achieve a sense of expansiveness and personal power through becoming the animals, and then explore living their lives from that place.

Relating to Others

Relating to others in the group from the higher state also encourages the deepening and bridging process. One powerful way to do this is through "honoring." Often at the end of an exercise which has been done in pairs, people make eye contact with their partner and silently honor them from the higher state that has been reached. In Child and Higher Self this is actually done from three different places, the internal child, the adult self, and the higher self. In Opening the Heart and in Acceptance, the honoring is done from loving and accepting states. In fact honoring can be added as an ending to any exercise which involves a significant amount of work in pairs.

When people have achieved an energetic and powerful state, it can be deepened by having each person declare something about themselves to the group and receive support and encouragement (Affirmations, Manifesting Your Intention). This enhances the empowerment for both the person declaring and for the respondents. This declaring can also be added as an ending to any appropriate exercise.

You may use a variety of other ways to deepen a higher state by relating to the group. In Opening the Heart people practice opening their hearts to the group as a whole. In Surrendering the Heart, the group lovingly touches each person in order to take them further. In Envisioning a Healthy Society, people embody the excitement of their visions by dancing with each other.

Anchoring

People need to be able to access in daily life a higher state reached during an exercise. This possibility is enhanced greatly when the person has an image, body sensation, word, or sound to remind them of the experience. This is called anchoring.[2] Once learned, anchors such as these can be consciously used to help recapture the state.

In a projective exercise, the material that emerges serves as a naturally occurring anchor. For example, after the Flight of Empowerment, a person could re-access the experience by visualizing the empowering figure or by remembering what it felt like to be the great soaring bird.

In an exercise that is largely suggestive, you might add a small projective element at the end, so that participants can develop an appropriate anchor for themselves. For example, at the end of Surrendering the Heart, we say, "And now let an image come to you, . . . that represents to you the state you are now in. . . . Keep this with you as a way of returning to this time. . . ."

Movement is a way to anchor an experience kinesthetically so that it will be evoked naturally during everyday life. In some exercises, after people have reached a higher state through guided fantasy, they act out or embody that state through movement, thereby grounding the learning in the body. For example, in Reowning the Shadow, after becoming the shadow in the guided fantasy, they act out the transformed shadow in movement, thus owning it at a body level.

Affirming

While the participants are in a higher state, it is important to affirm this experience—that this is really who they are, that there

---

[2] Richard Bandler and John Grinder, *Frogs into Princes* (Moab, UT: Real People Press, 1979).

is a part of them that is wise or loving or powerful. This affirmation is necessary because for many people the state achieved may occur rarely, if at all, in their ordinary lives. They might easily discount the experience, feeling that the state is really an artifact of the exercise or is attributable to the power of the leader. People with self-esteem difficulties are especially prone to this. However, we all need this kind of affirmation; we all need to have our best selves confirmed and celebrated.

The obvious way is through direct verbal suggestion. For example, in The Child and the Higher Self, after the participants have experienced all three parts of themselves and the parts have related to each other, the leader says, "Rejoice in these relationships you have within yourself. . . ." At the end of the Naming Ritual, we say, "Knowing yourself named and confirmed as one who has a significant contribution to make to the world, . . ."

Another way to affirm the experience is to have the participants use self-affirming statements. For example in Reowning the Shadow, after a positive quality, such as assertiveness, has emerged from someone's shadow, we have the person affirm, "I recognize my assertiveness." The Affirmations exercise is built around this idea, of course.

Affirmation from one's partner is extremely potent, as in the Naming Ritual and all the exercises that end with honoring. I have designed a number of other exercises that involve verbal affirmation in pairs, and invariably people find them very rewarding. It warms my heart to see how willing and even eager people are to lovingly empower each other. This affirmation can also come from the group as a whole, as in the Group Naming Ritual or when the group supports each person's declaration in Manifesting Your Intention.

"Celebratory movement" is another way to affirm what one has gained from an exercise. People are encouraged to celebrate themselves through dance—to celebrate the positive part of themselves they have discovered (Reowning the Shadow), the higher state they have achieved (Expanded Body), or their vision of a positive future (Envisioning a Healthy Society, Manifesting Your Intention). Celebratory movement can also be added as an ending to any appropriate exercise.

Healing Pain from the Past

Not all of the exercises fit into the general schema described above. A slightly different schema is needed for those exercises which deal with healing psychological pain from the past. In these exercises, participants first access some kind of painful material and then go through a healing experience. In this schema Higher State and Accessing the Unconscious are replaced by the following three sections:

Desired State

We want to induce a state appropriate to accessing the painful material. This is often an unpleasant emotional state, such as sadness or need or pain, as in Nurturing Touch or the first part of Child and Higher Self. We use many of the same techniques for inducing these states as described before under Higher State. For example, in Child and Higher Self, we use sad music and voice tone for accessing the painful child memories. In Reowning the Shadow, we induce a shadow state by having people go down into a deep cavity and then we use heavy, eerie music. In Nurturing Touch, to encourage regression we have people lying in a fetal position for the induction.

Accessing Painful Material

The next step is for people to access unconscious material that highlights the painful situation we would like to heal. This may be a memory (Child, Nurturing Touch) or a negative self-image

(Reowning the Shadow). For healing to occur, the painful material must be experienced as fully as possible. It shouldn't be just a vague idea or a static image; the participants need to be fully involved with it emotionally. In the case of a memory, we encourage them to relive it in all its vividness. In Reowning the Shadow, to encourage full experiencing, we have them interact with the shadow figure and then become the shadow figure exploring shadow country.

The Healing Experience

Once the pain has been experienced fully, the person is open for new learning to take place. At this point we provide an experience that can help heal the pain. Usually, this means providing whatever was missing which caused the pain in the first place when the person was a child. In Nurturing Touch this is provided by another group member, and in Child and Higher Self it is provided by the adult part of the person. It could also be provided by an inner archetypal figure or by the group leader (during individual work).

This healing experience can't undo the old painful experience, but it does provide a counter-balancing experience of a positive nature, which helps to heal the effects of that pain in the present. The old pain will still be there, perhaps in diminished form, but its negative effects on current feelings and behavior will be altered.

In Reowning the Shadow, the healing experience is the discovery of the positive qualities inherent in the disowned shadow. This helps the person to develop a more accurate self-image and to redress low self-esteem.

During this part of the exercise, we use many of the same methods used for inducing a higher state, such as music, voice tone, verbal suggestion, and contact with others. Here the desired state usually involves feeling warm, loved, safe, and good about oneself.

Relating to Internal Figures

Many of the Inner Journeys exercises involve an internal relationship—with your higher self, with an archetypal figure, with your inner child, etc. I have mentioned in earlier chapters how some of these are for the purpose of strengthening and internalizing parenting functions. In some exercises you relate to another group member in a way that strengthens these functions. The following summarizes and organizes these various kinds of relating.

Each of these exercises is designed so that the participant has a chance to receive a particular kind of relating that will enable them to grow. In some cases it is that which a parent would provide, in some it is that which a friend or teacher might provide, and in some it comes from the higher self or a divine power. For the sake of simplicity I have included the friend or teacher functions in with the parenting. So there are two general headings: parenting functions and spiritual functions.

Parenting Functions

The parenting functions include nurturing, acceptance, understanding, protection, appreciation, empowerment, setting limits, and teaching about life.

Parenting from a Person

In some of the exercises the participant receives parenting directly from another member of the group (Nurturing Touch, Acceptance, the Naming Ritual). Since the giving comes from outside, this is the most effective method for participants who feel they have little to give to themselves. On the other hand, it is the most difficult for someone who is afraid of contact with a real person.

In many of the exercises, participants also receive these functions indirectly from the leader during the normal course of the exercise. Thus, in suggesting in a caring way that participants feel how much they deserve to be loved, the leader is indirectly nurturing them. They may also receive this directly or indirectly from the leader during individual work. This kind of relating is central to much of individual psychotherapy, which uses the therapist-client relationship as a major vehicle for growth.

Parenting from an Internal Figure

In some of the exercises the participant receives parenting from an internal figure, remembered or imagined. This might be:

1. A memory of someone giving to them (Acceptance).

2. An ideal parent figure (Mira's work under Nurturing).

3. An archetypal figure (Flight of Empowerment, Sally's work under Acceptance).

4. Imagining receiving from the person's real parents.

This is an intermediate level where the fear of real contact is removed, and some of the giving must come from within the person's own psyche. The four possibilities are listed above in order of difficulty. Remembering something that actually happened is easiest; next is receiving from an ideal or archetypal figure. Most difficult is imagining receiving something from one's actual parents which they didn't provide, because the person has to overcome the memory of how it really was (see Mira's work under Nurturing Touch).

Parenting from the Self

In some exercises, participants give this parenting to themselves (Child and Higher Self, Befriending Yourself). This is the most difficult because people have to experience themselves as having the strength and goodness to give themselves what they need. It is also potentially the most valuable because it explicitly internalizes the parenting function.

The Spiritual Functions

The spiritual functions include unconditional love, higher purpose, creativity, wisdom, and oneness. We will see the same three types of relating in the spiritual realm.

Spirituality from a Person

In a few instances people in the group give to one another from a higher place, so that what is received is not a parenting function, but a spiritual one. This happens at the end of the Child and Higher Self, when people are making eye contact in pairs from their higher selves. It also can happen in the Naming Ritual, and in Surrendering the Heart when the group members use physical contact to take each person deeper into surrender.

Outside Inner Journeys work, this classically happens in the relationship between spiritual teachers or gurus and their disciples.

Spirituality from an Internal Figure

In a number of exercises, the participant relates to an archetypal spiritual figure (Gaia, Finding Your Contribution, Surrendering the Heart, Journey to the Spiritual Realm). This is the easiest way for most people to receive spiritual functions because we are used to conceiving of the divine as transcendent and external to ourselves, and because it is difficult for many people to imagine themselves as possessing these higher faculties. This is the usual way of relating to the divine in spiritual systems that recognize a personal god (e.g. Christianity, Sufism).

I might also have included Flight of Empowerment here, instead of under parenting. In fact, in any of the exercises involving an archetypal figure, the functions received by a particular person may be spiritual or parenting or some mixture of the two, depending of what that person needs for their growth at that time.

Identifying with the Spiritual

In some exercises, instead of relating to a spiritual figure, the participant *becomes* the spiritual figure (Child and Higher Self, Expanded Body, some Journeys to the Spiritual Realm). This is the most difficult of the three, because the person has to have enough self-esteem to own the divine within. It is also according to some conceptions[3] the most developed of the three.

These six categories are presented roughly in developmental sequence, from needing to receive from the outside to owning the power within. Keeping this in mind can be helpful in designing exercises or making choices during individual work. However, it should not be taken too far. The Child and Higher Self exercise, for instance, is excellent for beginners even though it uses the most advanced category, Identifying with the Spiritual. In doing this exercise, people who are not very spiritually developed may simply have a beginning experience of their higher self, or they may learn something about how they block the experience. Similarly, a more developed person can very usefully do exercises that involve the less advanced kinds of relating.

The Design Process

Designing workshop exercises is an intuitive process whose essence cannot really be captured in a set of concepts and sugges-

---

[3] Ken Wilbur, "The Developmental Spectrum and Psychopathology," *Journal of Transpersonal Psychology*, Vol. 16, No. 1, 1984.

tions. In this chapter I have described those aspects that lend themselves to rational analysis, but the important part must come from your own creativity.

The process of exercise design seems to happen best in a relaxed or semi-trance state. I often come up with ideas for exercises during the middle of the night or upon first waking in the morning. At these times I'm more open to my own unconscious creative processes, and I'm also in a state similar to that of participants during the exercises. At these times I take myself through the experience of the exercise as I'm designing it, thus getting immediate feedback on its effects.

Exercises generally have to be tried out and modified a number of times before they reach a form where the kinks have been worked out and the exercise is most effective. After designing an exercise I usually try it out on a friend or colleague before using it in a group or workshop, modifying it based on their experience. Then I modify it further after its first use in a group situation. Some exercises work pretty well the first time and require few changes, while others need continual improvement over three or four trials as I learn how different groups and different people react to them. One of the most satisfying things about designing Inner Journeys exercises is the joy of gradually improving an exercise until I am proud of its depth and power.

Other Comments

Unless you are working with a very sophisticated group, limit yourself to three or four minutes of silence during a guided fantasy. Most people cannot maintain a focus for longer than that without additional instructions from the leader. After a while they will "space out" or start daydreaming about other things. If a longer time is needed, one can insert periodic suggestions or arrange the fantasy to be done in pairs, as in Journey to the Spiritual Realm. When people are creating a fantasy in pairs, they can go much longer without external guidance because the act of sharing the images keeps them focused.

Movement and dance are used in four different ways in inner journeys work. In summary:

1. Exploratory movement can be used to help access unconscious material kinesthetically (Expansive Movement).

2. Expansive movement can be used to induce feelings of personal power (many exercises).

3. Movement can be used to act out or embody a particular state or capacity in order to anchor it in the body (Reowning the Shadow).

4. Celebratory movement can be used to affirm positive aspects of a person (later in Reowning the Shadow, and many other exercises).

Whenever possible, present many different viewpoints or ways of understanding the key concept of an exercise so that it will be comprehensible to as many different people as possible. This can happen both in the introduction to the exercise and in the guided fantasy itself. For example, in Surrendering the Heart we suggest a number of ways of conceptualizing the higher power, and we include the possibility that there will be a general experience of letting go without a clear object. Thus, the exercise can accommodate people of various religious persuasions or lack thereof, people who can visualize and relate to archetypal figures, those who relate more to the physical sensations of opening the heart, and those who are not ready to relate to a divine figure. Similarly, in Journey to the Spiritual Realm, we present many different viewpoints on the spiritual realm in the introduction, and then during the exercise when we suggest that people actually enter the spiritual realm, we mention a variety of these in shortened form.

Conclusion

DESIGNING AND LEADING Inner Journeys workshops has been a source of joy and deep satisfaction for me. I also trust that it has been useful to the participants in their personal growth and search for life purpose.

I hope that you use this work in whatever way is right for you—doing the exercises on your own, creating a peer group, leading the exercises as described here, designing your own, integrating this work into whatever you already do. I wish you much pleasure and success in this endeavor.

Unlock your creativity, spread your love, and may we all truly grow into our potential, manifest our purpose for being here, and help to heal our troubled world.